A2-Level
English
Language

The Revision Guide

Editors: Polly Cotterill, Rob MacDonald, Jennifer Underwood.

Contributors: Najoud Ensaff, Heather Haynes, Tony Flanagan, Rachael Powers, Chris Reynolds, Elisabeth Sanderson, Michael Southorn, Luke von Kotze, Emma Warhurst.

Proofreaders: Paula Barnett, Barbara Brecht, Katherine Reed.

Acknowledgements
Page 26, Text B: www.growingkids.co.uk
Page 28, Text F: Jean Aitchison, The Language Web, 1997 © Jean Aitchison 1997, published by Cambridge University Press, reproduced with permission
Page 29, Text H: © Mark Sebba, http://www.ling.lancs.ac.uk/staff/mark/resource/creole.htm
Page 73, Text B: Liam Byrne, © Crown Copyright, reproduced under the terms of the Click-Use Licence.
Page 140, Text F: www.allotment.org.uk
Page 144, Text B: Cameron Self, http://www.literarynorfolk.co.uk/norfolk_dialect.htm

Every effort has been made to locate copyright holders and obtain permission to reproduce sources.
For those sources where it has been difficult to trace the copyright holder of the work, we would be grateful for information. If any copyright holder would like to make an amendment to the acknowledgements, please notify us and we will gladly update the book at the next reprint. Thank you.

ISBN: 978 1 84762 279 2

Published by Coordination Group Publications Ltd.

Groovy website: www.cgpbooks.co.uk
Jolly bits of clipart from CorelDRAW®
Printed by Elanders Ltd, Newcastle upon Tyne.

Based on the classic CGP style created by Richard Parsons.

Contents

Old and Middle English

For WJEC and Edexcel. English didn't come in a packet, ready for some Celts to "open and add water". It's evolved over thousands of years — mainly through lots of fighting and generally stealing words from every other language possible.

English came from **Abroad**

1) English began as a combination of **Germanic** languages belonging to tribes that first invaded England around 449 AD — the **Angles**, the **Saxons** and the **Jutes**, from Denmark and northern Germany.

2) The people who lived in Britain spoke **Celtic languages**. They were pushed **north** and **west** by the invaders and settled mainly in Wales, Scotland and Cornwall.

3) The name 'English' comes from *Engle*, which meant *the Angles*. The Angles were from part of the mainland and the islands of **Denmark**, which at the time was called *Angulus*, or *Angeln*.

4) **All the new settlers in England** became known as *Engles*. The Engles and their collective language became known as *Englisc*. It's usually called **Anglo-Saxon** in history books. Both terms refer to **Old English** — the language of England from 450 AD – 1150 AD.

The success of the Angles can be easily measured.

Some **Old English Words** are **Still in Use**

1) Some of the everyday words we use come from Old English.
   Modern nouns like *father* (Old English **fædre**), *love* (**lufu**), *wife* (**wif**) and *house* (**hus**).
   Adjectives like *bloody* (Old English **blodig**), *cold* (**cald**), and *black* (**blæc**).

2) Some English **place names** have Old English structures — for example *Brad* means *broad*, and *ford* means *crossing*. So *Bradford* originally meant *broad crossing*.

3) Some areas of England reflect the original **Anglo-Saxon kingdoms** — *East Anglia* (**East Angles**), and *Sussex* (South **Saxons**), *Essex* (East **Saxons**) and *Middlesex* (Middle **Saxons**).

Old English had a **Distinctive Grammar**

1) The grammar of Old English relied heavily on **inflections**, **prefixes** and **suffixes**, which showed person, number, mood or tense.

2) For example, in modern English you form **plurals** by adding an *-s* or *-es*. In Old English, depending on the **gender** of a word and **where** it was placed in a sentence, a plural could be formed by adding *-as*, *-a*, *-um*, *-e*, *-an*, or *-ena*.

3) Old English also provided a range of **functional** words such as the **prepositions** *in*, *on*, and *under*.

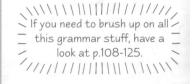
If you need to brush up on all this grammar stuff, have a look at p.108-125.

Old English **Spelling** and **Pronunciation** varied **Between Dialects**

1) By the ninth century, **four very different major dialects** had emerged. They were:

   - **Northumbrian** (the north of England and parts of present-day Scotland)
   - **Mercian** (the Midlands)
   - **Kentish** (present-day Kent)
   - **West Saxon** (the south of England down to Cornwall)

2) Words were pronounced very differently in each dialect due to **regional variation**, and they were also **written** differently.

3) Although hardly anyone could write anyway, the **lack** of a **standardised spelling system** meant it was extremely difficult to even try to learn. For example, the word *night* could be spelled *niht*, *neaht* or *neht*.

Old and Middle English

More Invasions *changed the language completely*

Viking Invasion (8th-11th centuries)
1) In the eighth, ninth, tenth and eleventh centuries, waves of **Scandinavian Vikings** invaded Britain. They settled in the north and east of England, and their language, **Old Norse**, had a significant influence on English.
2) Place names that end in -*by* (like *Whitby*) and -*thorpe* (*Mablethorpe*) show the influence of Old Norse. Both suffixes meant *settlement*.

Norman Conquest (11th century onwards)
1) After the Normans conquered England in **1066**, **French** became the language of the **aristocracy**, **law** and **government**. English remained the language of the **common people** though.
2) As you might expect, a lot of words derived from French can be found in **law** (*accuse, arrest*), **government** (*parliament, treasurer*) and the **military** (*soldier, lieutenant*).
3) Sometimes French words **replaced** English words — the Old English (OE) *wlitig* was replaced by the Old French (OF) *bealte* (which became modern day *beauty*). Sometimes both OE and OF words with **similar meanings** survived, e.g. *wood* (OE) and *forest* (OF).
4) French wasn't the only language that affected English. **Latin** was widely spoken in the **church** and among **educated people**. French contained lots of **borrowed** words from Latin, so Latin borrowings were also passed on to English. Latin words that became part of English include *distract, genius, interrupt, script* and *testimony*.

The Transition *to* Middle English (1150 Onwards) *changed everything again*

1) The most significant change to English grammar was the **loss of inflections**. As they were lost from the language (thought to be as early as the end of the twelfth century), **word order** became much more important.
2) In OE the **subject** of the sentence could be placed in **different positions**, but you could tell it was the subject due to its inflection. Middle English (ME) needed a basic word order, which became **subject-verb-object**.
3) As in OE, there were still huge **variations in spelling**. Writers who spoke one dialect would spell words differently from those who spoke another, e.g. *meadow* could be either *medwe, meede* or *medoue*.
4) Certain consonants and vowel sounds were **written down differently**, e.g. OE *sc* (pronounced *sh*) started to be written as *sh*. In OE the word for *shoe* was spelled *scoh* but in ME it became *sho*. Some **long vowels** in OE came to be spelled with an extra vowel in ME — e.g. *rot* in OE became *root* in ME.

English made a comeback in the mid-14th century

- By the end of the thirteenth century, there had been a lot of **integration** and **inter-marriage** between the **English** and people of **Norman descent**.
- The major **literary figure** of the Middle English period was **Geoffrey Chaucer**, a 14th century poet. Chaucer's poetry shows a **rich variety** of language, at times with strong French and Anglo-Saxon influences.
- During the ME period, the four OE dialects developed into **five** — Northern, East Midlands, West Midlands, Kentish and Southern.

Practice Questions

Q1 How did 'Englisc' come to Britain?

Q2 Name two differences between Old English grammar and Present Day English grammar.

Q3 What is the major grammatical difference between Old English and Middle English?

Essay Question

Q1 Explain the influences that the Viking invasions and the Norman conquest had on the English language.

Ye Olde Tea Shoppe — *not strictly an example of Old English, I'm afraid...*

And so a flurry of small independent cafés up and down Britain rush to change the little sign out front... it's just not authentic folks, sorry. I'm sure your scones are excellent though. Anyway, a nice straightforward start to the section... Angles + Saxons + Jutes + Vikings + Normans + Latin = English. Sort of. It equals Middle English. So still a bit to go yet.

Early Modern English

These pages are for WJEC and Edexcel. There's also some good background stuff for AQA A. This wasn't when people started using words like "tape recorder", or calling things "new-fangled". It was actually about 500 years ago.

The **Printing Press** helped to **Standardise English**

1) In 1476, **William Caxton** established the first **printing press** in Westminster — the centre of **political administration** and **law**.

2) This was an important step towards **standardising English**. Producing **identical copies** of a text meant that everyone was reading the **same** thing, written the same way.

3) However, it was pretty tricky for Caxton. In Old and Middle English, words were often spelled **differently** according to **dialect** or the **personal choice** of the writer, so he had to **decide** which **spellings** to use.

4) Caxton also had to choose an appropriate **punctuation system** as there was no uniform system in place.

The **East Midland Dialect** created the **Standard**

1) Caxton chose the type of English being used in the **courts**, the **universities** (particularly Cambridge) and in **London** at the time, which was pretty similar to the **East Midland dialect** of Middle English.

2) This dialect was already associated with **political authority**, **learning** and **commerce**. Using it in printed books gave it a feeling of **permanence** and **prestige**.

3) However, English wasn't standardised overnight. The spelling in Caxton's printed books still **wasn't consistent**, e.g. the word *things* might be spelled *thynges* in one text and *thingis* in another. Different forms of the same word, e.g. *booke* and *boke*, might appear across just a few lines.

4) At the end of the sixteenth century, the first **guides to spelling** were published, e.g. *Elementarie* (*1582*) by Richard Mulcaster contained around **8000 words** of recommended spelling (but no definitions). In the seventeenth century, more guides were published, attempting to **standardise** English even further.

Punctuation was **Much Simpler** than it is today

1) The early printed texts of this period used **three basic punctuation marks**. These were the **punctus** (•), which functioned like a full stop, the **colon** (used for a variety of purposes) and a forward slash sign known as a **virgule** (/) which functioned like a comma.

2) The **exclamation mark** and **semi-colon** started to be used in the sixteenth century.

3) In the sixteenth and seventeenth centuries, a printer had **more punctuation** to choose from. These included full stops, commas, question marks, semi-colons, quotation marks and parentheses (brackets).

English Vocabulary continued to **Expand**

English carried on **borrowing** words from all over the world.

1) There was a surge of interest in Roman and Greek **art**, **architecture** and **literature** in the 16th and 17th centuries. New words **derived** from **Latin** and **Ancient Greek** were introduced into English:

> **Latin** — *encyclopedia* (first recorded usage in 1531), *temperature* (1533) and *conspicuous* (1545).
> **Greek** — *catastrophe* (1540), *larynx* (1578) and *pneumonia* (1603).

2) Latin and Greek also gave English lots of **prefixes**, like *anti-* (e.g. *antibody*, from Greek), or *bi-* (as in *bilingual*, from Latin). English also took **suffixes** like *-ism* (as in *idealism*), found in both languages.

3) Increased international **trade links**, **travel** to and **communication** with other countries also brought new words into English, mainly from **Italy** and **Spain**:

> **Italian** — *rocket* (recorded 1611), *volcano* (1613) and *opera* (1644).
> **Spanish** — *tobacco* (recorded 1588), *hurricane* (1555) and *guitar* (1621).

Early Modern English

This period saw a **Significant Change** in **Pronunciation**

Between 1400 and 1600 there was a big change in the pronunciation of all **long vowels**.

1) The **Great Vowel Shift** (GVS) was the major phonological difference between Middle English and Early Modern English.

Middle English		Early Modern English
naam	became	*name*
hoos	became	*house*
teem	became	*time*

2) No one really knows for definite what brought about this change but **various theories** have been put forward.

3) One theory is that the new vowels were a way of **rejecting** French pronunciation patterns and adopting ones that were associated with a **prestige form** of English.

became pronounced as

i → ai   e.g. 'teem' to 'time'

e → i   e.g. 'sae' to 'see'

a → ei   e.g. 'naam' to 'name'

o → u   e.g. 'rote' to 'root'

u → au   e.g. 'hoos' to 'house'

Grammar was also Changing

1) Early Modern English (EME) used **verb forms** such as *art* (now just *are*) and **second** and **third person inflections** -*st* and -*th* as in *lovest* and *loveth* (which is now just *loves*).

2) **Double negatives** such as <u>not in sport</u> <u>neither</u> and **double comparatives** such as <u>more elder</u> were grammatically acceptable.

3) In Middle English people asked a question by **inverting the subject and verb**, as in *Hadst thou?* In the Early Modern period, people started to use the auxiliary verb *do* instead. Shakespeare, who wrote in EME, used both *do* and subject-verb inversion to **form questions**, as in *Do you know what you say?* and *Didst thou?*

Their relief at avoiding the Great Owl Shift was palpable.

4) People also started to form **negative questions** with and without *do*, as in *Know you not?* and *Do you not know?*

5) Latin had an influence on **sentence structures**. Middle English relied a lot on **conjunctions** such as *and* and *then*, but Early Modern English showed more **complex sentence structures** — using **subordinate clauses** and **subordinating conjunctions**.

Practice Questions

Q1 Why was William Caxton significant to the development of Early Modern English?

Q2 What developments in punctuation were there in this period?

Q3 Why did the East Midlands dialect gain more status than other dialects of English?

Q4 What was the Great Vowel Shift?

Q5 Give three examples of Early Modern grammar that are different from Present Day English.

Essay Question

Q1 Discuss the factors that led to English first being standardised.

Can you tell what it is yet...

With the vowel shift and the grammatical transitions of Early Modern English, everything suddenly starts to look a lot more familiar. BUT it's important to remember that there were marked differences between Early Modern and Present Day English. Think about it this way — Shakespeare wrote in Early Modern English, and he can still be pretty confusing.

Late Modern English

For AQA A, AQA B, WJEC and Edexcel. Late Modern English (1700-present) saw more standardisation. New words entered the language and dialects were "diluted" by influences from all over the place.

Prescriptive Books *had a major impact on* Grammar

Prescriptivism is an **attitude** towards language that assumes there are a set of 'correct' **linguistic rules** that English should follow (see p.24).

1)   Although **grammar books** had existed since the 16th century, they became really **popular** in the **18th century**, when they were written to lay down **rules** about language and **prescribe** the **correct usage**.

2)   For example, a rule that's still taught today is that *whom* should be used when *who* is the **object** of the sentence:

'Incorrect'	'Correct'
Who did you see today?	**Whom** did you see today?

3)   18th century **grammarians** were also **proscriptivists** — they outlined rules on the types of language people **shouldn't** use (while **prescriptivism** involves stating what types of language people **should** use). For example, one **proscriptive rule** states that sentences **shouldn't end** with a **preposition**, e.g. the sentence *where do you come <u>from</u>?* should be *<u>from</u> where do you come?*

4)   A lot of these rules were **invented** by 18th century grammarians like **Robert Lowth** (see p.24). Some were imposed on English from **Latin** or **Ancient Greek**, because these were seen as **superior languages** — they weren't spoken any more, so they couldn't 'decay' like English could (see p.24).

The first Dictionaries *had a strong influence on* Standardising Spelling

One of the most important publications in the history of the English language was Samuel Johnson's *A Dictionary of the English Language (1755)*, which contained about 40,000 words.

1)   **Johnson's** *Dictionary* laid down rules for the **spelling** and **meanings** of words. He stated that his **aim** was to **tame** the language because he felt that it was **out of control**, despite also saying that he wanted 'not to **form**, but **register**' the language.

2)   The dictionary was so important because it helped **standardise spelling and meaning**. If someone needed to know the meaning of a word or how to spell it, the dictionary could be used as a standard **reference point**.

Grammatical Change *was* Gradual *and* Subtle

1)   In Early Modern English, different **second person pronouns** were used depending on a person's status. *You* was used to address someone of a **higher social rank**, and *thou* was used for someone of **lower rank** (see p.13).

2)   In a process that started in EME, the auxiliary *do* took the place of **verb-subject inversions** in interrogatives, e.g. we now say *what do you know?* instead of *what know you?*

Syntax has gradually become **less complex**. Modern writers tend to avoid very long sentences with **multiple subordinate clauses**, like in this example from *Barnaby Rudge* (1841), by Charles Dickens:

> Indeed, the bird himself appeared to know his value well; for though he was perfectly free and unrestrained in the presence of Barnaby and his mother, he maintained in public an amazing gravity, and never stooped to any other gratuitous performances than biting the ankles of vagabond boys (an exercise in which he much delighted), killing a fowl or two occasionally, and swallowing the dinners of various neighbouring dogs, of whom the boldest held him in great awe and dread.

This sentence is **long** and **complex**. It contains several clauses — there are six **commas**, a **semi-colon** and a set of **parentheses** (brackets). Using **less complex** punctuation, the text can be split into **3 simpler sentences**.

This is what a more **modern version** might look like:

> Indeed the bird himself appeared to know his value well. Though he was perfectly free and unrestrained in the presence of Barnaby and his mother, he maintained in public an amazing gravity. He never stooped to any other gratuitous performances than biting the ankles of vagabond boys (an exercise in which he much delighted), killing a fowl or two occasionally, and swallowing the dinners of various neighbouring dogs, of whom the boldest held him in great awe and dread.

Late Modern English

The **Vocabulary** of English continued to **Grow**

1) The expansion of the **British Empire** brought new words into English from the countries that came under British rule. For example, the following words came from **India**: *bangle* (1787), *dinghy* (1810) and *thug* (1810).

2) During the Late Modern period, advances in **science** and **medicine** led to the invention of new words like: *centigrade* (1812), *biology* (1819), *laryngitis* (1822), *antibiotic* (1894), *chemotherapy* (1907), *penicillin* (1929), *quark* (1964) and *bulimia* (1976).

3) **New inventions** brought more **new words and phrases** into the dictionary such as *typewriter* (1868), *motor car* (1895), *radio* (1907), *video game* (1973) and *podcasting* (2008).

4) **Social**, **cultural** and **political developments** have contributed to the **lexis** (vocabulary), e.g. *hippie* (1965), *airhead* (1972), *grunge* (1980s), and *credit crunch* (2000s).

5) New words also emerged through **international conflict** and **war** — *Blighty* (to refer to Britain, 1914-18), *blitz* (1939), and *kamikaze* (1945).

Accents and **Dialects** changed in the **Twentieth Century**

Improved **communication** and increased **mobility** in the Late Modern period meant that people were exposed to a **wide range** of accents and dialects for the **first time**.

COMMUNICATION

- Radio, films and television have affected regional pronunciation.

- For example, **Estuary English** (see p.15) is a relatively new accent that is **spreading**, partly because it's used by a lot of people on **TV** and the **radio**. It originated in south-east England and London, but some people think it's **influenced speakers** as far away as Glasgow and Manchester.

- **International** soap operas (e.g. Neighbours) may have affected **younger speakers'** accents, too.

- Inventions like the **telephone** have meant that people from **different regions** can communicate much more easily.

Misinterpreting "Push here for change",
Jim imprisoned six innocent people.

MOBILITY

- The invention of the **railway** and **cars** meant that people began to **travel** more around Britain. This means that **regional dialects** aren't as **self-contained**, so they're becoming '**diluted**'.

- **Very strong accents** have tended to get **softer**, so people from different regions can understand each other better than they could.

- **International travel** has also affected English. **Non-native** speakers from different countries use Standard English or American English to **communicate** with each other and with **native** English speakers (see p.20-21).

Practice Questions

Q1 What influence did Johnson's dictionary have on spelling?

Q2 Give three examples of how grammar changed in the Late Modern period.

Q3 How has punctuation become simpler compared to the early nineteenth century?

Q4 Which factors contributed to the expansion of vocabulary during the Late Modern period? Give examples.

Q5 Explain why regional accents and dialects began to change during the Late Modern period.

Essay Question

Q1 Discuss how advances in transport, technology, science and medicine affected English in the Late Modern Period.

Prescriptive English — for standard eyes only...

You might remember a Blackadder episode where Johnson turns up with his dictionary. You might also remember Blackadder throwing in some words like 'pericombobulation', as if they were real words that Johnson had overlooked. Think that's funny? Just imagine what a pain it would be if you'd spent years on the dictionary only to find you'd forgotten to include "knitting".

Lexical Change

For AQA A, AQA B, WJEC and Edexcel. These pages are all about how the words we use change over time. You might have noticed that yourself — if you started this book saying 'I will revise,' I bet it's now changed to 'I can't be bothered...'

New Words have been created throughout History

New words are **always** being **created**.

1) For example, people think that Shakespeare invented over **1700 words**, some of which are still used today, including *assassination*, *courtship* and *submerged*.

2) In recent years the following new words have been accepted into the Oxford English Dictionary: *fashionista*, *wussy* and *twonk* (a stupid or foolish person).

3) The **creation** of new words is known as **coinage** and the new words themselves are called **neologisms**.

Hank didn't know it, but he was seconds away from coining 'flame-grilled steak'.

New Words are Created in Different Ways

There are many **different ways** of forming new words. Here are some of the methods:

Borrowing	A simple way to create new words is to 'borrow' a word from **another language**. Many of the words used frequently in everyday language are **borrowings** or **loan words**. For example, *barbecue* comes from **Spanish**, *bungalow* comes from **Hindustani** and *robot* comes from **Czech**. A lot of borrowings relate to **food** or **objects** not traditionally found in the UK, e.g. *spaghetti* from **Italian**.
Scientific Progress	Advances in **medicine**, **science** and **technology** cause new words and phrases to be invented. For example, *in vitro fertilisation* is a term that emerged in the **1970s**.
Affixation	Words can also be created by **affixation**, where **new prefixes** or **suffixes** are added to existing words. Many words in the English language have been created by adding **Latin** or **Greek prefixes** or **suffixes**. For example, the **Greek** word *hyper* is found in the words *hyperactive*, *hypersensitive* and *hypertension*.
Compounding	Sometimes a new word is created by **combining** two separate words to create one word. This is known as **compounding**. For example, *thumb* can be **combined** with *print* to create *thumbprint* and *hand* can be combined with *bag* to create *handbag*.
Blending	**Blending** is when two separate words are actually **merged together**. For example, *netiquette* is a **blend** of *net* and *etiquette*. Similarly, *infotainment* is a blend of *information* and *entertainment* and *satnav* is a blend of *satellite* and *navigation*.
Conversion	New words are also created when an existing word **changes class**. This is known as **conversion**. For example, many words that started off as **nouns** are now also used as **verbs**: *text/to text*, *chair/to chair* (a meeting), *mail/to mail*. Note that the word **doesn't** change its **form** (it looks the same), only its **function** (it does a different job).

New Words can also be created by Different Forms of Shortening

1) **Clipping** — this is when you drop one or more syllables to create an **abbreviation**. For example, *demo* is often used rather than *demonstration* and, more recently, *rents* rather than *parents*. Abbreviations are a common form of **word creation**.

2) **Initialism** — this is where the **first letter** of a word **stands for** the word itself. For example, *FBI* takes the first letters of the words in *Federal Bureau of Investigation*, *OTT* takes the first letters of *over the top*, and *FYI* takes the first letters of *for your information*. **Initialisms** are always pronounced **letter by letter**.

3) **Acronyms** — **initial letters** of words also **combine** to **create** a completely **new word**. For example, *NASA* stands for *National Aeronautics and Space Administration* and is pronounced as a word in itself rather than letter by letter. The acronym *WAGS* refers to the **wives and girlfriends** of footballers.

4) **Back-formation** — this is a **less frequent** form of word creation. It occurs when a word looks like it has been created by adding a **suffix** to an existing word, but actually, the suffix has been **removed** to create the new term. For example, the noun *baby-sitter* came **before** the verb *baby-sit*, *word-processor* came before *word-process*, *burglar* came before *burgle*, and the verb *enthuse* is a back-formation of *enthusiasm*.

Lexical Change

Many **New Words** come from the **Names** of **People**, **Places** or **Things**

1) **Words** can also be **derived** from people's **names**. Words that develop in this way are known as **eponyms**. For example, the word *nicotine* comes from **Jean Nicot**, a French ambassador to Portugal in the sixteenth century who sent **tobacco seeds** back to France.

2) **Brand names** are a source of new words too. Two examples (both taken from American English) might be asking for something to be *Xeroxed* rather than *photocopied* or asking for a *Kleenex®* rather than a *tissue*.

3) Sometimes words are derived from a particular **place**. For example the word *limousine* derives from **Limousin** (a French province). This came about because the car designers thought the shape of the driver's compartment was **similar** to the kind of hoods historically worn by shepherds in that area.

Words can Disappear

"No, grandpa, I'm not courting. I'm just using him for his private jet..."

1) Just as new words enter the language, old words **disappear**. Words that have become **obsolete** (are no longer used) are known as **archaisms**. For example, these words aren't used any more in modern English: *durst* (dare), *trow* (think).

2) Other words might still be used, but have fallen out of fashion, e.g. *courting* (dating), *wireless* (radio).

English Spelling hasn't always been fixed either

The English spelling system (its **orthography**) is notoriously complicated and is actually quite random — although you might expect this from a language that has borrowed words from almost everywhere.

The letters *-ough* are probably the most famous example of a segment that can represent a lot of **different sounds** in spoken English. The spelling of words with *ough* originated in **Middle English**, but probably sounded something like the *-och* part of *loch*. Here are a few **variations**:

through (an 'oo' sound)	*though* (an 'oh' sound)	*tough* ('uff')
cough ('off')	*plough* ('ow')	*hiccough* ('up')

One reason for **idiosyncrasies** like this is that changes in **pronunciation** occurred **during** and **after** standardisation of the system. This meant sounds were lost from spoken English, while their **original historic spellings remained** in written English.

Practice Questions

Q1 What is a neologism? Suggest three ways they can be formed.

Q2 What is the difference between an acronym and an abbreviation?

Q3 What is orthography?

Essay Question

Q1 Describe the ways in which different forms of shortening can be used to create new words.

All this cramulation is shoodling my thoughtbox...

Personally, I can't think of a Shakespeare play that takes place under water, but he must have had a reason for inventing the word 'submerged.' Maybe Juliet drowned in the first draft of R&J — he was probably right to scrap that idea, bit tacky, don't you think? Anyway, learn how words come and go over time, and pass me the wireless from betwixt those knaves yon

SECTION ONE — LANGUAGE CHA

Semantic Change

For AQA A, AQA B, WJEC and Edexcel. *Here's an idea — try thinking of this section in life cycle terms. The previous two pages covered the birth and death of words. These pages are about the lucky words that manage to get reincarnated...*

Semantic Change *is when a word's* Meaning Changes

1) Words which **remain** part of a language for many years often **change their meaning** over time. This is known as **semantic change**.

2) Language **changes** all the time without you really noticing, e.g. **metaphors** like *surfing the net* are now used without thinking, as are words like *rip* (to copy from a CD), *burn* (to copy files to a CD) and *cut* (a record).

3) **Slang** and **colloquialisms** give **new meanings** to **established words**. For example, the following words are used to **express approval**: *cool, buzzing, safe, mint*.

A word can Develop *a more* Positive *or* Negative Meaning

Amelioration

1) Amelioration is when a word develops a more **positive meaning**.

2) For example, *nice* used to mean *foolish*. *Tremendous* used to mean *terrible* but is now used to say something is *very good*. *Mischievous* used to mean *disastrous* but now means *playfully malicious*.

Pejoration

1) Pejoration is when a word **develops** a **negative meaning**.

2) For example, *hussy* used to have the same meaning as *housewife* but now refers to *an impudent woman of loose morals*. *Notorious* used to mean *widely known* but has come to be associated with being **well known** for **doing something bad**.

1) Some words change their meaning **altogether**. For example, *tomboy* used to mean a *rude, boisterous boy* but is now only used to refer to girls who act in what is perceived to be a **boyish way**. *Porridge* used to refer to *soup containing meat and vegetables* but now means *cereal made of oatmeal and milk*. *Bimbo* was originally a term for *fellow* or *chap*. It then took on negative connotations and came to mean *stupid man* before eventually being a term aimed **exclusively** at **women**.

2) Sometimes a word ends up making **less** of an **impact** than it used to. This is known as **weakening**. For example, the word *terrible* used to mean *causing terror* but now it's used to say that something is **very bad**. *Glad* used to mean *bright, shining, joyous* but now it means *pleased*.

The Meaning *of a word can get* Broader *or* Narrower

1) A word that has a **specific meaning** can develop a **broader meaning** over time. This process is known as **broadening, generalisation, expansion** or **extension**.

2) For example, the word *bird* used to mean a *young bird* or *fledgling* but now refers to **birds in general**. *Place* used to refer to an *open space in a city, market place, or square* but now means a *portion of space* anywhere. *Arrive* used to be a term that was connected with *landing on shore* after a long voyage. Today, it means to come to the end of any kind of journey, or to **reach a conclusion** (*I have finally <u>arrived</u> at a decision*).

3) A word that has a general meaning can develop a **narrower meaning**. This process is called **narrowing, specialisation** or **restriction**. For example, the word *meat* used to mean *food* in general but now specifically refers to *animal flesh*. *Girl* was a term used to refer to a *young person* generally and *liquor* used to mean *liquid* but now refers to *alcoholic drink* specifically. You still see the old meaning of *liquor* in a cooking context, e.g. you cook something then *pour off the liquor*.

4) Words can go though **multiple semantic changes**, e.g. *silly*:

> **Silly:**   *blessed > innocent > pitiable > weak > foolish*

Who are you calling 'girl'?

Semantic Change

Political Correctness can Cause Semantic Change

1) In the last thirty years, **political correctness** has had a major impact on how language is used. Its purpose has been to **remove** words and phrases that have **negative connotations** from the language.

2) For example, *old people* are referred to as *senior citizens*, and *disabled people* as *people with disabilities*. The term *half-caste* is no longer used for people who are *mixed race*.

3) **Trivialising suffixes** such as *–ess* and *–ette* are **no longer used** in many cases. The word *actor*, for example, now refers to either a **male or female performer** and the word *actress* is gradually becoming **redundant**.

4) Many people feel these types of **semantic change** are **positive** and that they remove negative connotations from the language. However, some people feel it's gone a bit too far when the changes begin to **obscure meaning**, e.g. using the job title *sanitation consultant* instead of *toilet cleaner*.

Figurative Expressions give New Meanings to Old Words

METAPHOR

1) Metaphors describe things as if they were actually **something else**.

2) For example, the following phrases were originally associated with the sea, but are now used metaphorically: *plain sailing*, *high and dry*, *clear the decks*.

METONYMY

1) Metonymy is when we use a word **associated** with an **object** instead of the object itself.

2) For example, *cash* used to mean *money box* but over time it came to mean the **money itself**.

IDIOM

1) Idioms are **sayings** that don't make sense if you **literally interpret** the meanings of the words.

2) E.g. you **can't tell** from the words alone that *it's raining cats and dogs* means *it's raining very heavily*.

3) Idioms **don't appear** out of **nowhere**. They usually have some **factual**, **literary** or **historical** basis.

4) For example, the expression *to have a chip on your shoulder* comes from nineteenth century America. A young man would challenge others to a fight by inviting them to knock a wood-chip off his shoulder.

EUPHEMISM

1) Euphemism is the use of **alternative** words or phrases to **avoid offending** someone or to make something **appear less unpleasant**.

2) E.g. there are lots of euphemisms for **death**, like *kicking the bucket*, *pushing up daisies*, or *popping your clogs*.

CLICHÉ

1) If idioms are used a lot, they may become **clichés** — **overused phrases** which fail to excite the imagination.

2) The **business world** has many **clichés**, such as *pushing the envelope* and *blue-sky thinking*.

Practice Questions

Q1 Explain the terms amelioration, pejoration and weakening, giving an example for each one.

Q2 What do narrowing and broadening mean?

Q3 How do metaphor, metonymy and euphemism contribute to semantic change?

Essay Question

Q1 Giving examples, discuss the impact that political correctness has had on semantic change.

Where do words go if they want to get narrower? Word Watchers...

It's all fun and games, this, isn't it? If you don't know what kind of figurative expression that last sentence is, go back and read these two pages all over again. Twice. As for me, I'm off to invent myself a new job title. Maybe I could be a 'Learning Aid Perfectioning Operative,' a 'Revision Expert' or, as someone has just kindly suggested, an 'office monkey.' Nice.

Grammatical Change

AQA A, AQA B, WJEC and Edexcel. Just as you thought it was safe to head off to the 'Land of a Thousand Euphemisms' after p.11, here's some grammar to tug irritatingly on your trouser leg and remind you it's not all a walk in the park.

There used to be **Loads** of **Inflections** in English

Inflections are **affixes** (prefixes or suffixes) which give **extra information** about the **base** word they're attached to. Inflections can indicate **number**, **tense**, **person** or **mood**, but a lot of them aren't used anymore.

1) **Present Day English** (**PDE**) contains some inflections, but there used to be a lot more in Old English (450–1150).

2) Most of these inflections had disappeared by the end of the **Middle English period** (1450):

Nouns — For example, in **Old English** you'd form the plural of *stan* (stone) by adding the inflection *-as*, *-a*, or *-um*, depending on its **function** in the sentence. These inflections have been **lost** in **Present Day English** — all regular **plurals** are now formed by adding the inflection *-s*.

Verbs — During the **Early Modern** period (1450–1700), the *-est* and *-eth* inflections on verbs were still used, e.g. *sittest* (second person singular form of *sit*) and *sitteth* (third person singular).

However, this usage **quickly faded**. The third person *-s* inflection found its way into the language through **Scandinavian settlers** in the north of England, and gradually spread southwards. The old Anglo-Saxon *-eth* inflection was **replaced** by an *-s* so *sitteth* became *sits*. This form is the one that survived into PDE.

Adjectives — Adjectives didn't escape the loss of inflections either. **Comparative** and **superlative** inflections (i.e. *greater* and *greatest*) exist in PDE as they did before, but the form of **some adjectives** has changed. In the **nineteenth century**, the superlative *properest* was **grammatically acceptable**, but in PDE it isn't — it's *most proper* instead. The two ways of forming superlatives **aren't combined** in PDE either — you don't say *most cleverest* for example, although **Shakespeare** used constructions like *the most unkindest cut of all* (in *Julius Caesar*).

There are **Reasons** why **Inflections Disappeared**

1) Inflections were often **unstressed** when they were pronounced, so they were **less obvious** in spoken English — and when they stopped being **pronounced** they stopped being **written**.

2) The system of inflections was **pretty complicated**, so moving to a **simpler** system could have just been a **natural development**.

3) **Different dialects** (see p.2-3) used **different inflections**, so the loss of inflections made it **easier** for people from **different areas** to **understand** each other.

The **Loss** of **Inflections** changed how the language was **Constructed**

WORD ORDER
- In Old English, it was possible to have **different** subject, verb and object word orders. The **inflections** on each component would show **who was doing what**.
- In PDE there's a fairly rigid **subject-verb-object** (S-V-O) order. If the word order was **changed** this sentence wouldn't make sense:

S	V	O
[The girl]	[kicked]	[the stone]

INCREASED USE OF AUXILIARY VERBS
- Increased use of auxiliary verbs like *do*, *have*, *be* (see p.114), in the **Early Modern** period also affected word order.
- For example, questions used to be formed with the **verb** at the **start**:

V	S	O
[Spake]	[you] with	[him]?

- In PDE, the **subject and verb** are **inverted** from the old construction to S-V-O. Auxiliary verbs like *do* are now used at the **start** of the question, e.g. *Did you speak to him?* **Questions** are also often formed with *wh*-words (see p.121).

NEGATIVE CONSTRUCTIONS
- In PDE, the negative *not* is placed **before** the verb rather than after it.
- Phrases like *I do not deny it* or *I don't deny it* **gradually replaced** the older constructions like *I deny it not*.

Grammatical Change

The use of Second Person Pronouns became simpler too

Using *you* as we do now wasn't common until the **sixteenth century** (in the EME period).

1) The **earliest forms** of the second person pronoun were *thou* and *thee*.

2) The huge influence of **French** on English meant that the next development reflected French forms. In French, *tu* is an **informal** form of *you*, while *vous* is the **polite, formal equivalent**.

3) **Thirteenth century English** reflected this by using the **old singular forms** *thou, thee* and *thy* to address people of a **similar** or **lower social standing**. The plural forms *ye, your* and *you* were used **respectfully** to address people who were **higher status** than the speaker.

4) In the EME period the old singular forms **fell out of use** and the more respectful *ye, your* and *you* became **the standard**. *Ye* then also disappeared, so now only *you* and *your* are used.

EME = Early Modern English

Ted was right to look worried. It was the second person pronoun he'd lost that week.

Double Negatives used to be Common in English too

1) Today, double negatives such as *I don't want nothing* are considered **non-standard**.

2) In **Middle English**, double negatives were used to give **emphasis** to a statement. For example in the 14th century, **Chaucer** wrote *Ther nas <u>no</u> man <u>nowher</u> so vertuous*.

3) The authors of 18th century **prescriptive grammar books**, trying to standardise English (p.6), decided that double negatives were 'incorrect' and shouldn't be used.

4) Robert Lowth's ***A Short Introduction to English Grammar (1762)*** was very influential (see p.24). He used **mathematical logic** to make the case that double negatives weren't acceptable: *"Two negatives in English destroy one another, or are equivalent to an affirmative,"* i.e. two negatives make a positive.

The Function of Words can change over time

1) As people use more and more **new technology** like mobile phones and the Internet, the **function** of the words associated with it has changed — **nouns** like *text, email* and *Facebook®* have become **verbs**.

2) In **Standard English**, the **adverb** *well* is used with **past participles**, e.g. *the meal was <u>well</u> cooked*. In contemporary English it's also common to see *well* as an intensifying adverb before an **adjective**, e.g. *that was <u>well</u> good*.

3) *Innit* used to be a shortened version of the **tag question** *isn't it?* In **urban slang** it's become interchangeable with a **variety** of other tag questions too, e.g. *we can do that tomorrow <u>innit</u>?* where *innit* means *can't we?*

4) In the 1990s the **intensifying adverb** *so* started to be used with not, e.g. *I'm <u>so</u> not ready for this*.

Practice Questions

Q1 Outline an example of the loss of inflections in English.

Q2 How has word order changed in negatives and questions since the Middle English period?

Q3 Give three examples of grammatical change since 1900.

Essay Question

Q1 Describe the main features of grammatical change in English since the Middle English period.

I've just had the most horrible cold — it was a superlative infection...

You'd think that the fact that grammar is constantly changing would make it a bit more exciting. Poof! That was an inflection vanishing. Bang! There goes another second person pronoun, lost forever in the depths of time. It promises so much, and yet in reality it's about as interesting as fourteen rice cakes and a kilogram of houmous. Tastier, but no more inspiring.

Phonological Change

For AQA A, AQA B, WJEC and Edexcel. Phonology is the study of sounds in a language. Phonological changes affect the pronunciation of individual sounds, as well as how certain sounds are acquired or lost over time.

Pronunciation is Always Changing

1) The most **significant shift** in pronunciation occurred between 1400 and 1600. During this period the **long vowels** of Middle English changed a lot. This transition is called the **Great Vowel Shift** (see p.5).

2) Between **1700** and **1900**, following the **GVS**, the long *a* vowel sound in words such as *path* (pronounced *parth*) came to be used in **southern parts** of Britain. Before this it would have been pronounced in its **shorter form**, as it is in **Northern** and **Midlands** accents.

3) In Present Day English (**PDE**), the **schwa** ([ ]), is a **generic vowel sound** we use instead of **fully pronouncing** the vowel. It's become more common in **everyday speech** than it used to be, even in **RP** (Received Pronunciation, see p. 33).
For example, we tend to say *uhbout* rather than **a**-bout, and *balunce* rather than *bala*nce.

4) **Consonants** have also changed. For example, before the nineteenth century, -*ing* was generally pronounced *in*, (as it is in many regional accents today), even by the **middle** and **upper** classes.

5) Today, some speakers **replace** the *th* sound with *f* (saying *fink* rather than *think*, or *vem* rather than *them*). This is a feature of **Estuary English** (see p.15) called **th-fronting**.

Intonation Patterns have also changed over time

1) A specific change in intonation since the early 1990s is **uptalk** or **upspeak**. Usually, intonation **rises** when people ask a question. With uptalk, intonation rises when you're **making a statement**.

2) The following sentences demonstrate how uptalk might come across in conversation:

> I was going to town? And I saw this man? He was acting really strange? Then he came up to me? Asked me for a cigarette?

3) At first uptalk was a feature of **teenage speech**, but it's now found in a **wider range** of age groups.

4) One theory is that it's been picked up from **Australian intonation patterns** that are heard in soaps like *Neighbours* and *Home and Away*.

5) There are different theories about people's **reasons** for using it. Some linguists say it's used because speakers don't want to sound **aggressive** or too sure of themselves. Others claim that it's only used when speakers are telling someone **new information**.

Pronunciation changes for Lots of Reasons

1) **Social factors** can affect pronunciation — people often change the way they talk depending on the **context** and who they're talking to.

2) Your pronunciation probably changes when you're being formally **interviewed**, compared to when you're talking with **friends**, e.g. you might be more **careful** about pronouncing *h*s in words like *how* and *have*. This is known as **upward convergence** — making everyday language sound closer to **RP**:

> A study in Norwich by **Trudgill (1983)** showed that women were more likely to speak closer to RP when they knew their language was being observed.

3) **Other languages** can have an impact on pronunciation — e.g. in Old English the stress was usually on the **initial syllable** of a word. The **French** words that became part of the language had a different **stress pattern**.

4) **American English** has also affected British English pronunciation. For example, the traditional British English pronunciation of *harass* stresses the **first syllable** (*harass*), but in PDE people might stress the **second syllable** (*harass*), as in American English.

5) The **media** can influence pronunciation. The BBC has a **Pronunciation Unit** which guides broadcasters on how to pronounce words. This is to make sure that the presenters are **consistent**, but **viewers** then often **copy** the pronunciation of **unfamiliar** or **foreign** words, and they become seen as the **standard** pronunciation.

6) **Aitchison (1991)** suggests that phonological change is a **process**. First, the accent of one group differs from that of another. The second group is **influenced** by the pronunciation of the first group, a **new accent** emerges and the process continues.

Phonological Change

Received Pronunciation *has changed significantly*

1) **Received Pronunciation (RP)** was seen as the standard English accent and is sometimes called the **Queen's** English. It's a **prestige** accent — it's associated with a good standing in **society** and with being **well-educated** (see p.33).

2) The emergence of RP in the **twentieth century** also caused **regional accents** to be seen as socially inferior.

3) RP was adopted as the **official accent of the BBC** in 1922, because they thought it was the accent that everyone would be able to **understand**. This added to its **prestige value** — as all the news and public broadcasts were in RP, it became the accent of **authority**. This is why RP is also sometimes called **BBC English**.

Stephen only bought the book so Maureen would stop RPing on about her crossword.

4) From the late **1950s onwards**, RP changed quite significantly. For example, in RP before the 1960s the word *hand* was pronounced more like *hend*, *often* was pronounced more like *awften* and *tissue* was pronounced as *tisyu*.

5) In the 1960s, with **working-class** teenagers going to **university** in larger numbers and the emergence of **celebrities** who spoke with **regional accents**, RP lost some of its desirability. Emerging pop stars, actors and artists had regional accents (e.g. Paul McCartney, Mick Jagger), and young speakers wanted to **imitate** them.

6) Today, RP has been **toned down** and is rarely heard. For example, broadcasters will use **Standard English** when they are speaking, but might have a **regional accent** rather than RP.

New Accents *have emerged*

Nowadays very **few** people actually use **RP** in its 'original' form. Even the Queen's accent has changed a bit from when she was first crowned over 50 years ago.

Estuary English

1) Some linguists claim that **RP** is being replaced as the most 'acceptable' English accent by **Estuary English**. This is an **accent** that has roots in the speech found around the **Thames Estuary** area in **London**.

2) It contains many similar features to the **Cockney** accent, e.g. dropping *h*s at the beginning of words (pronouncing *hit* like *it*), and pronouncing *th* like *f* (so *tooth* becomes *toof*). For example, estuary speakers will use a **glottal stop** instead of *t*, so *bottle* is pronounced *bo-ul*. They'll pronounce *tune* as *choon* rather than *tyune*, *wall* as *waw* and *north* as *norf*.

3) It's used by a lot of people in the **entertainment industry**, as it's seen as a **commercially acceptable** accent.

4) Because of the **influence** of the **media**, Estuary English is becoming quite common **outside** London. You can't necessarily tell where someone's from if they use Estuary English — it's become a **widespread accent**, probably a result of people **copying** the speech of **radio** and **TV presenters**.

Practice Questions

Q1 What is the *schwa*? Give an example of when it's heard.

Q2 What is Received Pronunciation?

Q3 What is Estuary English? Give three examples of how an Estuary English speaker's pronunciation would differ from that of an RP speaker.

Essay Question

Q1 Discuss some of the reasons why English pronunciation has changed.

So there are vese free pieces of string, right...

And they're trying to get into a bar. But the door policy is 'strictly no pieces of string allowed'. So one piece of string says to his mates, "Leave this to me lads, I'll get us in". He folds his arms, ruffles up his hair and walks to the door. The bouncers see him and ask, "Hang on, aren't you a piece of string?" And he says, "No, I'm a frayed knot." Phonology — always hilarious.

Graphological Change

For AQA B, WJEC and Edexcel. Graphology involves looking at things like layout, typeface (what you'd normally call 'font') and handwriting. It's about how the visual features of a text can have an impact on the overall meaning.

The way that Letters are Formed Changes over Time

Texts written hundreds of years ago look very **different** from modern day texts. This is partly because the way that some of the **letters** are written has changed.

1) The letter *u* only appeared in the **tenth century**. Before then, the letter *v* was used as a **vowel** and a **consonant**, e.g. the word *dough* would have been spelt *dovgh*. Then both letters were used as vowels **interchangeably** until *u* was established as a **vowel** and *v* was established as a **consonant** during the late **17th century**.

2) The letter *j* appeared in the **fifteenth century**. Before then, *i* was used as a **vowel** and a **consonant**, e.g. *justice* would have been written *iustice*. You might still see an *i* instead of a *j* in texts up until the **mid-17th century**.

3) From the **17th century** onwards the letter *s* was often written as *ſ* (like an *f* without the cross-bar), e.g. *ſit* instead of *sit*. This was based on the **handwriting style** of the period, and it appeared like this in **printed texts** until the early **19th century**. It wasn't written as *ſ* if it was at the end of a word though, and was often written alongside an *s* if a word contained a double *s*, e.g. *claſses*.

1) Up to the middle of the twentieth century, **serif** typefaces were usually used. They have a fine 'stroke' attached to the tops and bottoms of letters.

2) From the mid-twentieth century onwards **sans-serif typefaces** (ones **without serifs**) became fashionable.

3) Typefaces with serifs tend to seem **traditional**, while sans-serif typefaces look more **modern**.

A — serif

A — sans-serif

4) Modern **printed material** has a wider range of typefaces than in the past. Print advertising, newspapers, leaflets, posters, and books will use different fonts for **different purposes**.

5) For example, *The Sun* newspaper mainly uses a **sans-serif** typeface for **headlines**, and **serif** typefaces for **articles**. It also uses a wide **variety** of **typefaces** in the headlines on its entertainment and gossip pages to attract attention and make the pages **visually stimulating**.

Newspaper Layout has Changed

Newspaper designs have **changed** a lot in the last 100 years.

1909 newspaper

- The **leading** (line spacing) is very **dense**.
- The **text** is **small**.
- There are no **photos** or **illustrations**.
- It's all **black and white**.

2009 newspaper

- The **leading** is quite **wide**, so the text isn't very dense.
- There's a range of **colour**, including **colour photos**.
- There's **non-standard typography** (e.g. lower case name).
- There's **information** about what's **inside** the newspaper.

Graphological Change

Magazine Layout has also Changed

1) Modern magazines are very different from those of the eighteenth century.

2) In the past, the front page of a men's magazine, e.g. **The Gentleman's Magazine (1736)**, consisted of a **decorative illustration** at the top of the page, a title and then two **dense** blocks of print, black on white.

3) In contrast, the cover of a **modern** men's magazine such as *FHM* has a full page **glossy photograph** in the background. This is **overlaid** with print, indicating the main features to be found inside the magazine. The print has different **font types**, **colours**, and some of the text is presented in unconventional angles and styles.

The editors were less than impressed with Paul's choice of 'long legged stunner'.

The graphology of Modern Books is Varied

1) The earliest books often had **two columns** to a page, justified text and large margins for making notes. Modern books, like novels and textbooks, tend to have **one column** of print.

2) However, modern books can show a great deal of **variety** in terms of **layout**, **typeface** and **colour**. Non-fiction books in particular often show a lot of **innovation** and **creativity** with **colour** and **graphics**.

3) In children's books you might see blocks of print at **unusual angles**, and different **shapes** of text boxes (e.g. circles or speech bubbles). There's often a variety of **font colours** and **background colours**, and sometimes text **superimposed** on **background images**.

Electronic Media has changed the appearance of Written Communication

1) **Electronic media** allows writers and publishers to be more **creative** with graphology.

2) Web developers can use different **layouts**, **typefaces** and **colours** without having to think about printing costs. Web pages tend to contain **small chunks** of text broken up with **headings**, **subheadings** and **links** because this is **easier to read** on screen.

3) Web pages can also incorporate **animated text** and **images**. **Audio** is also used as part of **interactive videos**, **games** and **adverts**.

4) **Word-processing software** has given ordinary people access to loads of different **typefaces** and styles. You can **choose** which style to use depending on the **purpose** of the writing, for example:

This is Times New Roman PS   This is Litterbox ICG

5) You'd use these typefaces to create **different effects**. For example, you might use Times New Roman PS if you were writing a serious newspaper article, and Litterbox ICG in a text for children.

6) **Mobile phones** have also had an impact on **graphology**. People can send photos and videos along with small amounts of text, which often contains abbreviations, numbers and emoticons (see p. 82).

Practice Questions

Q1 What is graphology?
Q2 Outline three ways in which the graphology of newspapers has changed over the last 100 years.
Q3 How do books today differ from the first printed books in terms of typeface and layout?

Essay Question

Q1 Describe the impact of electronic media on the graphology of the English language.

Just remember to label your axes...

X and Y — along the corridor and up the stairs. That's pretty much all the maths I remember— something to do with people living in houses made of graphs I think. It all sounds hideously impractical. The squares on that graph paper are too small even for a box room, let alone an open plan kitchen-diner. Still, mathematicians aren't exactly known for their logic, are they...

Causes of Language Change

AQA A, AQA B, WJEC and Edexcel. The last few pages have covered the ways that language can change, but it's never down to just one single reason. These two pages bring all the different causes together, making them 24 carat essay gold.

Language often needs to be **Simplified**

Sometimes language changes because it has become too **complex** to use easily.

1) For example, the complex system of ending many words with **inflections** that was characteristic of **Old English** was gradually lost and replaced with a simpler system (see p.12).

2) Similarly, in Early Modern English, the **second person pronouns** (*thee, thou, thy, ye*) were reduced to just *you* and *your* (see p.13).

> • However, sometimes languages become **more complex**. For example, in Caxton's time, the **punctuation** system consisted of three main punctuation marks (see p.4). By the end of the **seventeenth century**, the range of punctuation that we have today was in use.
>
> • This range of punctuation marks enabled writers to be more **expressive** (using exclamation marks and question marks, for example) and gave them more options when organising their writing.

Phonological Change tends to make **Pronunciation Easier**

Omission and **assimilation** are **trends** of phonological change that make things easier to pronounce.

Omission

1) Omission is when sounds are **lost** from the language. Part of the reason why inflections were lost from Old English was because they weren't **pronounced** with any **stress** or **emphasis**.

2) In Old English the [*l*] sound used to be pronounced in words like *folk*. This was **dropped** in the ME period.

3) More recently (in about the last fifty years), **RP** speakers have dropped the *y* sound in words like *tune*, which used to be pronounced *tyune*. It now sounds more like *choon*.

Assimilation

1) Assimilation is where one sound in a word is affected by an **adjacent sound** to produce a new pronunciation.

2) For example, some people pronounce the word *sandwich* as *samwich*.

3) Assimilation also occurs across **word boundaries**, e.g. *What do you want / whatju want* or *Get it? / geddit?*

Standardisation has caused a lot of **Change**

You might need to talk about language from **different periods** in your answers. If you're writing about how **standardisation** influenced language change, you need to bring together some points from earlier in the section:

SPELLING	1)	The first major development was **Caxton's printing press (1476)** (see p.4). It helped to establish the **East Midlands dialect** as the 'standard', as well as making texts more **readily available** to people.
	2)	It also marked the beginning of the standardisation of **spelling**. Caxton had to choose one of a number of different **dialect spellings**, though he wasn't always **consistent**.
	3)	It wasn't until the eighteenth century that spelling began to look fully standardised. **Johnson's *A Dictionary of the English Language*** (see p.6) laid a firm foundation for the spelling system we have today.
GRAMMAR	1)	People also tried to standardise grammar in the eighteenth century. A number of scholars published books **prescribing** how English should be **constructed**, e.g. **Robert Lowth's *A Short Introduction to English Grammar* (1762)** (see p.24).
	2)	These ideas have influenced what people consider to be 'good' English. This has meant that there's **less variety** in Standard English.
PHONOLOGY	1)	Teaching a standardised form of **pronunciation** was a key feature of private school education. The main person behind this was the actor and educator **Thomas Sheridan** in the **mid-eighteenth century**.
	2)	He believed there was a **correct** way to speak and that this could be acquired through **elocution** lessons.
	3)	Like the other prescriptivists, Sheridan published books, including *A General Dictionary of the English Language* in **1780**, which outlined how to pronounce words 'properly'.

Causes of Language Change

Other Languages have Influenced English language change

A lot of language change has been brought about by the **influence** of **foreign languages**, especially because of **loan words** (**borrowings**). The table below shows just **some** of the languages that have influenced English over the centuries.

Period	Influence	Examples
8th-11th centuries — invasions from other countries.	Scandinavian	*skirt, cog, skip*
	French	*accompany, department, tax*
16th-17th centuries — words brought into English from Latin and Greek by writers.	Latin	*benefit, temperature, the prefixes sub and trans*
	Greek	*catastrophe, pneumonia*, the affixes *auto and pan*
18th-19th centuries — words borrowed from colonised countries during the expansion of the British Empire.	Malay	*amok*
	Hindi	*shampoo*
20th century — immigration to the UK.	Cantonese	*wok*

Language change can be Internal or External

1) **External** language change is a result of **outside influences** on a group of speakers. For example, English has been influenced by things like **invasions**, **immigration** and the **media**.

2) **Internal change** happens because of a need for **simplification** and **ease of articulation**. For example, **Old English inflections** were lost because they weren't pronounced with any stress and gradually became unnecessary.

Technology has influenced language change

1) **Industrialisation** in the eighteenth and nineteenth centuries introduced new words and phrases relating to labour, such as *productivity*, *shift work*, and *clocking-on*.

2) **Scientific advancement**, **new inventions** and **brand names** have resulted in new words entering the language (e.g. *spacesuit, microwave, PC, chatroom, MSN®, email, download, hard drive, web page*).

It took Margaret a while to get the hang of phonetic spelling.

Practice Questions

Q1 Give two examples of how English has become simplified over time.
Q2 Explain the terms omission and assimilation in the context of language change.
Q3 What have been the major factors in the standardisation of English?
Q4 How have new words been brought into the English language?
Q5 What impact have science and technology had on the langauge we use today?

Essay Question

Q1 Describe how standardisation, technology, and the influence of other languages have contributed to language change.

Learning all this stuff might seem like a bit of omission...

But if you like, I'll give you a-ssimilation of how it should be done. See that section on standardisation? Read it. Then cover it up. There are three points on spelling, two on grammar and three on phonology. Write them down... did you get them all right? Excellent. Well done. But 'tis only a fifth of this double page spread, so eyes down and look in for the other four...

World English

For AQA A, AQA B, WJEC, OCR and Edexcel. That'll be all of you then. Which is quite fitting really because these pages are about people from all over the world coming together in the spirit of the English language. Or something like that.

English is a World Language

English is spoken by about a **quarter** of the world's population. The number of **native speakers** is estimated to be between **350 and 400 million**. English is the **dominant** language in **75** countries — it's the language used in their legal and administrative documents.

1) English is so widespread because of Britain's **colonial past**. The **British Empire** used to cover about **25%** of the world (including America, Canada, India and Australia), so English spread to all of these countries.

2) English came to be seen as the language of **international trade** and **business**. It became the **lingua franca** — the language that speakers of different languages often used to communicate with each other.

3) Use of English also spread because of **academic**, **scientific** and **technological advances**. Documents outlining important scientific breakthroughs were often published in **English**, so **foreign scientists** needed to have a good knowledge of the language.

There are lots of International Varieties of English

Some parts of the world that used to be **British colonies** use varieties that differ from Standard English.
Here are a few examples (the **Standard English** equivalent is shown in brackets):

Country	Variations in Lexis	Variations in Grammar
Australia	*cobber* (mate)	Diminutives (shortened nouns), e.g. *arvo* (afternoon), *barbie* (barbecue).
South Africa	*takkies* (trainers)	Object nouns or pronouns omitted, e.g. *I shall have* (I shall have <u>it</u>).
Jamaica	*duppy* (ghost)	Verb 'to be' not used as an auxiliary, e.g. *him nice* (he is nice).
India	*dicky* (boot of a car)	Use of the **present continuous** tense *I am wanting this* (I want this).
Canada	*fire hall* (fire station)	Use of *am* instead of *have*, e.g. *I am finished my drink* (I have finished my drink).

Obviously there are a lot more examples of variation than this, and people's language **differs** within countries depending on their **regional** and **social background**.

Pidgins and Creoles form when Two Languages Meet

1) A **pidgin** is a language that develops so that speakers of **different languages** can communicate. It originally referred to the language that Chinese and English traders used to communicate in the nineteenth century — *pidgin* was how the Chinese traders pronounced *business*.

2) There are **no native speakers** of Pidgin forms of English, because they only develop so that speakers of different languages can understand each other.

3) Features of **Pidgin English** include a **limited vocabulary** (e.g. few function words) and **simplified grammar** (e.g. only one verb form).

4) For example, in **Nigerian Pidgin** (a pidgin form of English spoken in Nigeria), *watin dey happen* means *what is happening*. The **vocabulary** is **simplified** — *dey* is used for *is* and *are*. The **grammar** is also **simplified** — the *ing* inflection isn't used for the present participle verb *happening*.

1) When a pidgin is used as the **main language** in a community, it develops into a **creole**. It has **native speakers** (people who are brought up using it as their first language). The lexis and grammar **expand** to fit the needs of all speakers.

2) **Creoles** have their own **grammatical rules**. For example, in **Jamaican creole**, *mi* is used as a first person pronoun rather than Standard English *I*.

Insert pigeon joke here.

World English

American English is Widely Spoken

1) In the 20th century, **America** developed into a **superpower**. Its **political**, **economic** and **cultural influence** has maintained the importance of **English** as a **world language**.

2) **American English** can be accessed all over the world, especially because of the influence of **music**, **films** and **TV**. **Advertising** means that American **brand names** are **internationally recognised**.

3) **Standard American English** has a few specific lexical, grammatical and orthographical (spelling) differences from **Standard English**. For example:

Lexis	
American	**British**
trash	rubbish
sidewalk	pavement
soccer	football
gas	petrol

American Grammar
- More frequent use of the **subjunctive**, e.g. *I wish I were taller* instead of *I wish I was taller*.
- Omission of *on* in reference to days of the week, e.g. *see you Tuesday* instead of *see you on Tuesday*.
- Noun phrases ordered differently, e.g. *a half hour* instead of *half an hour*.

Orthography	
American	**British**
meter	metre
color	colour
organize	organise
gray	grey

Lots of Non-native speakers Learn English

English as a foreign language

1) Many students in non-English speaking countries learn English at **school** or through **English as a Foreign Language (EFL)** classes.

2) Students are taught different varieties of English. For example, students in many **European** countries are taught **Standard English** and **Received Pronunciation**. However, their English is often influenced by **American** TV and music.

3) In other parts of the world, such as parts of **South America** and **Asia**, people are taught **Standard American English** with a **General American** accent. American English has now overtaken British English as the variety most used by **second language speakers**.

English as a second language

1) Many **immigrants** in English-speaking countries speak English as a **second language**.

2) Their English often contains features of their **first language**. For example, the speech of **Mexican immigrants** in **North America** might contain some **Spanish** pronunciation features. Initial *th* sounds may be pronounced as *d* (*dese* rather than *these*). In terms of grammar, a **Hispanic** speaker might miss out the **third person singular** (*is good to be on time* rather than *it is good to be on time*).

3) People with English as a second language may have learnt English through **formal education**, but much of their language **develops** naturally through **interaction** with **native English speakers**. Speakers often pick up some of the **dialect** features of the region they live in.

Practice Questions

Q1 What's the difference between a pidgin and a creole?

Q2 Outline three differences between Standard American English and Standard English.

Q3 What's the difference between English as a foreign language and English as a second language?

Essay Question

Q1 Discuss the different factors that have helped make English a world language.

ME NO SPEAKY FOREIGN...

Ah, the unending tact of the British tourist. It's amazing how much people understand when you shout very loudly at them. Of course, the people on these pages do actually already speak English, so it's not really an issue... Sorry about that, everything seems to have suddenly got very confusing and painful. How can it still not be the end of this section...

English in the Future

AQA A, AQA B, WJEC, OCR and Edexcel here. *Come inside, and I will reveal the terrifying truth about what English will be like in the future. But first, you must cross my palm with silver... No? Well, it was worth a try I suppose.*

English has an Uncertain Future

1) English has the **fourth highest** number of **native speakers** in the world.

2) More people speak it as a **second language** than any other language, and this number is **growing** all the time.

3) With so many people speaking English, there are **various possibilities** for how the language will change in the **future**.

English might become more Uniform

1) It's necessary for **international trade** to have a **lingua franca** (a language that people from different countries can all understand). English has taken this role.

2) As well as this, some **countries** (such as Nigeria) that weren't originally English-speaking have adopted English as their **official language**. They feel that it's necessary to have a **standardised language** that **everybody** in the country can **understand**. This has happened especially in countries that have a lot of different **tribal languages**.

3) This shows a **trend** towards **uniformity**, and it suggests that eventually other languages may **die out**.

> 1) **American English** may become the **global standard** (the variety of English spoken by everyone in the world). It's already the **dominant** form, and the number of English speakers is **increasing**. People want to learn American English because it's the language of **world trade** and has global **prestige** and **authority**.
>
> 2) American English is also **growing** because of the global presence of American **films**, **music** and **brands**. As more people in less economically developed countries gain access to **TV** and the **internet**, they'll have **more exposure** to American English, so they'll be more likely to use it.
>
> 3) As the **importance** of American English grows, other varieties might **lose status** and gradually die out. This is called **dialect levelling**.
>
> 4) **Differences** between world **varieties** of English are **decreasing**. It's possible that one day this will lead to the emergence of a **World Standard English** — one that becomes the **official international language** of business and takes the place of all other varieties.

Technology might help make English more Uniform

1) English has been established as the language of **scientific** and **technological advancement** for a long time, so it's been an important language for **foreign scientists** and **academics** to learn.

2) The **internet** has spread English even further. It's been estimated that **90%** of computers connected to the internet are in **English-speaking** countries. Because of this, around **80%** of the **information** stored on computers **worldwide** is in **English**.

3) Technology has already had a dramatic impact on English usage (see p.82-83). Computer software usually uses **American spelling**, such as *programs* and *fav*o*rites*. This is helping to establish American English as a **global standard**.

Janet was thrilled. Finally she could combine her two loves — technology and uniforms.

4) Computers are **changing** English in other ways too, for example:

> - **Spell check** programmes mean people don't need to know how to spell unusual words **correctly**. This could lead to less emphasis being put on **teaching spelling** at **school**, because it isn't considered necessary.
> - **Web addresses** don't contain **capital letters**, so they might gradually **die out** in **other written texts**.
> - **Punctuation** isn't needed when you look something up on a **search engine**, so some marks might **die out**.

5) As **internet access** grows around the world, more people will have access to this **electronic variety** of English, so it could end up being the **World Standard English** that everyone uses.

English in the Future

English *might become more* Diverse

1) Another possibility is that different **varieties** of English around the world could develop into **separate languages**, e.g. American English would be completely different from Indian English. This is what happened to **Latin**, which was once spoken across a lot of **Europe**, but then **split** into **romance languages** like **Italian**, **French** and **Spanish**.

2) These separate varieties of English could then become a way of displaying **national identity** and **independence**. People might see it as a way of **rejecting cultural imperialism** from countries like America and Britain.

3) As the varieties became more different from each other, **localised national standard Englishes** might emerge, e.g. a particular form of Indian English. These forms of the standard would then become the **official language** of the country, rather than Standard English or Standard American English.

4) As well as this, **America's** economic, political and cultural **dominance** might be **challenged** by countries like **China** or **India** in the future. If this happens, then American English might not be the most useful or powerful language to learn any more.

Technology *might make* English *more* Diverse

1) English isn't the only language of the internet. As more people in **less economically developed countries** gain **internet access**, English might stop **dominating** the web. As **online translation software** improves, people won't have to be able to speak English to look at British or American websites. As well as this, there are already lots of versions of American and British websites and search engines in **other languages**.

2) Countries like **India** and **China** are likely to have much more of an impact on **science** and **technology** in the future. This could mean that languages like **Mandarin Chinese** become more important to learn than English.

If you're writing an essay about the impact of technology on the future of English, you can make it more balanced by discussing both the arguments for technology making English more diverse, and the arguments for technology making English more uniform on p. 22.

Bidialectism *means speaking* Two Dialects

1) Another thing that could happen in the future is that people will be able to **switch** from one **dialect** of English to the **standard**, depending on the **context** and **purpose**. Switching between two dialects is **bidialectism**.

2) This scenario imagines the possibility that **standard** forms of English will become more **uniform**, while **regional** and **social** varieties will become more **diverse**. People will have to learn the **standard** form for **formal** situations and for communicating with people from **other countries**.

3) This is **already happening** to a certain extent. For example, a Nigerian business executive might use a **regional** form of Nigerian English when speaking **informally** with **local** customers, but use a more standard English or American form with **international** customers.

Practice Questions

Q1 What is a lingua franca?
Q2 What factors might help American English become the global standard?
Q3 How might the internet lead to greater uniformity in English?
Q4 How might the internet lead to greater diversity in English?
Q5 What is bidialectism?

Essay Question

Q1 'The strength of English as a world language is set to grow and grow.' How far do you agree with this statement?

In the future we won't need English — we'll just read each other's minds...

Oh, English. Just like Pocahontas, you must choose your path. One may be steady, like the river. The other may be rapid and exciting, like the river... This isn't really working out. Perhaps Pocahontas wasn't the best comparison to use. Basically what I'm trying to say is that no one knows where English is going in the future, so just learn the different arguments and move on.

Attitudes Towards Language Change

This is for everyone. If there's one subject that's likely to cause a row down at the annual linguists' convention then it's language change. More people have got more bees in more bonnets over this than anything else. Time to get stuck in...

Attitudes towards Language Change can be Prescriptivist or Descriptivist

There are **two** main approaches to language change:

Prescriptivism

1) Prescriptivism involves stating a **set** of **rules** that people should follow in order to use language '**properly**' (**prescribing** what the language **should be like**).

2) Prescriptivists believe that language should be **written** and **spoken** in a certain way — in English this means using **Standard English** and **RP** (see p.32-33). Other **varieties** of English are seen as **incorrect** and **inferior**.

3) Prescriptivists argue that it's **essential** to stick to the rules of the **standard** form, so that everyone can **understand** each other.

4) The prescriptivist view is that language **decays** as it **changes**, and the only way to stop **standards falling** further is to try and **stop linguistic change**.

Descriptivism

1) Descriptivism involves **describing** how language is actually **used**.

2) Descriptivists **don't** say that aspects of language are '**correct**' or '**incorrect**'. They believe that different **varieties** of English should all be **valued equally**.

3) The idea is that language **change** is **inevitable**, so it's a **waste of time** to try and **stop** it. Instead, descriptivists record **how** and **why** change occurs, rather than assuming all change is bad.

4) Some descriptivists see **language change** as **progress** — they believe that English is becoming more **accurate** and **efficient**. E.g. they'd say that Old English inflections were lost because they no longer served a purpose.

5) Other descriptivists, like **David Crystal**, argue that language change is **neither** progress nor decay, as all languages **change** in **different** ways (e.g. some languages gain inflections).

Prescriptivist Attitudes have been around for a Long Time

1) In the second half of the eighteenth century there was a sudden flourishing of **grammar books** that outlined what the **rules** of grammar should be. The most influential was Robert Lowth's *A Short Introduction to English Grammar (1762)*. He argued that some constructions were grammatically **wrong**, e.g. split infinitives:

> **THE SPLIT INFINITIVE**
> * The infinitive (*to + verb*) should not be split by an **adverb**. The most famous example is *to boldly go*, from *STAR TREK™*.
> * Lowth argued that the construction *to + verb* is a **complete grammatical unit** and that's how it should remain.
> * However, the **meaning** isn't affected whether you say *to boldly go* or *to go boldly*, so **descriptivists** would argue that it's a **pointless** rule.

He was going to split an awful lot more than an infinitive if he didn't get up quick-smart.

2) Other prescriptivist texts have been more flexible about certain grammar rules, e.g. Henry Fowler's *A Dictionary of Modern English Usage (1926)*. Fowler argued against some of Lowth's rules, because he thought that constructions should be used if they **sounded comfortable**, e.g. ending a sentence with a preposition:

| Fowler would argue that: | *That depends on what they are hit <u>with</u>* |
| Sounds much better than: | *That depends on <u>with</u> what they are hit* |

3) However, many people still argue that certain rules **shouldn't** be **broken**, even though they **don't** affect the **meaning** of a sentence. For example, people often complain about constructions like *different to* and *different <u>than</u>*. They claim it should be *different <u>from</u>* because that's what you'd say in **Latin**, even though it's not the way that most English speakers say it.

Attitudes Towards Language Change

Descriptivism has become much more Popular in Recent Times

1) **The Oxford English Dictionary** (OED) was first published in the early **20th century**.

2) The editors of the dictionary were **descriptivists** — they stated in the **preface** that their **aim** was to **record** the language as it was, **not** to **prescribe** rules. Lots of other modern dictionaries have the same aim.

3) However, most people look words up in the dictionary to **make sure** they get a **meaning** or **spelling** 'right'. This shows that most people think of dictionaries as **prescriptive rule books**, not just records of the language.

> Many linguists are completely **against** prescriptivism. In the 1980s **Milroy and Milroy** argued that language change is **inevitable** and shouldn't be fought against. They also argued **against** the **high status** of **Standard English**. They claimed that fears about **falling standards** meant that people are often **discriminated** against, e.g. by employers, if they **don't** follow the **arbitrary** rules that were set out by grammarians in the **18th century**.

4) However, **Cameron** (**1995**) argued that prescriptivism **shouldn't** be **discounted** as just people being **fussy** or **pedantic** about something that doesn't really matter.

5) She's a **descriptivist**, but argues that **prescriptivism** shows that people realise that **language** is an important **social tool** and **care** about how it's used.

6) She also argues that **fear** about **language change** often **symbolises** fear about **social problems** — people worry that **declining** standards of **language** mirror **declining** standards in **behaviour** and **education**.

7) This means that people **focus** on **language change** because they want to **make sense** of **bigger problems** in **society**. She argues that this should be used to **start** a **debate** about what **attitudes** towards language change **symbolise**, rather than just being discounted as an **illogical belief**.

There are Different ways to Study Language Change

You can use different **methodologies** to **study** language change. You could look at:

Lexis	Grammar
New words are constantly being **added** to the language. You could focus on **borrowings** from **other languages** or the **impact** of **technology**. To do this you could look at the **etymology** (origin) of new words in the **OED**.	For example, you could look at how **syntax** has become a lot **less complex** since the **19th century**. You could do this by **comparing** the syntax in a page of a **Dickens novel** with the syntax in a page of a **contemporary** one.

Phonology For example, you could analyse how **accents** have **changed** in **broadcasting** by looking at how **newsreaders** spoke in the **1950s** compared to **today**. You could **transcribe** recordings from the different periods and **analyse** how their **pronunciation** has changed, using the **phonetic alphabet** (see p.60).

Practice Questions

Q1 What is the difference between the prescriptive and descriptive approaches to language change?

Q2 What was the purpose of 18th century grammar books and dictionaries?

Q3 Outline one method you could use to study language change.

Essay Question

Q1 "Something must be done to halt the rapid decline in standards of English."

How far do you agree with this statement?

Refer to prescriptivist and descriptivist views in your answer.

Some of these prescriptivists have got a real attitude problem...

...I mean, really, fancy telling people that the way they use language is wrong. Except, of course, everyone does it all the time. So maybe we're all prescriptivists at heart... Anyway, enough thinking, just try and force this into your brain — prescriptivism lays down rules about how the language should be, and descriptivism describes how it actually is. The clue's in the name really.

Sources and Exam Questions

Here are some exam-style questions, with sources like the ones you'll get in the real paper.
The exact question style will vary depending on your exam board, but these will still be good practice.

Text A is from *The First Book of Manners* (1856), a guide to polite behaviour for young people.
Text B is taken from a page of a modern website, www.growingkids.co.uk, which offers advice to parents about their children.

1. With reference to both texts, analyse what they show about changes in written language over time.   [48 marks]

Text A — from *The First Book of Manners* (1856), by Felix Urban

When the hour for meals draws nigh, take care to be ready, properly dressed and washed, so as not to be behind time; it is a breach of manners to keep others waiting.

Shew no unbecoming haste to sit down; but take your place as you are desired. Wait until a blessing has been asked: the head of the family (or a clergyman, when present) usually does this; not unfrequently, however, the youngest present is called upon: should it be your duty, perform it reverently, with a due feeling of devotion, remembering that it is the offering up of a solemn prayer to Almighty God.

It is not proper to sit either so close to the table as to touch it with the body, nor too far back; the right distance is that at which the wrists can rest naturally upon the table's edge.

Sit upright, not throwing yourself back, nor yet sitting upon the edge of the chair. To place the elbows on the table, is a most unmannerly act. When a table-napkin is put for you, unfold it, and place it securely before you upon your knees.

You will find the knife and spoon at your right hand, and the fork at your left; they are to be so used.

It is unmannerly to ask to be helped before others, or to shew signs of impatience by moving about the plate or the body; such behaviour may be ascribed to greediness. Await your turn; be assured you will not be forgotten.

Text B — from www.growingkids.co.uk/TableManners.html

If a child has an assigned seat, it is easy for him/her to get into the routine of eating at the table from the moment they sit down. When comfortable and calm, encourage children old enough to eat at the table to:

- Scoot their chair in so that they can easily reach the table without having to rest their elbows on it.
- Put their napkins in their laps, not tucked into their shirts.
- Understand that their plate is in the middle, forks are to the left and knives/spoons are to the right.
- Know that their glass is up to the right of their plate.

Chow Down

When it's time to eat, even the most mild mannered of children can turn into ravenous monsters! Ask your children to:

- Politely request the dish they would like to spoon onto their plate (if you have not already served them).
- Serve food onto their plates using the serving utensils provided, not their own utensils.
- Serve only one helping of food at a time. Assure your children there will be seconds if they so desire.
- Give each foodstuff a separate space on the plate. Piling a plate with a mountain of food is a recipe for frustrations!

Chew and Chat

Some table manners have survived for centuries with good reason. Remind your kids:

- Not to chew with their mouths open. No one wants to see what's in their mouths.
- Not to talk while eating. Again, no one wants to see what's in their mouths.
- If they need to remove something from their mouth (such as a pit or a bone), remove it the same way they ate it. If they ate fish from a fork and discovered a bone, have them remove it with their fork...

No matter how crazy mealtime can get in your house, a few basic table manners will serve you (and your kids!) well. Find out which rules work for you, and which you are willing to bend every now and then.

Sources and Exam Questions

Text C is a letter written in 1819 by Lord Byron, to a woman he was in love with.

Text D is a letter written in 1972 by an engineer working in Saudi Arabia to his wife.

2. With reference to both texts, analyse what they show about the development of language over time.   [48 marks]

Text C — a letter to the Countess Teresa Guiccioli (1819), by Lord Byron

My dearest Teresa-

I have read this book in your garden; - my love, you were absent, or else I could not have read it. It is a favorite book of yours, and the writer was a friend of mine. You will not understand these English words, and *others* will not understand them, - which is the reason I have not scrawled them in Italian. But you will recognize the handwriting of him who passionately loves you, and you will divine that, over a book which was yours, he could only think of love. In that word, beautiful in all languages, but most so in yours - *Amor mio* - is comprised my existence here and hereafter. I feel I exist here, and I fear that I shall exist hereafter, - as to *what* purpose you will decide; my destiny rests with you, and you are a woman, seventeen years of age, and two out of a convent. I wish that you had stayed there, with all my heart, - or, at least, that I had never met you in your married state.

But all this is too late. I love you, and you love me, - at least, you *say so*, and *act* as if you *did* so, which last is a great consolation in all events. But I more than love you, and cannot cease to love you.

Think of me, sometimes, when the Alps and the ocean divide us, - but they never will, unless you *wish* it.

B.

Text D — a letter written from a husband to his wife (1972)

Dearest Julia,

        I arrived here in Riyadh on Monday evening after the most awful flight. I should be feeling really happy and excited, I suppose, but I am already missing you. Back in England, the thought of being separated from you for three months didn't seem so bad but now just the thought of being without you *even for a week* makes me feel desolate.

I suppose I'm just feeling a bit homesick, jetlagged and, dare I admit it, even a bit lonely. Yes, that's *me* talking, the person who always says he likes his own company!

I've met a few people so far and they seem really nice. I start work tomorrow – Saturday – so I expect that I won't feel so bad once I get stuck in to things. All I know is that already I can't wait till March when I'll be back home with you in our nice little house that has a garden and trees and rain! Yes *rain*, can you believe it?

I know you'll be thinking I'm a terrible wimp but I do hope you're missing me the same. Give my love to all the family and tell them I'm fine (even though I'm not!).

Will write again soon.

All my love
Toby x

Sources and Exam Questions

Text E is from the Preface to Samuel Johnson's *A Dictionary of the English Language* (1755).
Text F is from the linguist Jean Aitchison's book *The language web* (1997).

3. Analyse and evaluate the way these two texts use language to communicate their ideas about language change. Evaluate these ideas using your knowledge and study of language change. [45 marks]

Text E — from the Preface to *A Dictionary of the English Language* (1755), by Samuel Johnson

I have, notwithstanding this discouragement, attempted a dictionary of the *English* language, which, while it was employed in the cultivation of every species of literature, has itself been hitherto neglected, suffered to spread, under the direction of chance, into wild exuberance, resigned to the tyranny of time and fashion, and exposed to the corruptions of ignorance, and caprices of innovation.

When I took the first survey of my undertaking, I found our speech copious without order, and energetick without rules: wherever I turned my view, there was perplexity to be disentangled, and confusion to be regulated; choice was to be made out of boundless variety, without any established principle of selection; adulterations were to be detected, without a settled test of purity; and modes of expression to be rejected or received, without the suffrages of any writers of classical reputation or acknowledged authority.

Having therefore no assistance but from general grammar, I applied myself to the perusal of our writers; and noting whatever might be of use to ascertain or illustrate any word or phrase, accumulated in time the materials of a dictionary, which, by degrees, I reduced to method, establishing to myself, in the progress of the work, such rules as experience and analogy suggested to me; experience, which practice and observation were continually increasing; and analogy, which, though in some words obscure, was evident in others.

In adjusting the ORTHOGRAPHY, which has been to this time unsettled and fortuitous, I found it necessary to distinguish those irregularities that are inherent in our tongue, and perhaps coeval with it, from others which the ignorance or negligence of later writers has produced. Every language has its anomalies, which, though inconvenient, and in themselves once unnecessary, must be tolerated among the imperfections of human things, and which require only to be registered; that they may not be increased, and ascertained, that they may not be confounded: but every language has likewise its improprieties and absurdities, which it is the duty of the lexicographer to correct or proscribe.

Text F — from *The language web* (1997), by Jean Aitchison

Naturally, language changes all the time. This is a fact of life. In the fourteenth century, Geoffrey Chaucer noted that *in forme of speche is chaunge* 'language changes' (see figure I.I), and the same is true today. But change is one thing. Decay is another. Is our language really changing for the worse, as some people argue?

Of course not. Over a hundred years ago, linguists — those who work on linguistics, the study of language — realised that different styles of language suit different occasions, but that no part of language is ever deformed or bad. People who dispute this are like cranks who argue that the world is flat. Yet flat-earth views about language are still widespread. As the Swiss linguist Ferdinand de Saussure said over seventy-five years ago: 'No other subject has spawned more absurd ideas, more prejudices, more illusions or more myths.' Things have not changed very much since then.

On inspection, the web of worries surrounding change turns out to be largely traditional, somewhat like the worries each new generation of parents has about its offspring. Laments about language go back for centuries.

A fourteenth-century monk complained that the English practise *strange wlaffyng, chyteryng, harryng, and garryng grisbittyng* 'strange stammering, chattering, snarling and grating tooth-gnashing'. And the complaints continued. 'Tongues, like governments, have a natural tendency to degeneration', wrote the lexicographer Samuel Johnson, in the preface to his famous *Dictionary of the English language* published in 1755.

Eighteenth-century worries are perhaps understandable. Around 1700, the seemingly fixed grammar of Latin aroused great admiration, at a time when English itself was in a fairly fluid state. Many people hoped to lay down similar firm precepts for English, and assumed that somebody, somewhere, knew what 'correct English' was. Jonathan Swift wrote a famous letter to the Lord Treasurer in 1712 urging the formation of an academy to regulate language use. He complained that 'many gross improprieties' could be found in the language of 'even the best authors'. But 'correct English' was as hard to define then as it is now. In practice upper- and middle-class speech was often praised as 'good', artificially supplemented by precepts from logic and imitations of various Latin usages.

Sources and Exam Questions

Text G is from a blog written by a 26 year-old American man.

Text H is from a story written by a London school pupil of Caribbean descent.

4. Evaluate how the different contexts might have shaped the language of the texts and the ways the ideas are communicated. [45 marks]

Text G — from a blog written by a 26 year-old American man

So now I'm gonna tell you about the crazy thing that happened to me yesterday.......

It was about quarter after 4 and I was headed to the store to pick up some groceries. Nothing so weird in that right? Well, I'd only walked a couple of blocks when I heard this woman screaming in the park. I looked round and saw two people in a tussle. The guy was on top of her kinda holding her down, and she was yelling "get off of me!" REAL loud. At first I thought they might just have been play-fighting - you know how couples do sometimes. And it was a sunny afternoon and I thought maybe they were just goofing around having a wrestle on the grass. Anyway, you don't wanna just start interfering in someone else's relationship right?

So I was watchin this for a few seconds from the sidewalk thinking "what do I do", when she yelled again "call the cops!!!".

That's when I knew they weren't just fooling around.

I ran over as fast as I could and hollered "GET THE HELL OFF OF HER!!!!!". And then it was like slow motion.... The guy turned around, looked up at me and yelled "back off!". But I guess the adrenaline was pumping then, cuz next thing I know I've grabbed him and pulled him off her. He stumbled up and that's when i saw what a big guy he was. I dunno why but at the time I wasn't scared at all. Anyway, he stands up straight and lunges at me with his fist. God knows how but I manage to duck out of the way and punch him in the stomach. I must have hit a real good shot cuz he goes down hard. By now all the noise has drawn a lot of attention, so some guys ran over and we sat on this guy while someone called 911.

The girl was real shaken up, so some people took her inside for a drink while we waited for the cops. The dude was kicking up like crazy, but there was no way we were gonna let him go.....

Now I think about it I can't believe I did that, cuz I had no clue what was gonna happen to me. I'm no hero or nothing, but it was like something just took over me and I couldn't just stand and do nothing while this girl was being attacked.

Text H — from a story written by a London school pupil of Caribbean descent

One manin in January me and my spars dem was coming from a club in Dalston. We didn't have no donsi so we a walk go home. De night did cold and di gal dem wi did have wid we couldn't walk fast. Anyway we must have been walking for about fifteen minutes when dis car pull up, it was this youthman ah know and him woman. We see sey a mini cab him inna. Him sey "How far you ah go"?

Me sey "Not far, you ketch we too late man".

Anyway before me could close me mout de two gal dem jump inna de car, bout sey dem nah walk no more. Me an Trevor tell dem fi gwan. And de car pull way.

Next ting me know me is about 50 yards from my yard and is the wicked dem just a come down inna dem can. At first me wanted fi run, but Trevor sey "run what" "After we no just kool". We don't have no weed or money pon us. Dem can't do notin.

Next ting we know dem grab we up anna push we into dem car. Me and Trevor put up a struggle but after a few licks we got pushed in. "Now then you two "Rastas" been ripping off mini cabs haven't you?". "We aren't "Rastas" and we don't know what you are talking about". "Save all that until we get to the station Rastus my son". Den him get pon him radio, and tell the station that him ketch the two responsible for that hold up of the mini cab. Trevor luk pon me I could see that he was worried.

manin — morning
spar — friend
donsi — money
gwan — go on
yard — home
weed — marijuana
Rasta — Rastafarian

Accent and Dialect

These two pages are for everyone apart from AQA B. Regional dialects and accents can be a bit confusing if you're not from that area of the country. It's not always just the pronunciation that changes, the lexis can change too.

Accents are Variations in Pronunciation

1) **English** words can be **pronounced** in different ways.
The different **patterns** of pronunciation are called **accents**.

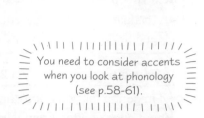
You need to consider accents when you look at phonology (see p.58-61).

2) An accent can be a feature of a dialect. But it's **different** from **dialect** because it just refers to **how** you say words, not the words themselves.

3) Accents can be affected by the speaker's **regional** or **social** background:

> 1) You can tune in to **regional variation** over **large geographic areas**.
>
> 2) For example, in **England**, most people can tell the difference between **northern accents** and **southern accents**. The main differences between them are the **vowel sounds**, e.g.
>   - Someone with a **northern accent** would say *grass* with a short vowel sound, to sound like *c<u>a</u>t*. This can be written **phonetically** as /græs/ (see p.60).
>   - Someone with a **southern accent** would say *grass* with a long vowel sound, to sound like *c<u>a</u>rd*. This can be written **phonetically** as /grɑːs/.
>
> 3) People who live **near** each other can tune in to **smaller** differences in each other's accents, to the point where you can sometimes tell if someone's from your town or one a few miles away.
>
> 4) A **social accent** is the result of someone's **class** or **background**, rather than the region they're from. The most **recognisable** English social accent is **Received Pronunciation** (see p.33). If somebody speaks with this accent, it's often **not possible** to tell which part of the country they're from.

Dialects are Variations in Language

1) A **dialect** is a **variation** in a language, with its own distinctive features of **vocabulary**, **grammar** and **pronunciation**.

2) The term **dialect** is usually used to describe language that's particular to a specific **geographical region**.

3) It's also sometimes used as a **general** term for variations in language that are the result of **social background** (**sociolect** — see p.34) or **personal differences** (**idiolect** — see p.35).

Lexis

Different dialects have different words for things, e.g.

- Someone from Yorkshire might say *anyroad* for *anyway*.
- People in Lancashire might call a *bread roll* a *barm*.
- In the West Country *acker* means *friend*.
- In East Anglia to *mardle* is to *gossip*.

Grammar

The way that people form sentences can depend on their dialect. Regional dialects often contain **non-standard** grammar, e.g.

- *them* as a demonstrative adjective — *look at **them** books*
- Double negatives — *we **don't** want **none***
- Missing plurals — *it costs four **pound***
- Missing the *-ly* suffix off the end of adverbs — *I walked **slow***

Some grammatical variations are **specific** to a **particular** dialect, e.g. people from **Yorkshire** might miss out the definite article *the*, so they might say *I cleaned car* rather than *I cleaned **the** car*. The **Scouse** dialect has *youse* as the plural of *you* — e.g. *what are youse doing?*

Phonology

1) Most regional dialects have an **accent** to go with them. So you'd probably expect a **Geordie** (someone from Newcastle) to say the word *town* like *toon*, or someone from **Cornwall** to pronounce the *r* in *water*.

2) But don't forget — accents are just **one feature** of a dialect. You can use words and constructions from one dialect but speak in the accent of another.

Accent and Dialect

Contact with other dialects causes Regional Variations to Change

Accents and dialects aren't fixed. They're often exposed to other variations and can end up changing and sharing linguistic traits as a result of this **contact**. Here are a few theories about how they can change:

Dialect Levelling	Levelling is the gradual **loss of differences** between distinctive dialects or accents. When nearby dialect forms come into **contact**, some features might **transfer** and become present in both. For example, features of **Estuary English** such as th-fronting have spread into neighbouring regions and become part of the dialects there as well (p.15).
Code-switching	Sometimes speakers use different forms of English depending on **where they are** or **who they're with**. Being able to use **different varieties** like this is known as **code-switching**. For example, schoolchildren of different ethnic minorities who go to school in England might use **Standard English** (see p. 31) in school, a **pidgin** or **creole** (see p.20) when with friends, and another language when they're **at home**.
Status and solidarity values	Status and solidarity are two sets of values that people use to **judge speakers** according to how they sound. Accents that carry **high status** might imply things like **education**, **wealth** and **intelligence**. Accents that are rated as **high solidarity** might imply that the speakers are **trustworthy**, **friendly**, **kind** and **good-natured**. Accents that are high status are sometimes low solidarity, and vice versa. **Received Pronunciation** (see p. 33) is widely recognised as **high status**, whereas **regional variations** are generally found to be **high solidarity**.
Koineisation	A **koine** (coy-nay) language is produced when two **existing dialects** come into contact with one another and create a **new variety** with influences from both. However the koine remains **distinct** from the original dialects and all three can exist in a community **at the same time**. This is how **Liverpool English** arose — in the nineteenth century as the port expanded, elements of the **north-west England** dialect and elements of the newly arrived **Irish-** or **Hiberno-English** created what people now recognise as Liverpool English (or 'Scouse').

There are also factors that affect Individual Speakers

Geography
You might move to another part of the country and therefore **hear less** of your own accent, or encounter a **mix of accents** (e.g. at university). You might **alter** your speech so you can be **more easily understood**, or **adopt** elements of the **broader accents** you encounter in order to fit in or become less noticeable.

Alternatively, if a region is quite **isolated**, speakers are more likely to **retain** their regional dialect as there won't be a big influence from other accents coming into the area.

Media
The media can also have a major influence on the way people speak, as they end up **imitating popular catchphrases** or **presenters** on the TV or radio.

On the other hand, it might also make you want to **emphasise how you speak**, if it becomes fashionable.

Attitudes of others
Professional environments can affect speakers. You might try to adopt a more **formal** way of speaking, or try to **suppress** elements of a regional accent, depending on how formal your workplace is.

Some regional accents appear to be associated with **straightforward**, **honest** people (see p.38) — many companies locate **call centres** in areas with **distinctive accents** for this reason.

Practice Questions

Q1 Explain what the term 'accent' means.
Q2 Give three examples of variations in grammar in different regional dialects.
Q3 Describe people's attitudes to different accents in terms of status and solidarity values.

Essay Question

Q1 Describe the lexical, grammatical and phonological features of a regional dialect of your choice.

The media can affect speakers — but I always check they're plugged in first...

Different regional accents can cause a lot of bother. You'd think that because we live on such a tiny island, we could all get along quite nicely speaking the same way and understanding each other perfectly. But no, that would be too easy. And after all, variety is the spice of life, so quit yer mitherin, stop yer chelpin and wind yer neck in. There now, that's better.

Standard English and RP

This is for AQA A, WJEC, OCR and Edexcel. There comes a time in everybody's life when they must learn the secrets of Standard English and RP. This is your time. Your quest begins now. But be warned — it's not for the faint-hearted...

Standard English *is a* Social Dialect

Standard English is a dialect of English. It has distinctive features of **vocabulary**, **grammar** and **spelling**.

1) A **standard** form of a language is one that is considered to be **acceptable** or correct by **educated** speakers.

2) In **medieval England** people in different parts of the country spoke very different **dialects**. They were so varied that people from different regions would have had **difficulty understanding** each other.

3) The **Standard English** used today started off as the **regional dialect** of the East Midlands (see p.4). Its influence spread around the country, and it became the dialect that was used in print.

4) As more books were printed, **variations** in spelling and grammar were ironed out — the language started to conform towards a **standard**.

5) People began to **codify** the language (decide how to write it) in **dictionaries** and try to regulate it by writing books of **grammar rules**. Johnson's dictionary, printed in 1755, aimed to standardise spellings and meanings.

6) The standard form of the language became associated with **education**, **class** and **power**, rather than any particular region — making it a unique sub-variety of English.

Standard English *is used in* Lots *of Situations*

Standard English is the most widely understood version of English, so it's used in lots of different fields:

1) **Education** — Standard English is the variety of English taught in schools, and it's what people are taught when they learn English as a foreign language.

2) **Media** — it's used in newspapers and by newsreaders on the TV or radio.

3) **Formal documents** — it's the language used in essays, business letters and reports.

4) **Formal speech** — you'd expect people to speak using Standard English in formal situations like business negotiations and public announcements.

In some fields, mind you, Standard English is blindingly inappropriate.

Standard English *can be a* Tricky Concept

It's difficult to give examples of **Standard English** as a dialect, because it's what other dialects are usually compared with. This book is written in Standard English — it mostly contains **standardised vocabulary**, **spellings** and **syntax**.

It's important not to confuse Standard English with different levels of formality. For example:

> *1) Mother appeared exceedingly fatigued following the intense culinary efforts required to satiate her offspring.*
>
> *2) Mum looked bloody shattered after cooking tea for the kids.*
>
> *3) Mum were tired having made us all dinner.*

These three sentences are in very **different styles**.

- The first is **excessively formal**. It contains lexis like *fatigued* and *satiate* that you wouldn't often use in normal conversation or writing, but **prescriptivists** (see p.24) would say that the syntax, grammar and spelling are 'correct'. This sentence is in Standard English.

- The second contains **swearing** (*bloody*) and **informal terms** like *shattered*. However, the **syntax, verb forms** and **spelling** would be considered 'correct' from a prescriptive point of view. These elements (like the first sentence) are **consistent** with what you'd expect from Standard English.

- Even though it might not seem as unusual as sentences 1) and 2), the third sentence would **not** be classed as Standard English because of the use of the verb *were*. Using the **plural form** instead of the **singular** *was* to refer to one person (*Mum*) means that grammatically this sentence is 'incorrect'.

Standard English and RP

Received Pronunciation (RP) is a Social Accent

1) **Received Pronunciation** is an **accent**, traditionally associated with **educated** people and the **upper classes**.

2) This means it's **different** from other accents, which normally indicate which **region** the speaker's from.

3) Traditionally **RP** and **Standard English** are linked — the most **prestigious** way of speaking would be Standard English using RP. While lots of people speak Standard English (or something close) with regional accents, you don't generally hear people saying dialect words and phrases in RP.

How now...

4) The most recognisable examples of RP are how the **Queen** speaks, and the traditional speech of **BBC presenters**. Because of this, people sometimes refer to RP as the **Queen's English**, or **BBC English**.

5) Because RP has been seen as the standard, accepted way of speaking English, it's the accent many people are taught to use when they learn English as a **foreign language**.

> **Some features of RP**
> - **Long vowel** sounds in words like *grass* (grarss) and *castle* (carstle).
> - **Long vowel** sound in words like *come* and *under*.
> - Pronouncing **h**s and **t**s in words like *hat* and *letter*.

RP hasn't Stayed the Same

BBC newsreaders still use **Standard English**, but they now speak it in a range of **regional accents**. RP is still associated with educated and upper class speakers, but its association with **authoritative voices** (like newsreaders) has diminished.

1) Only a very **small percentage** of the population of Britain (less than 3%) still uses RP in its traditional form.

2) There has been a **downward convergence** and **levelling** (see p.31) of RP over the years. Speakers may have modified the accent because it's so distinctive. Levelling helps them to **integrate** with the other language varieties in society.

No one knew what Tommy was so unRP about...

3) The decline of RP is linked to the **rise** of **Estuary English** (see p.15). Estuary English has become increasingly widespread because Cockney speakers use it as a **higher status** variety, and RP speakers **converge** on it as a **standard variety** in order to fit in.

4) Estuary English is viewed as a **classless variety** of English which has also helped it to **spread further** than other varieties — very **few prejudices** exist about an accent that can be heard all over the country.

Practice Questions

Q1 What is Standard English?

Q2 List three situations in which you might find Standard English being used.

Q3 In what way are RP and Standard English linked?

Q4 Describe two features of RP.

Essay Question

Q1 Explain how RP has developed and describe the factors that influence its usage.

I heard the Queen's English — funny, I always thought she was German...

For something that's generally acknowledged to be the 'standard', Standard English has had its share of controversies. It pretty much boils down to the prescriptivists / descriptivists debate — whether some language use is just plain wrong. All I'll say is they'd have a total meltdown if they knew we just spent all day 'superpoking' each other on Facebook®.

Sociolect and Idiolect

This bit is for AQA A, WJEC, OCR and Edexcel. The way you speak is influenced by loads of things, like your age and who you hang around with. So choose your friends wisely — you might end up speaking like them. Scary thought.

Sociolect is the Language of Social Groups

Sociolects (or **social dialects**) are **varieties** of language used by particular **social groups**, e.g. middle-aged lawyers speak differently from schoolchildren. The sociolects of different groups help to give them their own **identities**.

The language people use depends on different social factors:

> The points in this section are generalisations, so they're not true for everyone.

Socio-economic status

- Studies have shown that **middle** and **upper class** people tend to use more **standard forms** than **lower class** people.
- The language of lower class people is more likely to contain features of **regional dialect** (p.30-31).

Education

- Studies show that **well-educated** people are more likely to use **Standard English** and **RP** (see p.32-33) than less well-educated people.
- They're usually less likely to use words and sentence structures from **regional dialects**.

Age

- Sociolects used by teenagers tend to include more **non-standard** forms and **slang** (p.36-37) than language used by adults.
- They also include more influences from, and references to, **popular culture**.

Occupation

- Every occupation has its own specialist terms and technical vocabulary, known as **jargon**.
- You might expect a lawyer to talk about *tort* (a civil wrong) or *GBH* (grievous bodily harm), and a doctor to talk about *prescriptions* or *scrubs*.
- Sometimes these **sociolects** also have distinctive **grammatical** features, e.g. legal documents often contain **complex** sentences with lots of subordinate clauses.

Belief system and culture

- **Religious groups** use lots of **specialist vocabulary**, e.g. *Diwali* (the Hindu festival of light), *kosher* (food prepared in accordance with Jewish law), *salah* (Islamic daily prayers).
- Because UK society is **multicultural**, lots of words from other languages and cultures have become part of other sociolects.
- For example, the word *kosher* isn't just used by members of the Jewish community. It's taken on a **broader** meaning in the English language, so people often use it to mean *genuine* or *legitimate*.

The Way you Speak can Depend on the Situation

Language that's **appropriate** in one social group might not be appropriate in another. People **adapt** the way they speak depending on the **situation** they're in, and how they want to present themselves. For example:

1) **Politicians** tend to use **Standard English** when they're making a political speech, because they're in a formal situation. But when they're talking to individuals on the street they might use **non-standard** language and features of **regional dialect**, so that they seem down-to-earth and approachable.

2) Lots of people find that the way they speak to their **friends** is different from how they speak to their **parents**. They might use more **slang** with their friends, or speak in the same **regional dialect** as their parents when they're at home.

3) Some people have a **telephone voice** — a different voice that they use on the phone. Usually it involves using more **standard** forms and an accent that's closer to **Received Pronunciation**.

"I find my speech changes more than my spots."

Sociolect and Idiolect

Idiolect *is the* Unique Language *of an* Individual

1) The word choices that people make, and the way they form sentences, are specific to them.

2) This means that the way you use language can **identify** you, like a **fingerprint**.

3) Your **idiolect** is the result of a **unique combination** of **influences**.

Where you're from
- Where you're from affects how you speak. You might expect a person from Newcastle to have a Geordie **accent** and use **dialect** words like *gan* for *go*.
- But not everyone from the same **area** speaks in exactly the **same** way.
- A person could have **moved** from somewhere else and so **retained** aspects of **other** regional accents and dialects.

Social background
- The way you speak is also influenced by your **social background** (**sociolect** — see the previous page).
- Your sociolect is the **product** of lots of different **factors** such as socio-economic status, age, religious beliefs, education and gender.
- It's also affected by influences from **smaller** social groups, e.g. schools, sports teams and groups of friends.

Some idiolects involve neighing and whinnying.

Personal characteristics
- The language a person uses could be affected by aspects of their **personality**.
- For example, a **nervous** person might use sentences with lots of **fillers** (*um, like, sort of* etc.).

Practice Questions

Q1 How might a person's age affect the language they use?

Q2 Name three other social factors that might affect the way someone speaks.

Q3 What is a telephone voice?

Q4 What is a person's individual use of language known as?

Q5 Give an example of how someone's personality could affect the way they speak.

Essay Question

Q1 Explain some of the possible differences between the language used by a 45-year-old surgeon and the language used by a 17-year-old A level student.

Verbal chameleons...

Politicians definitely vary the way they speak a lot. There was the time when Margaret Thatcher used the Lincolnshire dialect word 'frit' (= frightened) during a debate in the House of Commons, to goad a member of the opposition. And Tony Blair often spoke 'Mockney' (= mock Cockney) to make himself sound like one of the people. In fact, we all do it to some extent. We each have a lot of linguistic features at our disposal, and it's the sum of these that gives us our idiolect.

Slang

Ignore these pages if you're doing AQA B. In the olden days, a lesson on slang would consist of everyone sitting around swearing at each other as if they were in a charity swear-a-thon. Not so now. There's slang for everything...

Slang is Informal Vocabulary

1) **Slang** refers to **informal**, **non-standard** words and expressions that tend to be used in the **vernacular** (casual, everyday speech).

2) It's often **inventive** and **creative**, and enters the language in lots of different ways.

New meanings for existing words	Shortening existing words	New words
• *cool, wicked* — good • *sad* — pathetic • *chick* — girl	• *telly* — television • *rents* — parents • *mare* — nightmare	• *moolah* — money • *yonks* — a long time, ages • *snog* — kiss

Slang has Different Purposes

1) People tend to use slang to **identify** that they're part of a particular **social group** — it's part of their **sociolect**. Using particular slang shows that you **fit in** and suggests **shared values**.

2) Slang can act as a code to **exclude outsiders**, e.g. groups of teenagers might use slang to establish a sense of identity which is separate from the adult world. It can be **exclusive** and **secretive**.

3) Two of the main **purposes** of using **slang** are to be **rebellious** or **entertaining**.

Slang and social taboos

• There's lots of **slang** for **taboo subjects** — things that are thought of as **inappropriate** or **unacceptable** to talk about in formal social situations, e.g. words for sex, sex organs and bodily functions.

• Some of the most common and most offensive slang words are **swear words**.

• It's seen as **taboo** to swear in some situations, e.g. in class at school. In this case the purpose of swearing is to be **rebellious**.

• In other situations swearing is an **accepted** part of a group's **sociolect**, and people do it to **fit in** and be **entertaining**, e.g. when they're talking with a group of friends.

• Not all **slang** is **taboo language**, but there's a lot **more** slang for **taboo subjects** than for any others.

Slang is Specific to Social and Regional Groups

1) Some slang words are **familiar** to **lots of speakers**, e.g. most people in the UK probably know that **tenner** is short for **ten pounds**.

2) However, slang also **varies** depending on which **region** speakers are from. Sometimes it's difficult to distinguish **slang** words from **regional dialect variants**.

3) One example of **regional slang** is **Cockney rhyming slang**, e.g. *butcher's hook* — **look**.

4) The slang a person uses also depends on **social factors**, e.g. a middle class speaker will probably speak something close to **Standard English** and use fewer slang words than a working class speaker.

5) Some slang is only used by very **small social groups**, like a particular school or group of friends.

6) Slang reflects **multiculturalism**, as slang terms can come from lots of different cultures, e.g. **tucker** — an Australian slang word for food.

7) The **media** also influences slang and gives people **access** to different subcultures.

> • British **youth** culture has been particularly influenced by **African American** slang, through popular music and TV.
>
> • **Hip hop culture** has introduced black American slang that lots of English speakers now recognise, e.g. *sick* — good, *bling* — flashy jewellery, *crib* — house.

Slang

The use of slang **Depends** on the **Context**

1) The **amount** and **type** of slang that people use depend on the **situation** they're in.

2) **Who you're with** can have a **big impact** on the kind of language you use. For example, you might want to give a **different impression** of **yourself** to your **friends** than you do to your **grandparents**, so you might use more **specific slang** and **taboo language** with your **friends** than with your **grandparents**.

3) **Time** and **place** can also have an effect on the type of language that's seen as **appropriate**. For example, in a **formal context** like a business meeting, people are **unlikely** to use much **slang** or **taboo language**. This is because it would be seen as **unprofessional** in that context, and the people in the meeting might **not** be **familiar** with each other. In an **informal context**, like having dinner with friends, people are **more likely** to **swear** and use **slang** words.

Paul desperately hoped it wasn't too obvious that he hadn't understood a word.

Slang is used in **Written Language** as well as casual speech

- Slang is **especially** used in **multi-modal texts** (see p.125). These are texts that have **elements** of **spoken** and **written** language, like **emails** (p.82-83).

- The **amount** and **type** of slang used **depend** on the **purpose** and **audience** of the text, e.g. a **text message** to a **friend** would probably include **more slang** than an **opinion column** in a **newspaper**.

- The **reasons** for **including** slang in writing can be to appear **informal** and **accessible** to audiences. **Taboo language** can be included to **shock** the audience.

Slang is always **Changing**

Slang changes very quickly as words go in and out of **fashion**.

1) Lots of slang words used to be popular, but you wouldn't hear them any more, e.g. *cove* — man, *beak* — magistrate, *viz* — face, *cits* — citizens.

2) Slang terms can quickly start to sound **dated**, e.g. *mega* (good), or *dweeb* (someone who isn't cool). This happens especially with **teenage slang**. When adults and young children start using it, the slang becomes more **mainstream** and then teenagers stop using it.

3) Sometimes slang terms become so **widely** used that they become part of **Standard English**, e.g. *okay*, *phone* and *bus*. These words were once considered **informal**, but now it would seem formal to say *telephone*, and very unusual to say *omnibus*.

4) The **opposite** can also happen — words can go from being formal or acceptable to being classed as vulgar. An example of this is the word *arse*, which wasn't thought of as informal until the 17th century.

Practice Questions

Q1 What is slang?

Q2 Explain what is meant by the term 'taboo'.

Q3 How can the context affect someone's use of slang?

Q4 Why does teenage slang change quickly?

Essay Question

Q1 Discuss the use of slang for two different purposes, referring to context and mode in your answer.

S'lang time since I heard anyone say mega...

It can get a bit confusing, all this slang. I mean, if someone tells you you're looking fierce, do you take it as a compliment or should you try and look less angry? And if you hear someone saying that one of your friends is sick, does it just mean they like them, or should you send a get well soon card? I'm almost surprised anyone manages to communicate at all.

Attitudes Towards Language Variation

These pages are for everyone. The thing you have to remember about English is that everyone who speaks it has an opinion about it. Fortunately a lot of people have quite similar opinions, otherwise you'd be in for a very long night...

People have **Different Attitudes** towards **Standard English**

1) As one variety of the language became standardised (see p.6), other varieties became seen as **less prestigious**.

2) **Standard English** is a **social dialect**. It's usually associated with **educated**, **middle** and **upper class** people. It's the way that you're taught to use English at school, and the language of **formal speech** and **writing**.

3) **Regional dialects** were associated with the **uneducated** and the **lower classes**, so it was seen as important to be able to use English '**properly**' if you wanted to be successful.

- Prescriptivists see **Standard English** as the '**correct**' or '**pure**' form of the language.
- Other varieties are sometimes thought to be '**corruptions**' of it.
- There's a view that if you use another dialect, you're not using English '**properly**'.

- However, **descriptivists** argue that all varieties of English should be **valued equally**.
- There's **no reason** why Standard English should be seen as better than any other dialect.
- They claim that people shouldn't be considered **uneducated** if they **don't** use Standard English.

4) Whether it's **appropriate** to use Standard English depends on the **mode** and **context**. You'd expect a **formal text** to be **written** in Standard English, but you wouldn't necessarily expect people in an **informal** setting to **speak** to each other using Standard English.

People Have **Different Attitudes** towards **Accents** and **Dialects**

Someone's **accent** or **dialect** is often a good indication of **where they're from**. But it can also influence attitudes about a speaker's **social background** and **education**.

1) Some people **assume** that people who use **regional dialects** are **poorly educated** or **lower class**.

2) On the other hand, **regional varieties** of English are often associated with being **down-to-earth** and **modest**, e.g. because regional accents are seen as being more **accessible** to audiences, they are used more in voice overs in adverts (to **sell things**) and by presenters (on **national** as well as **local** radio or television stations).

People sometimes make assumptions about others based on the variety of English they use, e.g. people from the **north** of England often think that people with **southern accents** sound '**posh**'.

1) **Workman (2008)** studied people's **perceptions** of different **accents**. Participants listened to recordings of different accents while they looked at photos of people.

2) It was found that participants rated the **intelligence** of the people in the photos differently, depending on which accent they thought they had.

3) **Yorkshire** accents were rated as sounding the **most intelligent**. When a recording of a **Birmingham** accent was played, the people in the photos were rated as being much **less intelligent**. Obviously this **isn't** actually **true**, but it shows how strong the **stereotypes** about different accents can be.

People have **Different Attitudes** towards **Slang**

Slang is sometimes seen as **low level**, **vulgar** language, which shouldn't be used in **writing** or in **formal situations**.

1) Some people think that if you use slang you're **undermining standards** by not using the language '**properly**'. They assume that people who use lots of slang are lower class and uneducated.

2) Slang is seen as the language of **informal speech**, so it's considered **inappropriate** to use it in a **formal context**, e.g. you'd lose marks if you wrote an essay using slang words and phrases.

3) This is because slang has a reputation for being **rebellious** and **subversive**, so it isn't formally accepted as a variety of English. Some people worry that it doesn't follow the 'proper' **spelling** and **grammar rules** of **Standard English**.

4) However, most slang words and phrases **do** follow the rules of Standard English — they're just more flexible.

5) People who are interested in slang argue that it's an **intelligent** and **creative** variety of language, which **changes** and **develops** very quickly. It also serves an important purpose in **social contexts** — people use it to **identify** themselves as part of a **group**.

Attitudes Towards Language Variation

There's **Debate** about **Regional Varieties** and **Slang** in **Education**

People have different attitudes towards the role of **standard** and **vernacular** varieties of English in education.

1) Linguists like **Milroy and Milroy** (1985) have argued that it's **not fair** to correct children for using **non-standard** varieties of English.

2) Children who use regional varieties of English can end up **struggling** at **school** because **Standard English** is **unfamiliar** to them. Because regional dialects are linked to **social class**, it's often **working class** children who are put at an immediate **disadvantage** because they're told that the language they use is **wrong**.

3) The Milroys argued that all varieties of English should be **valued equally** and children **shouldn't** be **discouraged** from using non-standard English.

"Henry VIII were a proper mardy bum..."

1) However, people such as **John Honey** (1997) argue that children **should** be taught **Standard English** at school, because this is the only way to make sure that all children have **equal opportunities**.

2) Because Standard English is the **prestigious** form of the language, children will be **disadvantaged** if they **don't** learn how to use it.

3) For example, they might miss out on **job opportunities** because they fill in applications using non-standard spelling. Employers might assume that they're unintelligent, and not give them the job. Therefore, it's important to teach all children the **writing skills** they need to succeed.

4) This viewpoint sees non-standard varieties as **barriers** to **universal communication**. Non-standard varieties are appropriate for informal speech, but **Standard English** should always be **favoured** because it ensures that **everyone** will be able to **understand** each other. This is called **bidialectism** — children end up using **two dialects**.

There are **Different** Ways to **Study Language Variation**

Different **methodologies** are used to **study** language variation, depending on the linguistic features you're focusing on:

Lexis
For example, researchers look at poetry written in **dialects** and focus on **regional vocabulary**. They might also record **informal speech** and look at the amount of **slang** used by people of different ages.

Phonology
Phonemic transcriptions (p.60) from recordings of people with different **accents** are the best way to study different phonological features. They are compared and contrasted, highlighting **distinctive features** in particular accents.

Grammar
For example, researchers might compare transcriptions of the speech of a **Standard English** speaker with someone with a **regional dialect**. A good place to start looking is the **verb forms**, e.g. whether a speaker says *the dog wants fed* or *the dog wants feeding*.

Practice Questions

Q1 Name a mode and context that the use of Standard English might be associated with.

Q2 Outline the negative associations that some people might have with regional varieties of English.

Q3 Outline the two different viewpoints on the use of slang.

Q4 What did Milroy and Milroy argue about the role of Standard English in education?

Q5 Why do some people feel that it would be unfair not to teach children how to use Standard English?

Essay Question

Q1 Discuss whether non-standard varieties of English should have the same status as Standard English.

Deer sur, Oi would loik to apploi forra jab with yow...

Those poor Brummies, always getting a hard time about their accent. Personally, I think it's a lovely accent — and it doesn't seem to have done Cat Deeley's career any harm, or Jasper Carrott's, or Adrian Chiles'... Anyway, you need to know what other people think about language variation, whether you agree with them or think it's a load of twaddle.

Language and Gender

AQA A, WJEC and OCR (Language, Power and Identity option). These pages are about how men and women use language differently from each other. Or maybe how they don't use language differently, and people just think they do...

Men *and* Women *use* Language Differently

Studies have shown that women tend to use **accents** from a **higher social class** than men.

Dear, I do wish you'd say 'wuff', not 'woof'.

- **Trudgill (1983)** studied men and women's **social class accents**. He found that women's pronunciation was closer to **Received Pronunciation (RP)**, the accent that's usually seen as the most **prestigious**.

- **Cheshire (1982)** studied the speech of adolescent girls and boys, and found that boys tended to use more **non-standard grammatical forms**, e.g. *ain't,* than girls.

1) Using **Standard English** and **RP** gives a person **overt prestige** — the prestige of being associated with a respectable, well-off section of society. **Women** tend to seek **overt prestige** more than men.

2) Using **non-standard** English gives a person **covert prestige** — they seem a bit rebellious and independent. **Men** are more likely to seek **covert prestige** than women.

Women *may use more* Prestigious Forms *for* Several Reasons

There are several **possible explanations** for why **women** use more **prestigious** language than **men**.

1) Women might be **less secure** than men in terms of their **social status**. If they feel that they have an **inferior position** in society, then they might use more **prestigious** language to **overcome** it.

2) Society generally expects **higher standards** of **behaviour** from **women** — they're expected to behave like 'ladies' and use 'ladylike' language. This includes things like not swearing or arguing.

3) Men already have a **higher social status** than women, so they don't need to use prestigious forms to improve it. Instead, they seek **covert prestige** by using non-standard language that seems tough and rebellious.

Remember — these explanations are based on studies of a few men and women. You can't generalise them to all men and women. There have also been changes in gender roles since the 1980s, when these studies were done.

4) **Non-standard language** is traditionally associated with **working-class** men, so men might use it to show that they share **traditionally masculine** qualities, like being '**tough**' and '**down-to-earth**'.

Women's Language *is usually* More Polite *than* Men's

The researcher **Robin Lakoff (1975)** identified features that she felt were characteristic of women's language:

> **Hedges and fillers** — fragments of language like *sort of, kind of, maybe.*
> **Apologetic requests** — e.g. *I'm **sorry,** but **would you mind** closing the door?*
> **Tag questions** — e.g. *this is nice, **isn't it?***
> **Indirect requests** — e.g. *It's very noisy out there* (meaning — *could you close the door?*)

1) **Lakoff** also pointed out that women tend to **speak less** than men, use **fewer expletives** (swear less), and use more **intensifiers** (words like **so** and **very**).

2) She argued that these features of women's language reflected women's **inferior social status**, and made it worse by making them seem **indecisive** and **needy**. She said that women's language is **weak** compared to men's language, and this **prevents** women from being **taken seriously**. This explanation is known as the **deficit model**.

3) **O'Barr and Atkins (1980)** suggested an alternative explanation to the **deficit model**. They analysed transcripts of **American courtroom trials**. They found that **male and female** witnesses who were of **low social status** and/or inexperienced with the courtroom practices both showed many of the linguistic features that Lakoff labelled **female**.

4) This suggests that the kind of language **Lakoff** describes as female isn't only found in women, and might be more to do with individuals feeling **powerless**.

> **Lakoff's** research is quite **old**. More recently, researchers like **Holmes (1984)** have suggested that 'women's language' doesn't show **weakness**, but a desire to **co-operate**. Linguists like **Cameron (2007)** argue that there are actually very **few differences** between men and women's language, and **situation** affects how people speak much more than **gender**.

Language and Gender

Language can be Explained in terms of Dominance and Difference

Linguists have come up with other models to explain the **differences** between men and women's language.

1) Dominance model

- Zimmerman and West (1975) recorded interruptions in conversations between men and women.
- They found that **96%** of the interruptions were by men.
- This suggested that men are **dominant** in **male-female conversations**. They argued that this reflects male dominance in society.

2) Difference model

Tannen (1990) described male and female conversational style in terms of **difference**.

- **Men** are concerned with **status** and **independence**, e.g. they interrupt a lot.
- They give **direct orders**, e.g. *pass me that*, and don't mind **conflict**.
- **Men** are interested in gaining **factual information** and finding **solutions to problems**.

- **Women** are interested in **forming bonds** — they tend to talk less and agree more than men.
- They usually give polite, indirect orders, e.g. *would you mind passing me that*, and try to **avoid conflict**.
- **Women** aim to show **understanding** by **compromising**, and offering **support** rather than **solutions**.

The **reasons** for these **differences** in male and female interaction could be to do with the **topics** that they talk about in **single-sex groups**, e.g. traditionally **male** topics of conversation have focused on **work** and **sport**, where **factual information** and **status** are important. Traditionally **female** topics have centred on the **home** and **family**, where **emotions**, **support** and **compassion** are important.

There are Problems with these Explanations

Other researchers have cast **doubts** on some of these explanations of differences in **male** and **female language**.

1) **Beattie (1982)** questioned **Zimmerman and West's** idea that men **interrupting** women was a sign of **dominance**. He suggested that interruptions can be **supportive** and show that the person is listening, e.g. if they **repeat** what the speaker is saying, or say things like *yes* and *mm*.

2) **Cameron (2007)** argues that a lot of research is **biased** because there has been more focus on the **differences** between male and female language, which are actually quite small, rather than the **similarities**.

Practice Questions

Q1 Give three reasons why women might use more prestigious forms of language than men.
Q2 How does Lakoff explain women's use of language?
Q3 Explain O'Barr and Atkins' alternative explanation to the defecit model.
Q4 What are the main features of Tannen's difference model?

Essay Question

Q1 Outline the deficit, dominance and difference models of gender differences in language use, and evaluate each model.

Boy meets girl, boy interrupts girl seventeen times, girl cancels date...

This stuff can sound obvious, but it's actually slightly tricky. The problem is, for every bit of research that says men and women use language differently, there's loads of research that says they don't. So the research cancels itself out in a way, which only helps to prove that gender can't be the only factor that determines how you use language... how very annoying.

Language and Gender

AQA A, WJEC and OCR (Language, Power and Identity option). Men and women are often spoken and written about very differently. Most people are so used to this that they hardly notice it, but you'll start to see it cropping up all the time.

Men and Women are Represented Differently

1) **Sexist language** is language that **insults**, **patronises** or **ignores** people on the basis of their **gender**.

2) There is a lot **more** sexist language about **women** than men.

3) Some language implies that the **male** version is the **norm**, and the **female** version is **different** or **wrong**:

> **Marked terms**
> - These are words that reveal a person's **gender**, e.g. *policeman, wife*.
> - **Unmarked terms** don't reveal the person's gender, e.g. *police officer, spouse*.
> - Some words are **marked** by a **feminising suffix**, e.g. *actress, usherette, comedienne*.
>   The suffix implies that the male version is the **original** or the **norm**, so it seems **superior** to the female version.

> **Generic terms**
> - This is when a **marked term** is used to refer both to men and women.
> - It's nearly always **masculine terms** which are used to mean **people** in general, rather than just **men**.
> - The most common example is the word *man*, e.g. the noun *mankind*, or the verb *to* **man** *the desk*.
> - **Generic terms** refer to everybody, but using them can make **females** seem **invisible** by **ignoring** them. When this occurs, women are said to be occupying **negative semantic space**.

> **Lexical Asymmetry** refers to **pairs of words** that appear to have a **similar meaning**, but aren't **equally balanced**, e.g. *bachelor* and *spinster* (unmarried man and unmarried woman).
> - The connotations of *bachelor* are usually **positive** — it's associated with a man living a carefree, independent life.
> - The connotations of *spinster* are usually **negative** — it implies that the woman has been unable to find a partner.

> **Patronising terms** are words used by speakers that imply **superiority** over the person they're talking to.
> - Terms that imply someone is **younger** than the speaker can be patronising, e.g. *girls, young lady*.
> - **Terms of endearment** can be **patronising** in some circumstances, e.g. *love, dear, sweetheart*.
> - Whether a word is **patronising** depends on the **context**, e.g. a male employee who addresses a female colleague as *love* could be seen as patronising, but boyfriends and girlfriends calling each other *love* might not.

Grammar can be Sexist

The idea that the **male** is the **norm** is also evident in English **grammar**.

1) **Pronouns** — the 3rd person masculine pronoun *he* or *his* is often used to refer both to men and women, e.g. **an employee** *who is absent for longer than five days must obtain a sick note from* **his** *doctor*.

2) **Syntax** — when one gender specific word is always placed before another, it's known as **order of preference**, e.g. *Mr and Mrs, men and women, Sir or Madam*. Usually the male term comes first.

There are More Insults for Women than Men

There are a lot **more insulting terms** for **women** than there are for **men**. This is known as **over-representation**.

1) Lots of insulting terms for **women** have an **animal** theme, e.g. *bitch, cow*.

2) There are lots of words to label women as **promiscuous**, e.g. *slag, slut, slapper*.

3) There are hardly any **equivalents** for men. Terms like *stud* tend to have **positive connotations**.
   Terms like *man whore* or *male slut* tend to be used **comically**, and imply that the **female** version is the **norm**.

4) The **lack** of an **equivalent term** for something — e.g. a male term for *slut* — is known as a **lexical gap**.

Language and Gender

Sexist Language can be Avoided and Changed

1) The **Sex Discrimination Act** was passed in **1975** to **protect** people from sexual discrimination and harassment, especially at work and at school.
2) It reflected the work of **feminist campaigners** who wanted to promote **equality** between men and women.
3) Part of this campaign was a push to get rid of **sexist language**.
4) The idea is that language doesn't just **reflect** sexist **attitudes** — it helps to **keep them alive**.
5) So if you change **discriminatory language**, then people's **attitudes** might change too.
6) This is often called **political correctness** (more on this on p.11).
7) **Sexist terms** can be avoided by **replacing** them with **gender neutral** ones.

Calm down, ducky.

For example...

1) **Marked terms** can be replaced with **unmarked terms**, e.g. *head teacher* instead of *headmaster* or *headmistress*, *police officer* instead of *policeman* or *policewoman*.
2) **Feminising suffixes** can be **dropped**, e.g. a female manager is called a *manager*, not a *manageress*.
3) Instead of *Mrs* or *Miss*, the title *Ms* is often used, so you **can't tell** whether a woman is **married**.
4) The generic use of **man** can be replaced by gender neutral terms, e.g. *humankind* instead of *mankind*, *workforce* instead of *manpower*.
5) The **generic** use of the masculine 3rd person pronoun (*he*) can be replaced by *he/she*, *s/he*, or *they*. Sentences can be made **gender-neutral** by using the **plural** instead, e.g. *Employees who are absent for longer than five days must obtain a sick note from **their** doctor.*

People have Different Views about Avoiding Sexist Language

1) The point of encouraging people to avoid sexist language is to ensure people will be treated **equally**, and not feel they're being **singled out**, or **ignored**, because of their gender.
2) Sometimes there are **problems** with trying to **control language** in this way. People can feel that it's **overbearing**, and find it frustrating because they feel they can't speak freely without getting into trouble. Some people argue that this can create **resentment** towards the group of people it's designed to protect.
3) It's hard to **enforce** the use of non-sexist language. Some people think that condemning all sexist language ignores **context** and **intent**, e.g. if everyone understands that a comment is a joke, and nobody is offended by it, then it's **pointless** to have laws that stop people from making it.

Practice Questions

Q1 What is a marked term?
Q2 Explain what is meant by lexical asymmetry.
Q3 How can pronouns be used in a sexist way?
Q4 What is the Sex Discrimination Act?
Q5 Give two reasons why people might disagree with having controls on language use.

Essay Question

Q1 Discuss how language can be used to change sexist attitudes.

So, boys, any more feminising suffixes and you really will be gender-neutral...

Some scare-mongering tactics for you there... sorry, don't let it put you off language and gender. It's not all marked terms, asserting superiority and political correctness, honest. I think this is one of the most interesting topics actually — does language that points out the differences between men and women actually end up making them more different...

Section Two — Language in Social Contexts

Writing About Language Issues

These pages are for AQA A, AQA B and Edexcel. 'Writing about language issues' can sound tricky, but it doesn't have to be. It's really just about looking at how people deal with language issues, and how important language is in society. Easy...

Language Issues aren't only for Linguists

1) Language issues are **frequently debated** in wider society.

2) Regional and national **media** — TV, radio, newspapers, magazines and the Internet — often conduct debates about the 'state of language' today. They discuss how it's **developing** and **changing** (for better or for worse).

3) Debates amongst linguists are sometimes brought to the **general public's attention** in this way.

4) While you might think that not many people are that bothered about how they and others **speak** or **write**, lots of non-specialist readers and writers care about **how** language is used. They think it reflects on the **individual** and on **society** as a whole, and they care **strongly enough** to join in the debate with their **own thoughts** or **examples**.

Some people complain that Language is Declining

Editorials in newspapers and magazines often have their say about the **state of language** today. They often link changes in language to a sense of **decline** rather than **development**. Some also link what they see as the deterioration of language with the **state of society** in general.

1) Writing for a non-specialist audience means you can get your point across in lots of different ways.

2) If you look at how these texts work according to **linguistic frameworks**, you'll have a better understanding of how to put one together **yourself**. This sample magazine editorial is about **language change**:

> "It's apparent that the English language in its purest form, having enriched itself with borrowings and loans from the world's most progressive and intellectual cultures, has peaked. Worst of all, and to our horror, it is now receding. From the summits of Johnson and Lowth, English has tumbled almost toward the Neanderthal — a series of (albeit now electronic) monosyllabic grunts and minimalisms that reek of laziness rather than meaningful or worthy contributions to a formerly rich tapestry. The biggest culprit — "text message speak", has no place in linguistic debate, unless we realise that *pmsl* means not so much *piss myself laughing* as *please murder some language*."

Semantics

- The author specifically aims to create a **pessimistic atmosphere** by using terms with very **negative associations** like *receding, tumbled, horror, reek, laziness, culprit, murder*.

- The author also **juxtaposes** an idealised form of English (*peaked,* Johnson's and Lowth's *summits*), with a **physical fall** or **collapse** (*tumbled*), and a **lack of civilisation** (*Neanderthal*).

- Constructing a **different meaning** to *pmsl* also aims to make fun of the number of abbreviations that are used in informal English but maintains a serious undertone by using the term *murder* — the author's aim is to make the readers feel as if the English language is in **danger**, and it's their **responsibility** to stop the changes.

Grammar

- **Superlative adjectives** like *biggest, purest, most progressive* and *worst* give the text an air of **authority** and make it (both the text and the situation of English) seem much more **serious**.

- **Declarative sentences** e.g. *It's apparent that the English language... has peaked* also make the writing sound **authoritative** and mean that the points made in the text seem **definite** and **unquestionable**.

- Using **collective address** e.g. *unless <u>we</u> realise* directly **involves** the reader in taking responsibility for the problems the author identifies.

Lexis

- The lexis is mostly **non-specialist terminology** — the author doesn't use any linguistic phrases, and even **sensationalises** the writing by describing current English as *Neanderthal* and **exaggerating** everyone's emails and text messages into *grunts and minimalisms*.

- The lexis creates **oppositions** between the *meaningful and worthy... rich tapestry* of English *in its purest form*, and **informal varieties** of English, using *culprit* and *murder* to highlight the author's judgement that non-standard English like the kind used in text messages has *no place in linguistic debate*.

Writing About Language Issues

Some writers *Embrace Language Change*

Not everyone has the same feelings about language issues. Writing about something you support or agree with sometimes requires a **different approach** from when you're criticising or complaining.

> "If English had been to school it would've been the small kid in first year that matured into the playground bully — always pushing French in puddles and stealing Latin's dinner money. But it is dismissive of teachers' discipline, and has never been fully tamed by its many adoring students. The English language is a living organism, assuming myriad forms, rebuffing invasions (both military and prescriptive), constantly changing and developing. It is at once beyond control and our one pervasive constant — our identity. Shouldn't we be celebrating it for the unique world force it has now become?"

The **tone** and **style** of this piece of writing are different from the one on p.44, as a result of the following techniques:

Personification

Writing that aims to highlight the good things about language change and variation often tries to give English a **personality** and make it appear **alive**. The aim is to make the reader feel like the language can't be **controlled** by prescriptivism, and that is exactly what makes it so great. Attributing the **qualities** needed to *rebuff* invasions also makes English seem **superior** to other languages.

Metaphor

The author places the concept of a 'living' English language into a **familiar human situation** — using a humorous metaphor of a school playground. This communicates the writer's message in a way that **non-specialists** can easily understand.

Rhetorical Questions

The rhetorical question at the end **leads** the reader into **agreeing** with the writer's opinion, by suggesting that there is no other possible logical answer.

Non-specialist Books *on Language are Popular*

Non-linguists are now quite **well informed** about language. This has resulted in lots of different opinions — everyone's got their **own view** on what constitutes 'good' or 'bad' English and whether they accept or understand certain phrases.

1) It's not only **textbooks** that discuss the various aspects of English.
2) **Linguists** write non-specialist titles, like David Crystal's *By Hook or by Crook: A Journey in Search of English* (2007) and *Txting: The Gr8 Db8* (2008), which are both very descriptive.
3) There are also books like the *How to talk proper in Liverpool: Lern Yersel' Scouse* or *Larn Yersel' Geordie* series, which are examples of **light-hearted** popular titles that document **regional variations**. There are also plenty of books about the differences between men and women in terms of **language and gender** too.
4) **Journalists / broadcasters** — who aren't necessarily experts on linguistics — sometimes write about language too, for example Melvyn Bragg's *The Adventure of English* (2003).

Practice Questions

Q1 How does the general public become involved in debates about language change?
Q2 How might you use lexis, semantics and grammar to convince people that language is deteriorating?
Q3 What devices could be used to make the issues accessible to a non-specialist reader?
Q4 Apart from textbooks or revision guides, what sort of texts about English are available to a non-specialist reader?

Essay Question

Q1 Discuss the different styles you could adopt to get your views about English language across to a reader in a persuasive article.

Writing about language issues can give you writing about language issues...

My problem with it is the sheer wastefulness of the operation. It seems such a shame to use up so many precious words just writing about other words. They should be out there living the dream in marriage proposals, song lyrics and great political speeches, not cooped up in stuffy essays and newspaper articles. They'll probably run out one day, then we'll be sorry.

Sources and Exam Questions

Here are some exam-style questions, with sources like the ones you'll get in the real paper.
The exact question style will vary depending on your exam board, but these will still be good practice.

1.   Study Texts A - D below.

     The texts illustrate different viewpoints on accent and dialect.

     Analyse and compare the use of language in these texts.
     You should explore:

-    The writers' attitudes and opinions about accent and dialect.
-    How their language choices convey these attitudes.   *[45 marks]*

Text A — An extract from *Sons and Lovers* (1913) by D H Lawrence

At half-past eleven her husband came. His cheeks were very red and very shiny above his black moustache. His head nodded slightly. He was pleased with himself.

"Oh! Oh! waitin' for me, lass? I've bin 'elpin Anthony, an' what's think he's gen me? Nowt b'r a lousy hae'f-crown, an' that's ivry penny—"

"He thinks you've made the rest up in beer," she said shortly.

"An' I 'aven't—that I 'aven't. You b'lieve me, I've 'ad very little this day, I have an' all." His voice went tender. "Here, an' I browt thee a bit o' brandysnap, an' a cocoanut for th' children." He laid the gingerbread and the cocoanut, a hairy object, on the table. "Nay, tha niver said thankyer for nowt i'thy life, did ter?"

As a compromise, she picked up the cocoanut and shook it, to see if it had any milk.

"It's a good 'un, you may back yer life o'that. I got it fra' Bill Hodgkisson. 'Bill,' I says, 'tha non wants them three nuts, does ter? Arena ter for gi'ein' me one for my bit of a lad an' wench?' 'I ham, Walter, my lad,' 'e says; 'ta'e which on 'em ter's a mind.' An' so I took one, an' thanked 'im. I didn't like ter shake it afore 'is eyes, but 'e says, 'Tha'd better ma'e sure it's a good un, Walt.' An' so, yer see, I knowed it was. He's a nice chap, is Bill Hodgkisson, e's a nice chap!"

"A man will part with anything so long as he's drunk, and you're drunk along with him," said Mrs. Morel.

"Eh, tha mucky little 'ussy, who's drunk, I sh'd like ter know?" said Morel. He was extraordinarily pleased with himself, because of his day's helping to wait in the Moon and Stars. He chattered on.

Mrs. Morel, very tired, and sick of his babble, went to bed as quickly as possible, while he raked the fire.

Text B — [Sir Toby], *Twelfth Night* by William Shakespeare — Act 3 Scene 4

SIR TOBY: ...swear horrible; for it comes to pass oft, that a terrible oath, with a swaggering accent sharply twanged off, gives manhood more approbation than ever proof itself would have earned him.

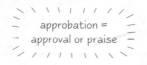

approbation = approval or praise

Sources and Exam Questions

Text C — Comments in response to a blog on the use of Standard English in teaching

county_teacher1947 at **11:44** on **13/04/09**

Are you seriously suggesting that we should be teaching children English based on the geographical location of the schools they go to? Standard English is the necessary consistent factor in the education system — you can't dismiss it as strictly prescriptivist when the alternative is diversifying the education system so that ultimately one region would struggle to communicate with another. I am totally receptive to the fluidity of spoken English across regions but written English — in a standard form — is necessary in education as it provides our children with the necessary skills to communicate effectively in adult life (imagine writing a letter to the bank in your dialect — ridiculous).

i_love_lamp at **12:27** on **13/04/09**

i have 2 agree. what sort of -ve effect wud this have on pupils that moved school... how would that work?!

jasondonovanssocks at **12:31** on **13/04/09**

I think there's something in this. I don't like the thought of my kid being told that one way of using his native language is 'right' and another 'wrong'. He speaks how he speaks. Why should he be corrected all the time just because his teacher thinks he is wrong? He's not even familiar with 'standard english'.

bretty901 at **12:32** on **13/04/09**

er... jasondonovanssocks hv u eva bin 2school m8? dats sort of how it works ahhaaha!!!

lyssy20 at **12:40** on **13/04/09**

While im not enamoured with his written english, i think bretty is right. if your kid went to a maths lesson and asserted that 2 + 2 = 5 he would be corrected. Teaching a standard variety of a language ensures that everyone is learning the same thing. you might think its a bit draconian but schools need to have the concept of right and wrong in place otherwise they couldn't teach anything.

Text D — Transcript of a conversation between two male friends

R: did you see the footie last night

S: aye (.) I couldn't believe it (2) what a load of rubbish

R: total rubbish man (1) think you'll gan next week

S: aye (1) canna just give up like even (.) even though (.) why are you not

R: // aye suppose not   // aye no I probably will then

[the phone rings]

S: hang on (3) hello (4) right (3) nope (.) no sorry (.) she's (.) she's not here at the moment I'm afraid (5) no I'm not sure like (.) dunno (.) probably some time this afternoon (3) aye I will (.) get her (.) get her to give you a ring when she's back (2) all right (1) cheers then (2) cheers bye now (1) soz mate

R: and what was that

S: what (.) what was what

R: your phone voice (.) when you was on the phone like you was

S: // what phone voice (.) what do you (.) that's how I always talk

R: it is not man (1) no way like you sound well posh (.) posh like

S: // shut up will you (1) like you never talk proper on the phone

R: not like that man I don't no

Transcription Key

(.)	*Micropause*	//	*interruptions / overlapping speech*
(2)	*Pause in seconds*		

Sources and Exam Questions

2. Study Texts A - C below.

The texts illustrate different varieties of language in social contexts.

- Analyse how the language choices convey attitudes to men and women and their respective roles in society.
- Evaluate how the different contexts might have shaped the language of the texts and the ways the ideas are communicated. *[40 marks]*

Text A — An extract from *The Yellow Wallpaper* (1892) by Charlotte Perkins Gilman

John laughs at me, of course, but one expects that in marriage.

John is practical in the extreme. He has no patience with faith, an intense horror of superstition, and he scoffs openly at any talk of things not to be felt and seen and put down in figures.

John is a physician, and PERHAPS — (I would not say it to a living soul, of course, but this is dead paper and a great relief to my mind) — PERHAPS that is one reason I do not get well faster.

You see he does not believe I am sick!

And what can one do?

If a physician of high standing, and one's own husband, assures friends and relatives that there is really nothing the matter with one but temporary nervous depression — a slight hysterical tendency — what is one to do?

My brother is also a physician, and also of high standing, and he says the same thing.

So I take phosphates or phosphites — whichever it is, and tonics, and journeys, and air, and exercise, and am absolutely forbidden to "work" until I am well again.

Personally, I disagree with their ideas.

Personally, I believe that congenial work, with excitement and change, would do me good.

But what is one to do?

I did write for a while in spite of them; but it DOES exhaust me a good deal — having to be so sly about it, or else meet with heavy opposition.

I sometimes fancy that in my condition if I had less opposition and more society and stimulus — but John says the very worst thing I can do is to think about my condition, and I confess it always makes me feel bad.

Sources and Exam Questions

Text B — A table from a humorous magazine feature on men and women's language

Men		Women	
Say	**Mean**	**Say**	**Mean**
Mmm-hmm	There is a screen nearby and I'm watching it while you're talking	Yes	No
Of course I'm listening	It is unlikely I'm listening	No	No
That one looks really nice	Can you buy it so we can leave?	Maybe	No
Your hair looks really nice	I remembered you went to the hairdressers today but I can't tell the difference	It's OK	It's not OK
I just need some 'me' time	I want to go and watch the football with my mates tonight	I don't mind	I definitely do mind
Can we take your car?	My car is unfit for human beings	It's up to you	Agree with me or you'll be sorry

Text C — Transcript of a conversation between two male (1M and 2M) and two female (1F and 2F) friends

1M: did they say how long it would be when you ordered mate

2M: nope (1) I (.) I don't know

1F: // how are you complaining <u>already</u> (.) we've only been here

1M: // because I'm <u>starving</u>

2F: aw (.) are you hungry Jon

1M: yes I am (1) I am actually really am starving (1) didn't get a chance to have breakfast this morning did I

1F: what does that (.) why you looking at me then

2M: // didn't you (.) unlucky mate (1) you get forced into chores again

1M: // too right I did

1F: erm (.) just a minute there wait

2F: // yeah right be quiet Chris (1) good on you Kate (1) I should take a leaf out of out of your book right (.) get <u>this</u> one doing something useful for a change

1F: // too right

2M: // erm <u>excuse</u> me I am very useful

2F: I'll believe <u>that</u> when I see it shall I then

1M: // don't argue mate (.) you'll regret it (1) just say take it from me just say yes (2) oh brilliant (.) finally it's here

1F: thank you (2) oh yours looks really nice too

2F: // um (.) oh thanks (1) but erm (.) I don't think this is what I ordered actually

1F: oh no (1) what should it be (.) can you like see if they'll change it

2M: // what (.) yeah excuse me mate (.) I think this is wrong can you change it

2F: // no it's ok (.) um (.) I'm sure it's (2) well ok thank you

1F: // no I think you should get the right

Transcription Key

(.)	*Micropause*	//	*interruptions / overlapping speech*
(2)	*Pause in seconds*	<u>underlining</u>	*indicates stress / increased volume*

Spoken Language

These pages are for WJEC and OCR. Texting, mailing, blogging — have we forgotten the glorious art of conversation... the mechanics of a decent discussion... the joys of spoken language... no, we haven't. It's all right here on these pages.

Spoken language has **Two Main Purposes**

1) **To convey meaning** — when you need to **explain something** to someone, or **give orders** or **instructions**, you use language as a means of **clarification**, so that the listener will **understand** you.

2) **To demonstrate attitudes and values** — language lets you offer **opinions** on subjects, and get your **point of view across**.

Martin loved good conversation — but the logs remained unresponsive

The **Content** of spoken language **Depends** on its **Context**

Spoken language is usually the most **efficient** way for speakers to communicate with each other. As with written language, the way a spoken text is **constructed** can be affected by **external** features.

1) The **audience** or **person being addressed** — it could be someone the speaker has known for years, or thousands of people that they've never met before.

2) The speaker's **background** — this will affect their **word choices**, **grammatical constructions**, etc.

3) The **location** and **purpose** of the text — speakers use language differently depending on where the conversation is taking place, and what's being talked about.

Spoken language can be **Formal** or **Informal**

1) **Formal** speech is often used in situations when you **don't really know** the people you're talking to.

2) You might also use formal speech in a situation where you want to **show respect**, like a **job interview**.

3) It's most common in **prepared** speeches — the speaker is reading from **planned, written notes**.

4) Formal spoken language is more likely to use **complex** and mainly **complete grammatical structures**.

   1) **Informal** speech is generally used **among friends** or in situations where there's **no need** for formality or preparation.

   2) It includes mostly **colloquial language**, which is casual and familiar.

   3) It has **simpler** and often **incomplete grammatical structures**, **simpler vocabulary**, more **slang** words and **dialect** features.

Speech can be **Individual** or involve **More Than One Person**

Individual speech is often known as a **monologue**. Monologues convey **internal thoughts**, **opinions** or **experiences**.

1) The term 'monologue' is usually used for a **scripted performance** (a dramatic monologue), but it can also include any **individual** speaking for a longer period of time than normal.

2) Monologues are directed at listeners who make **no spoken contribution**.

3) They can be **prepared** or **spontaneous**.

Dialogue is **spoken** language that involves **more than one** speaker.

1) A dialogue is a **conversation** involving two or more people — they use language to **interact** with each other.

2) Dialogue exchanges can be **short**, but in longer conversations one of the speakers may take the **major role**, with the others mainly listening and only **contributing occasionally**.

3) Dialogue can be prepared or spontaneous. Most conversations between characters on TV or in plays or films are **scripted** by a writer, but conversations between you and your friends are **unprepared** — in spontaneous dialogue speakers **respond** to the different **cues and contexts** that come up as the conversation goes on.

Spoken Language

Spoken Language Functions *in different ways*

There are **five** categories of **spoken language**, which are used in different situations.

1) Interactional language
is the language of **informal speech**. It has a **social** function — its purpose is to **develop relationships** between speakers.

The speakers exchange personal information. →

> **A:** *so what're you studying when you get there*
> **B:** *I'm going to be doing astronomy*
> **A:** *no way (2) so am I (1) I'll see you in lectures*

← Asking a question guarantees a response and keeps the interaction going.

2) Referential language
provides the listener with **information**. It's used to **refer** to **objects** or to **abstract** concepts. The speaker **assumes knowledge** from the listener. The listener has to understand the **context** before they can make sense of the **references**.

> ***the parcel** is being delivered **here** at **two o'clock***

This wouldn't make sense to the listener unless they knew that a parcel was expected.

The listener wouldn't understand this reference unless they knew where *here* was.

This assumes that the listener knows what day the parcel is expected, and whether it's more likely to be delivered at two o'clock in the morning or in the afternoon.

3) Expressive language
highlights the speaker's **emotions**, **feelings** and **attitudes**. The language shows the speaker's judgements or feelings about another person, event or situation.

> *this **really** can't be allowed to continue my friends (2) it's a **total** disgrace*

It's likely to contain adverbs to make the statements forceful.

Emotive adjectives make the statements subjective.

4) Transactional language
is about **getting information** or **making a deal**, e.g. buying or selling. It has a specific purpose, so it's driven by **needs and wants** rather than **sociability**.

A direct request for information is followed by a direct answer. →

> **A:** *could you tell me where the soup is please*
> **B:** *it's on aisle 7 (.) right by the croutons*

5) Phatic language
is used for **social purposes** rather than to convey serious meaning, e.g. when someone comments about the weather as a means of **initiating a conversation**. They don't want to have a meteorological discussion with you, but it starts a conversation that (usually) quickly moves on to other subjects. Phatic communication is also called '**small talk**'.

The speaker doesn't expect these questions to be answered. →

> *did you see that rain before (.) it was unbelievable (2) I'm not too late am I*

Practice Questions

Q1   What are the two main purposes of spoken language?

Q2   What external factors can have an effect on spoken language?

Q3   Outline the differences between informal and formal speech.

Essay Question

Q1   Write five short passages that show the five different types of spoken language.
Analyse the linguistic features and function of each passage.

Spoken language? Never heard of it...

But apparently it's ideal for conversations and speeches. Well who knew? This book really is a revelation — time to go forth and spread the word about spoken language to all you meet. I'd start with something referential if I were you, then slip in a bit of interactional language if you like the cut of their jib, and finish with something expressive to really pack a punch.

Speech Features

These pages are for WJEC and OCR. *"Speech" features George Clooney, Jessica Biel and a Scottish kilted marching band who trek across the Andes in search of a new world language. These pages tell of their struggle to survive in a world where even their own language defies them. Actually, I'm pulling your leg. This page is about speech features though.*

Speech can be **Prepared** or **Spontaneous**

You can either know exactly what you're about to say, or you can make it up as you go along.

Prepared speech

1) Worked out **in advance**.
2) Designed for specific **audience and purpose**.
3) Needs to be **well written** (so is usually **formal** and in Standard English).
4) **Performed** or **delivered** to try and make an impact.
5) Needs to **maintain the interest** of listeners (who may or may not be known to the speaker).
6) Examples include **political speeches** and **sermons**.

Spontaneous speech

1) **Not prepared** or written down beforehand.
2) Delivered **on the spot** as soon as, or shortly after, the idea comes to the speaker.
3) Usually **informal** (depending on context).
4) Usually shared with people **known to the speaker**.
5) Mainly **in response to** another speaker.

"Shut your cakehole, speech features!" Jessica taunted.

Prepared and Spontaneous speech are Very Different

If you apply **language frameworks** to prepared and spontaneous speech, you can see how different they are.

Lexis
- **Prepared speech** — the lexis is likely to be **standardised** and formal. Speakers have time to think about their word choices, so the vocabulary is more **sophisticated** and **technical**.
- **Spontaneous speech** — the lexis is likely to be **non-standard**. The informal context means **slang** and **dialect** forms are used more.

Grammar
- **Prepared speech** — the structure of sentences follows standard **grammatical rules** and pauses in the speech are controlled by **punctuation**. Speakers don't tend to use many **contractions**.
- **Spontaneous speech** — non-standard **agreements**, non-standard or **irregular tenses**, and **double negatives** are common in conversation, e.g. *I done it, We was planning to, I never told him nothing.*

Formality / Audience
- **Prepared speech** — speeches are aimed at an **audience**. The language is carefully chosen to persuade the audience in some way. Prepared speeches usually **address** the audience **directly** (the speaker uses *I* or *we*, and *you*). They're often **formal** to create a feeling of **prestige**.
- **Spontaneous speech** — most spontaneous speech is only meant for the speakers involved. Conversations that take place in **public places** (over a shop counter etc.) or between strangers are usually more **formal** than private ones.

Prepared and spontaneous speech also have some features in common:

1) **Discourse structure** — a prepared speech has a beginning, middle, and end. **Themes** and **ideas** are introduced at different points, and the whole thing is usually written to end on a **positive note**, so that the audience go away with a **lasting impression**. Spontaneous speech also has **formulaic** beginnings and endings (see p.54).

2) **Non-verbal communication** relates to body language, gestures and facial expressions. It **emphasises** certain words or phrases in both prepared and spontaneous speech, but can also be **disruptive** if it's overdone.

3) **Prosodic features** — include stress, rhythm, pitch, tempo and intonation. They're useful in prepared speech, where a speaker can use the devices to keep an audience **interested** over a long period of time.

Speech Features

Spontaneous speech has many Unique Features

Even though **spontaneous speech** shares some features with prepared spoken English, it has lots of **specific features**. Look at the following **conversation** between two people:

> **Ellipsis** is where part of a grammatical structure is omitted without affecting understanding, e.g. *(Are) You going to come round later?* It makes the tone more casual than the full version.

> **Phatic expressions** play a key role in spontaneous speech, especially when you're initiating a conversation. The comments have no great meaning or interest in themselves, but are designed to help conversations get started.

> **False starts** regularly occur in conversation. The speaker changes their train of thought halfway through, and begins the utterance again.

> **Back-channelling** is used to feed back to a speaker that what they're saying is being understood, e.g. *I see* or another repeated utterance. You can also give feedback non-verbally e.g. nodding or shaking your head.

> **Deictic expressions** are pointers that refer the listener backwards, forwards or outside a text. Most common are words such as *this, that, here,* and *there*. You can't understand deictic expressions unless you know their context.

Speaker 1:	alright mate
Speaker 2:	hi Dan (.) how's it going
Speaker 1:	yeah not bad thanks how are you
Speaker 2:	good thanks (.) enjoying the sun
Speaker 1:	makes nice change dunt it (1) I mean
Speaker 2:	// yeah (2) you get my message the other day
Speaker 1:	um, yeah, I think so (.) about (1) er (.) you're having a party
Speaker 2:	// party yeah
Speaker 1:	// oh yeah
Speaker 2:	yeah on sat (.) er tomorrow night
Speaker 1:	// oh yeah
Speaker 2:	down at mine (.) d'ya know where that is
Speaker 1:	// yeah // yeah no um I know it
Speaker 2:	cool (.) gonna come down then
Speaker 1:	coursa will mate (.) sounds good
Speaker 2:	nice one (3) er, see you there then
Speaker 1:	yep, probably see you later

> **Hedging** shows uncertainty in a conversation — words like *perhaps* or *maybe* are used to weaken the force of what you're saying.

> **Elision** is the slurring together of sounds or syllables, e.g. *gonna* rather than *going to* — this saves time, and is less formal.

> **Non-fluency features** are devices that interrupt the flow of talk. Hesitation or repetition, fillers such as *er* or *um*, interruptions and overlaps are all non-fluency features.

Practice Questions

Q1 List the key differences between prepared and spontaneous speech.
Q2 How might non-verbal communication influence a conversation?
Q3 Describe the following unique features of spontaneous speech: ellipsis, non-fluency and back-channelling.

Essay Question

Q1 Outline the key features of spontaneous speech. Use specific examples to highlight their effect on a conversation.

The Elisionist — top new movie based on a slurring magician...

If you thought that hedging was something Bill the gardener pretended to do while he drank your entire supply of tea, think again. Everything on this page will be evident in any conversation you have today, so next time you find yourself in one, stop chatting and have a listen. And as if by magic... the faces of the people you've abruptly stopped talking to become hilarious.

Conversation and Turn-taking

WJEC and OCR again here. For some of us, conversation is just a case of opening our mouths and watching our peers marvel at the verbal gold that spills forth. Others, however, believe in something called 'taking turns'. Beats me...

Some features occur in All Conversations

No matter who you find yourself talking to, the devices for **starting** and **ending** conversations are usually the same.

1) **Openings** — an informal conversation may begin with a simple **familiar starter**. These are usually **greetings**, such as *hello*, or *alright?* More formal conversations often include **inquiries** like *I wonder if you could help me?* to get someone's **attention**.

> A: *good morning*
> B: *hello (.) can I help you*

2) **Responses** — familiar openings (see above) invite a particular response.

> A: *hello (.) can I help you*
> B: *I'm just browsing thanks*

3) **Adjacency pairs** — **short**, **familiar exchanges** of conversation that follow **predictable** patterns.

> A: *how are you*
> B: *I'm fine thanks*

4) **Signalling closure** — speech indicators and other non-verbal signs can be used to show that a conversation is **drawing to a close**.

> A: *he fell down a manhole once*
> B: *really (1) well (.) time I was off*

Some features depend on the Individual Speakers

Switching and turn-taking

1) The person speaking at any given time may be aware that **someone else** wants to speak.
2) In an orderly conversation they **invite** the switch to another speaker e.g. by **pausing**, or trying to make an **emphatic** final statement.
3) **Domineering** speakers sometimes choose to **ignore** this, meaning other speakers have to break into the conversation by **interrupting**, or just **stay silent**.

> A: *I can't believe he didn't see it*
> B: *why not (1) it wasn't a penalty (2) what do you think*
> A: *I think it probably was*
> B: *that's why you're not a referee*
> A: *it's pretty hard to work out*
> B: *// maybe if you weren't watching*

Tag questions

1) These are attached to the **end of statements**, and **invite responses** from other speakers.
2) They're used by speakers who are seeking some **feedback**.
3) This could be because they're feeling **uncomfortable**, or because they're trying to **control** the conversation by bringing other people into it.

> A: *this is an issue that we need to resolve quickly <u>isn't it</u>*

Topic Shifts

1) **Topic shifts** are when speakers **change** the **subject** of the conversation.
2) They move the conversation forward or **change** its **focus**.
3) They're usually started by the domineering speaker trying to control the **content** and **direction** of a conversation.

> A: *so I said carbonara*
> B: *right (2) did you ever hear back from Dave*

Feedback

1) When someone's speaking, people give **verbal** and **non-verbal** signs that they're **listening** to them.
2) For example, brief comments, nodding or shaking your head, smiling, frowning, etc.

> A: *no one told me it was a sponge*
> B: *mm-hmm*

Conversation and Turn-taking

Different Techniques are involved at different Stages of a Conversation

Getting involved / Initiating conversation

1) Most participants in a conversation will offer a contribution **without waiting** to be asked — if you waited to be asked to speak in every conversation, you might **never** speak at all.

2) You might get a conversation started by showing an **interest** in the other people involved.

3) If you're talking to an **unfamiliar person**, appropriate **phatic expressions** and **questioning** can help get things started, e.g. you can use **tag questions** to initiate **responses**.

Sustaining conversation

1) Fluent speaking (following **adjacency patterns** and **turn-taking rules**), showing an interest (**feedback**) and generally enjoying talking are all factors that help people **sustain** conversation.

2) **Speaker empathy** is important — if people are exploring **shared interests** or **opinions** then the conversation is more likely to be sustained. Listeners might make it clear that they share the speaker's views by using feedback, e.g. *mm* and *yeah*.

Ending conversation

1) **Social convention** makes us not want to appear rude, cut people short or walk away when they're not ready — so **phatic expressions** are used to **signal closure** in a socially recognisable way, e.g. *I should probably get going.*

2) There are also **non-verbal** cues that signal a speaker is about to end the conversation e.g. starting to **get up** from a seat, or increasing the **distance** between the speakers.

Judith signalled her intention to leave the conversation.

Participants Manage and Control conversations

In an orderly conversation, you take **turns** speaking with other people. However, not all conversations are orderly and it's rare to find one where each speaker actually waits their turn — it depends on the **individuals** involved.

Prepared / Formal situations

1) These are the types of conversation where there is a defined power relationship between the participants, e.g. conducting an **interview** with someone.

2) **Prepared situations** (like a tutorial, job interview or debate) have a **specific subject** or subject area on the agenda. You may not know precisely how the conversation will go, but you know what is **likely** to be discussed, and the level of **formality** you're expected to use.

3) There's usually a person **overtly** in charge of the exchanges, like an interviewer, lecturer or chairperson, whose **authority** to change the conversation at will is **already acknowledged** before it starts.

Unprepared / Informal situations

1) **Informal** social conversations are less likely to be prepared, and could involve any topic, but these still tend to be **controlled** by certain individuals.

2) People who are **louder**, **quicker** and more **forceful** than other speakers often **dominate informal conversations**.

3) It is easy for less confident and less assertive speakers to be **inhibited** or **intimidated**, and to end up contributing very little.

Practice Questions

Q1 Give an example of an adjacency pair and describe its purpose.

Q2 What is a phatic expression and how might it be used in conversation?

Essay Question

Q1 Discuss the ways in which an individual speaker might influence the course of a conversation.

Support the conversation movement — save the talking trees...

Conversation is a bit of a minefield really — sometimes people want you to gab on even when you've got nothing to say, and other times you're expected to shut up and listen when you've got loads of great words in your face just desperate for an airing. It's a tricky one all right, but if you remember one conversational rule then let it be this one — say it don't spray it...

Pragmatics

These pages are for WJEC and OCR. The words people say and how they say them are affected by social surroundings. People often don't say exactly what they mean because of politeness, or because they want something. Sly little foxes...

Pragmatics is about how Language is used in Social Situations

Pragmatics is the study of the part that language plays in **social situations**.

1) The meaning of what people say **isn't** always as **clear-cut** as it might seem.

2) There are lots of **unwritten social rules** that **prevent** people saying certain things, e.g. you probably wouldn't ask the Queen to '*put the kettle on, love*'.

3) There are also social conventions that make people say things in particular situations, e.g. saying *thank you* when somebody gives you something.

4) Pragmatics looks at **how** people get their **meaning** across within different **social contexts**. People often have to **imply** meanings rather than state them **directly**, so pragmatics concentrates on the meaning **behind** what's actually being said — the **subtext**.

> **EXAMPLE:**
>
> - In a meeting, an employee might say *it's a bit chilly in here*. What they actually mean is *can we close the window?* Saying it **indirectly** seems **less controlling** — it gives other people the opportunity to agree that it is chilly, and sets up a situation where **someone else** will offer to close the window.
>
> - Someone might say *I seem to spend all my time washing up* to their housemates. This is an **indirect request** for help, as what it actually means is *can someone else help?*

Prosody can Change the Meaning

Getting your meaning across isn't just about **what** you say, it's also about the **way** you say it.

1) Prosody is part of non-verbal communication (see p.52). It includes **pitch**, **volume**, **pace**, **pauses**, **intonation** and **stress**.

2) The way that something is said can completely change its meaning, so looking at **prosodic features** is really important in **pragmatics**.

Bert's speech had volume, pitch and stress, but he hadn't quite mastered pauses yet.

3) For example, there are loads of ways of saying this sentence that would **change** its **meaning**:

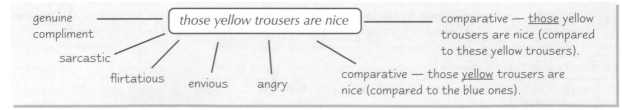

genuine compliment — those yellow trousers are nice — sarcastic — flirtatious — envious — angry — comparative — <u>those</u> yellow trousers are nice (compared to these yellow trousers). — comparative — those <u>yellow</u> trousers are nice (compared to the blue ones).

4) It can be really **difficult** to convey **prosodic features** in **writing**. Writers sometimes use **bolding**, <u>underlining</u> or *italics* to show where the emphasis should be. In fiction, they often have to **explain** how a character says something, e.g. *He answered quickly and angrily.*

The Words people Choose depend on the Audience and Context

This stuff is useful to know in your exam, because you can pick up on the **relationship** between speakers and the **context** they're in from how they speak to each other. For example:

1) If a speaker tells someone to *shut the door*, you might assume they were speaking to a **friend**, a **family member**, or someone they have **authority** over. You might also assume that they were in quite an **informal setting**.

2) If they said *I'm sorry but would you mind closing the door — there's a terrible draught* then you might assume that they were talking to a **stranger** or a **superior**. Friends or relatives would probably only speak to each other like this in a **formal setting**.

3) Any analysis like this is open to your **interpretation**, so it's good to discuss it even when speakers don't address each other as you might **expect** them to, e.g. family members might speak formally because they don't get on and feel uncomfortable around each other.

Pragmatics

Politeness Strategies ensure speakers Don't Cause Offence

1) There are lots of **different ways** to communicate an idea. The way you do it depends on the **situation** — where you are and who you're with.

2) You might need to be **tactful** and **diplomatic**, or very **forceful**.

3) People use different **politeness strategies** depending on how they want to come across, even if the **underlying meaning** is still the **same**.

4) Here are some of the possible strategies for saying *no* in response to the question *would you like to go and see a film tonight?*:

Gregory desperately wished he'd thought of a way to politely refuse.

Politeness Strategy	Example
Definite with negative word (e.g. *no, not, never*)	*No / no way / not a chance*. This sort of direct response would normally just be used with friends or family, because it's generally thought to be a bit rude.
Definite without negative word	*Are you serious? / I'd rather die*. These could be used for humorous effect, or if you really didn't care about being offensive.
Excuse	*I'd love to but I'm busy / Tonight isn't a very good night*. Excuses are used to justify why the answer is no.
Evasive	*Can we talk about this later / Now's just not a good time*. Evasive responses are used to avoid having to say no.
Apologetic	*Sorry... / I'm afraid...* People often apologise when they're saying no to soften their negative response.
Inarticulate	*Erm / Ah / Hmm* This usually shows that the person feels awkward and is trying to think of an excuse or a way to say no politely. If they stall for long enough, the meaning will become clear anyway.

5) People often use **more than one** politeness strategy in their response, e.g. if they were saying no, they might say *erm sorry no I can't tonight, I'm really busy*.

6) Politeness strategies also act as **conventions** for what to say in certain situations, e.g. shop assistants and customers usually say *thank you* to **each other** when a transaction is carried out at a till. Some politeness strategies like this are used **more** in the **UK** than in other countries.

7) Sometimes following the rules of politeness can lead to strategies being used in **strange ways**, e.g. people often say *sorry* when someone else bumps into them in the street.

Practice Questions

Q1 What is pragmatics?

Q2 Explain why and how a person might alter the language they use depending on their social surroundings.

Q3 Describe and give examples of the six main politeness strategies we adhere to in the UK.

Essay Question

Q1 Explain how language might be altered to fit a certain social situation. Refer to prosody and lexis in your answer.

Now's just not a good time for a funny gag — can we talk about it later...

If you wouldn't mind awfully, I think it might be quite a good idea to read through these pages carefully and make some notes. If you're already a very pragmatic person, I suppose you'll find these pages terribly easy. On the other hand, if you're a bit challenged on the tact front, then perhaps you should spend slightly longer on them. My, I do pull off politeness rather well...

Phonology and Phonetics

AQA A, OCR and WJEC should all look at these pages. They're all about different sounds in English, and the effects that they can create. Lots to take in here — but it's nothing you won't have heard before, in AS and in real life too.

Phonology *and* Phonetics *are* Different

Phonology

1) **Phonology** is the study of the **sound systems** of languages, in particular the **patterns** of sounds.

2) It focuses on **units** of sound, called **phonemes** (see below).

3) Unlike phonetics, in phonology you **don't** look at **differences** of **articulation**, e.g. if someone pronounces *stupid* as *shtupid*, the *s* and *sh* are still classed as the **same phoneme**, because the different pronunciation doesn't create a **different meaning**.

Phonetics

1) **Phonetics** is the study of how speech sounds are **made** and **received**.

2) It covers all **possible sounds** that the human vocal apparatus (vocal chords, tongue, lips, teeth, etc) can make.

3) It focuses on **differences** in **articulation**, e.g. different accents.

Phonemes *are* Units *of* Sound

1) The **smallest units** of **sound** are called **phonemes**. There are only about **44** phonemes in English, and combinations of them make up **all** the **possible** words and sounds in the language.

> This is the International Phonetic Alphabet (IPA). It's used for writing all the possible phonemes (sounds) that humans can make in any language. Slanting brackets are used to distinguish between phonemes. See p.60 for more on this.

2) For example, the word *cat* has **three** phonemes — /k/ (like the *c* in *coat*), /ae/ (like the *a* in *bat*) and /t/ (like the *t* in *toy*). By **changing** one of these phonemes (e.g. /f/ for /k/) you can create a new word, *fat*.

3) The 26 letters of the **alphabet** can express **all** the possible sounds in English, e.g. **pairs** of letters (**digraphs**) like *sh-* and *ch-* can be used to represent **single phonemes**.

4) The study of phonemes is divided into **vowel sounds** and **consonant sounds**.

Vowel Sounds

1) There are about **twenty vowel sounds** in English, even though there are only **five** vowels in the alphabet.

2) E.g. the vowel *a* has a different sound depending on the word in which it appears. In *ape* it sounds different to when it's in *sat*, *care* and *saw*.

3) Vowel sounds are usually in the **centre** of a **syllable**, e.g. b*a*g, c*oa*t.

4) When a vowel sound is spoken, the **vocal tract** is always **open** — the **airway** is clear and your **vocal chords** rub together to 'voice' the sound. Vowel sounds are made by **altering** the **shape** of the **mouth**. The way vowel sounds are **pronounced varies** in **different** regions. This is how people can tell the difference between accents (see p.30-31).

Consonant Sounds

1) The number of **consonant sounds** in English is close to the **actual** number of **consonants** in the **alphabet**.

2) Consonants are mostly found at the **edges** of **syllables**, e.g. *b*oy*s*, *g*irl*s*. Sometimes they can appear in **sequences** of three or four consonants **together**, e.g. *str*ing or twel*fth*.

3) Unlike vowels, they're mostly articulated by **closing** the vocal organs.

4) Some consonants are formed by **vibration** of the vocal chords, e.g. /b/ and /n/. The amount of vibration depends on the **position** of the consonant within the word. At the end of the word, the consonant is less pronounced. Other consonants don't use the vocal chords at all, such as /p/ and /s/.

Words *are made up of* Syllables

Syllables are a word's **individual units** of pronunciation. They are normally **combinations** of consonants and vowels.

1) The **centre** of a syllable is usually a **vowel sound**, e.g. b*u*n, t*y*ke.

2) Syllables can have one or more **consonants before** the **vowel**, e.g. *b*e, *sl*ow.

3) Many syllables have one or more consonants **following** the **vowel**, e.g. a*nt*.

4) They can also have consonants before **and** following the vowel, e.g. *pl*a*y*, *r*ea*d*.

5) **Monosyllabic** words have **one syllable**, e.g. *plate, car*. **Polysyllabic words** have **more than one** syllable, e.g. *amazing* (*a-maz-ing*), *cryogenic* (*cry-o-gen-ic*).

Phonology and Phonetics

Words Sound Different when they're Connected

Words are often pronounced **differently** than you'd expect when you see them **written down**.
This is because spoken language **combines** and **runs** sounds together.

Elision is when sounds are **left out**.
1) It happens especially in **rapid speech**, with words that have **clusters** of **consonants** or **syllables**.
2) For example, *library* is usually pronounced *libry*, and *everything* can become *evrythn*.

Assimilation is when sounds that are next to each other become **more alike**.
1) This happens especially in **rapid speech**, because it makes the words **easier** to say quickly.
2) For example, in the word *handbag*, *hand* becomes *ham*, to make it **easier** to **pronounce** with the syllable *bag*.

Liaison is when a **sound** is **inserted between** words or syllables to help them run **together** more smoothly.
1) For example — pronouncing /r/ at the **end of words**. When a word ending with *r* is **followed** by a word that **begins** with a **vowel**, the /r/ is **pronounced**, e.g. *mother ate* sounds like *mother rate*.
2) This is to avoid a gap between the words, known as a **hiatus**.
3) Sometimes it's easier to link words with /r/ even if there's no r in the spelling — e.g. *media(r) interest*.

Phonological Frameworks are used to Analyse Sound Patterns

Part of **phonology** involves looking at how sounds can convey **meaning** and **association**.

1) **Rhythm** is very clear in **poetry**. Lines are often **constructed** so that the **stress** falls on **important** words, emphasising their meaning, e.g. *But to go to school in a summer morn, / Oh! it drives all joy away.* **Advertising** also uses rhythm, particularly in **slogans**, to help the audience **remember** the **product**.

2) **Rhyme** is when words have **similar endings**. It's usually associated with poetry and songs, but it's also used in planned speeches and in advertising. The rhyming words in a speech or text always **stand out**, and their meanings are often **linked**.

3) **Alliteration** is where two or more words close to each other **begin** with the **same sound**, e.g. <u>s</u>ix <u>s</u>izzling <u>s</u>ausages.

4) **Assonance** is when the **vowel sounds** in the middle of two or more words are similar, e.g. *spoke* and *hope*. When vowel sounds **clash** with each other it's known as **dissonance**, e.g. *ham-fisted*.

5) Alliteration and assonance are used in **creative writing** to **emphasise** words and show that the **meaning** is **linked** in some way. They're also used in **persuasive writing** to make phrases catchy and more memorable.

6) **Onomatopoeia** — this is when a word **sounds like** the noise it describes, e.g. *buzz, pop, bang, snap*.

7) Sometimes sounds can appear **symbolic** for other reasons, e.g. **closed vowels** in words like *chip* and *little* can suggest smallness, while **open vowels** in words like *vast* and *grand* can suggest largeness. It's not always the case, but it's worth noting **sound symbolism** like this when you're analysing a text.

Practice Questions

Q1 What is the difference between a phoneme and a syllable? Give examples of both.
Q2 Explain how words may sound different when they become connected in speech.
Q3 Define the following terms: onomatopoeia, assonance and alliteration.

Essay Question

Q1 Discuss how phonetics and phonology are relevant in any analysis of a written or spoken text.

Frank's late for his dinner — why doesn't he phoneme...

I mean, it's the third time this week. Anyone would think he doesn't like eel and mushroom baguettes — actually that's disgusting. Anyway, remind yourself what phonemes are, how syllables build words, how words are connected in speech, and of the importance of the phonological framework. Then, if you're lucky, I'll make you a sandwich... yum.

Phonology and Phonetics

AQA A, AQA B, WJEC and OCR. Here it is at last — the really meaty spoken language stuff, complete with all the funny symbols and everything. So fasten your chinstraps, put down that weasel, and all hail the International Phonetic Alphabet.

Phonemic Symbols express the Sounds of the language

Here is a list of the phonemic symbols that represent the **basic sounds** of the English language. You don't have to memorise them, but you should be **familiar** with the ones that are likely to be different across **regional accents** — mainly the **vowels**. This list gives you examples of the sounds of English as they would be pronounced in **RP**.

Consonants of English

/f/ = **f**riend, tou**gh**   /ʃ/ = **sh**ape, bru**sh**   /b/ = **b**id, ro**b**   /n/ = me**n**, **sn**ake

/v/ = **v**enue, **v**illain, ha**v**e   /ʒ/ = lei**s**ure, vi**s**ion   /d/ = ba**d**, **d**eman**d**   /ŋ/ = ha**ng**er, lo**ng**

/θ/ = **th**ink, **th**rough   /h/ = **h**aunt, **h**it, be**h**ind   /g/ = ba**g**, **g**ain   /l/ = **l**arge, be**ll**

/ð/ = ei**th**er, **th**em, **th**ough   /p/ = **p**ot, ti**p**, **sp**at   /tʃ/ = **ch**ur**ch**, hun**ch**   /j/ = **y**ou, **y**acht

/s/ = **s**ell, dot**s**, cro**ss**es   /t/ = **t**op, pi**t**, s**t**ep   /dʒ/ = **j**u**dg**e, **g**in, **j**ack   /w/ = **wh**at, **o**nce, s**w**itch

/z/ = **z**oo, dog**s**, squee**z**e   /k/ = **k**ick, **c**ope, s**cr**ew   /m/ = **m**iddle, s**m**ell   /r/ = **r**oad, d**r**y

Short vowels of English

/ɪ/ = t**i**p, b**u**sy, h**i**ss

/e/ = sh**e**d, **a**ny

/æ/ = c**a**t, h**a**d, b**a**nk

/ɒ/ = w**a**nt, rob**o**t

/ʌ/ = c**u**p, s**o**n, bl**oo**d

/ʊ/ = w**oo**d, p**u**t, b**oo**k

/ə/ = **a**bout, bal**a**nce

Long vowels of English

/iː/ = sh**ee**p, h**ea**t

/ɑː/ = c**ar**, b**al**m

/ɜː/ = b**ir**d, h**ear**d

/ɔː/ = p**or**t, t**al**k

/uː/ = f**oo**d, shr**e**wd

Diphthongs of English

/eɪ/ = gr**ea**t, d**ay**   /əʊ/ = b**oa**t, h**o**me

/aɪ/ = fl**y**, br**igh**t   /ɪə/ = h**ere**, n**ear**

/ɔɪ/ = b**oy**, n**oi**se   /eə/ = st**are**, **air**

/aʊ/ = c**ow**, h**ou**se, g**ow**n   /ʊə/ = m**ore**, p**oor**

There are different types of Vowel Sound in English

There are three **distinct types** of vowel sound in English — short vowels, long vowels and diphthongs (two vowels in one).

> *bin /bɪn/, ban /bæn/* and *bun /bʌn/* are examples of **short vowel sounds**.
> *bean /biːn/, barn /bɑːn/* and *burn /bɜːn/* are examples of **long vowel sounds**.

Two vowel sounds can also be fused together, making what is called a diphthong.

> *bite /baɪt/, bait /beɪt/* and *boat /bəʊt/* are examples of **diphthongs**.

Phonemic symbols provide a valuable way of demonstrating the **differences in sound** — something that you can't necessarily show by the way the **words** are **spelled** — think of *read* /riːd/ and *read* /red/.

You can use phonemic symbols in Language Analysis

The standard practice when you're including a phonemic transcription is to start it on a **new line** so it can be read easily, leaving spaces **between the words** as in normal writing.

To give you an idea, this is how the definition of phonetics from p. 58 would look in transcription:

> *Phonetics is the study of how speech sounds are made and received*
> fənetɪks ɪz ðə stʌdɪ ɒv haʊ spiːtʃ saʊndz ɑː meɪd ænd rɪsiːvd

And this is how part of the definition of phonology would look:

> *Phonology is the study of the sound systems of languages*
> fənɒlədʒɪ ɪz ðə stʌdi ɒv ðə saʊnd sɪstəmz ɒv læŋgwɪdʒɪz

Don't panic — you don't have to transcribe anything, OR learn all these symbols off by heart. If you've got time though, and it's appropriate, it'll do your coursework no harm to include them.

Phonology and Phonetics

Phonetics shows the Differences between Accents

Here's a sentence as an example:

> *How are you feeling today?*

A phonemic transcription of this sentence in **Received Pronunciation** (RP) would look like this.

> haʊ ɑ juː fiːlɪŋ tədeɪ

However, the same sentence spoken in a **Scottish accent** would appear like this:

> hɒʊ er ju fiːlɪn tɪdeː

A **Geordie accent** would be different again:

> hu: ɔ juː fiːlɪn tɪdɪə

And so would a **West Country accent**:

> aʊ ɑːr juː fiːlɪŋ tədeɪ

Today, Gemma was feeling how she always felt — funky.

You'd never be able to see all the **different variations** of *today* from a transcription that used **regular spelling**.

Phonemic Symbols can identify Specific Features of Pronunciation

If you're using a phonemic transcription in some analysis, you can record specific **linguistic features** very accurately. This is especially useful if you're looking at **accent** and **dialect**. Here are a couple of examples:

Glottal Stops — e.g. in the word *matter*

- The 't' sound in *matter* often **isn't articulated** with the tongue.
- Instead the speaker will use what is known as a **glottal stop**. This is technically a movement of the **vocal chords** that mainly (in English) acts as a **substitute** for the non-pronunciation of the 't'.
- The glottal stop is shown in phonemic transcriptions by a symbol that looks a bit like a **question mark** /ʔ/. So *matter* would look like this in transcription: /mæʔɒ/

Elision — e.g. in the phrase *Alright mate?*

- This greeting is likely to be said **quickly**, and this will result in **elision** (see p.59).
- Some sounds will be **left out altogether**, even though they're included when the phrase is spelled out.
- A phonemic transcription of what is actually spoken might look like this: /ɒwɔɪmaɪʔ/

Practice Questions

Q1 What are the three distinct types of vowel sound in English?
Q2 What is a diphthong?
Q3 What is a glottal stop?

Essay Question

Q1 Explain, with examples, why a phonemic transcription is more useful in highlighting the differences between regional accents than a direct transcription of a conversation or interview.

It's a shame no one coined 'diphthong' as an insult first...

Can you imagine if you were able to call someone a 'massive diphthong'? That would be brilliant. It's a real shame that it's a very technical term for two vowel sounds realised as one. Anyway, I'm sure you'll get over it. Phonemic symbols are really useful for highlighting the differences between regional speakers — so it's pretty handy to be familiar with them, at least.

Sources and Exam Questions

Here are some exam-style questions, with sources like the ones you'll get in the real paper.
The exact question style will vary depending on your exam board, but these will still be good practice.

1. Study Texts A, B and C below.

    Analyse and compare the use of language by the speakers in these texts.

    You should consider in your answer:
    *   how the speakers deal with and react to confrontation
    *   the pace of each of the texts
    *   the use of standard and non-standard English.

    [40 marks]

Text A — a manager (M) confronts an employee (E)

M: it's just not acceptable you know

E: sorry what's not acceptable

M: you know <u>precisely</u> what's not acceptable (2) what's not acceptable is you going off home at the end of the day leaving half of what you should've done unfinished (1) <u>and</u> it's not the first time

E: // yeah but I didn't have <u>time</u> (1) and I was given way too much to do anyway (.) like <u>far</u> too much (.) it's ridiculous

M: // [inaud]   // what's ridiculous is people like you leaving stuff unfinished so that <u>other people</u> have to pick up the slack (1) it's not on it's just <u>not on</u> that you think (.) you (.) right basically you need to pull your socks up <u>really</u> quickly (.) or you're going to be

E: // are you threatening me

M: don't be pathetic (.) I'm reminding you about the standards <u>I</u> expect from people in this company and you

E: // what

M: are falling way <u>way</u> below them <u>son</u> (.) so either you pull your weight properly or you'll find yourself out in the cold (.) get me

E: I'm not putting up with any more of this (.) it's absolutely

M: // great (.) best news I've had in a <u>long</u> time (.) now why don't you get out

E: you haven't heard the last of this right (.) <u>you</u> think <u>you</u> think you can just

M: // what's this (.) <u>you</u> trying to threaten <u>me</u> now are you right that's <u>priceless</u> that is

E: you should count yourself lucky I'm not <u>decking</u> you right here and now

M: // very scary mate

Text B — a manager (M) and an employee (E) have a discussion

M: err (.) okay sit down won't you

E: (2) thanks

M: (2) well (.) so (.) how are things

E: okay (2) well (.) I mean I think they're okay

M: no problems

E: (1) don't <u>think</u> so no

M: (2) right (.) okay Josh well basically (.) basically I've called you in today because I've been getting reports from one or two of the others about you (.) sort of err (1) well shall we say taking a <u>long</u> <u>time</u> over things and I (1) erm well <u>I</u> thought better have a few words with you about this (.) see see if we can't get to the bottom

E: // no one's said anything to me

M: no (.) no well they wouldn't really would (.) I mean the the people in this office wouldn't want to do that no

Sources and Exam Questions

Text B contd.

E: right (1) but they've spoken to you about it

M: yes (1) well err (1) one or two have yes one or two (.) they (.) err (.) they feel your <u>output</u> is (.) well not that it's but it's (.) it's <u>lower</u> than everyone else's really (1) so like I say <u>one or two</u> they've asked <u>me</u> just to have a word

E: // so they've gone behind my back

M: in a manner of speaking they have yes (2) but they (.) err they didn't want to confront you themselves

E: right (.) so what do you think (.) I mean do you think

M: // well I (.) think that everyone should be pulling their weight and

E: // and you think I'm not (.) is that it

M: that's not what I'm saying <u>exactly</u> Josh no I (.) I I (.) I all I'm saying is people are <u>expecting more</u> from you than you're actually giving (.) so that's all

E: (2) okay (1) well I'll try to quicken up a bit then

M: fine (.) and we'll (.) err review the situation again in a month or so

E: (1) cool

M: and (.) err do you think you could smarten up your appearance a bit

E: what's <u>wrong</u> with it

M: well (.) err (1) you always look unshaven and (.) err (1) well most of the time you seem to be wearing these <u>dirty</u> looking trainers and (.) well and <u>I feel</u> like it lowers the tone a bit (.) don't you think (2) I mean (.) just smarten up a bit (.) that's all I'm saying

Text C — a motorist (M) has returned to his vehicle to find a traffic warden (T) about to issue a ticket

T: is this your vehicle sir

M: looks like it doesn't it

T: right and <u>were</u> you aware that you left it parked on double yellow lines sir

M: (2) no (.) well I mean yes I was actually (.) <u>obviously</u> but I only popped into the bank for a couple of minutes mate you know

T: more like <u>ten</u> minutes if you ask me really

M: (2) yes (.) no well but it would have been a <u>couple</u> of minutes if I hadn't had to wait so long while they sorted out the guy in front of me so

T: // the thing is sir (.) there are plenty of places along here where you can park your car for a short time (1) but this isn't one of them and I don't know if you're aware but in this location you are in fact partially blocking an <u>access</u> road (.) which is is a

M: // come on only by a fraction (.) see (.) yeah and as you say (.) but when I <u>arrived</u> there weren't any so I (.) and and I mean no disrespect to <u>you</u> or anything but I didn't actually <u>expect</u> there'd be people like you snooping around you know

T: // just doing my job sir

M: right but in any case aren't you actually <u>allowed</u> to park on double yellows for a short time anyway

T: in some situations yes (.) but not

M: // it's not as if I've been here all day or anything I mean come on it's ten minutes (.) ten minutes is

T: // I <u>can</u> let you off with a warning <u>this time</u> sir

M: // ah good man (1) knew you'd see sense eventually

Transcription Key

(.)	Micropause	//	Interruptions / overlapping speech
(2)	Pause in seconds	<u>**underlining**</u>	Indicates stress / increased volume

Purpose, Audience, Genre

*These two pages are for **AQA B**, **WJEC** and **OCR**. They're really just a recap of things that you're probably dead familiar with from AS. Basically, texts can be put in groups depending on what they're about and who they're for.*

Texts usually have one of **Four Main Purposes**

1 *Informative Texts* are *Factual*

1) Informative writing needs to contain **knowledge** or **facts** that readers want to know, like the latest news in a newspaper.

2) Informative texts might include presentational features such as headings, bullet points, boxes and illustrations.

3) The tone is usually **serious**. Informative texts don't generally include **opinions** or **comments**. Some informative texts simply consist of times and dates, e.g. a train timetable.

4) Informative texts are usually written in the **third person**, using *he*, *she*, or *it*.

2 *Instructional Texts* tell you *How* to do something

Instructional texts have a **clear**, **structured** style:

1) They use graphological devices such as **bullet points** and **headings**.

2) The instructions are often given as **imperative** sentences e.g. *Add the butter, sugar and flour to the mixture.*

3) The text may use **second person** forms (e.g. *you do this*) to address the reader directly.

4) The lexis is **straightforward** and **uncomplicated**, but can be **subject-specific** (e.g. *beat*, *whisk*, *fold* in cooking).

3 *Persuasive Texts* aim to *Change Your Mind*

1) Persuasive texts try to **influence** the reader's opinions, or **persuade** them to do something.

2) They often use **first person address** (*I* and *we*) to communicate the writer's **feelings** and **include** the readers. Possessive pronouns like *our* and *your* also **personally** involve the reader in the views expressed in the text.

3) They often use **emotive adjectives** and **subjective judgements** to provoke emotional and intellectual responses.

4) They use facts, statistics and other **evidence** to support the main argument, linked together with connectives such as *therefore*, *because*, and *however* to create a **logical route** to a conclusion.

5) They might use eye-catching **graphology** (p.16-17), such as **logos**, **capitalization** and **colour**, to attract the reader's attention and **stress** the importance of a particular point or argument.

4 *There are lots of* **Different** *types of* **Entertainment Text**

1) Entertainment texts include novels, articles and plays. They tend to have **several features in common**:

- **Sophisticated** language
- **Figurative** language
- **Extensive** vocabulary
- Often **complex structure**
- Varied **sentence types**
- Eye-catching **layout**

2) Writers use these features to influence how the audience **experiences** the text. Entertainment texts can help audiences **escape** from reality, make them **laugh**, **frighten** and **shock** them or affect them **emotionally**.

The **Audience** is the group of people that the **Text** is **Aimed At**

Intended audiences can be **general** (e.g. 'adults'), or very **specific** (e.g. 'females over 30 with young children'). Whether the audience is **known** or **unknown** can also affect the kind of language used:

Known audience
- The writer might use **personal pronouns** like *I* and *you*. This is most often found in **stories**, **personal letters** and **diaries**.
- The writer might have a specific **target audience**, so they will choose language that they **expect** the target audience to **understand**.

Unknown audience
- This is the language of **academic** or **instructive texts**.
- The writer doesn't **acknowledge** the reader directly — the text is usually written in the third person.
- There's no expression of **personal feeling** and no use of first or second person **pronouns** (*I* or *you*).
- The text is quite **formal** — it may use formal lexis, imperatives (in instructive texts) or the **passive voice**.

Purpose, Audience, Genre

You can **Work Out** the **Intended Audience** of a text

To identify the **intended audience** of a text, you need to look at **style**, **content**, **lexis** and **tone**.

1) **Style** — **formal** and **serious** writing is usually for an **older audience**. If the text is **informal** and more **light-hearted** it's often aimed at a **younger audience**.

2) **Content** — the text might be about a **general topic** like global warming, or it might be something **specific** like the writer's new trainers. The first would have a **broad** audience, the second would be aimed at a smaller audience.

3) **Lexis** — if there are any **complex**, **specialist** or **technical** words, then the writer is assuming the audience will already be **familiar** with the jargon. If there are no specialist words, and the lexis is **uncomplicated** and easy to follow, this suggests a **younger** or **less specialist** audience.

4) **Tone** — the tone reflects the **purpose** of a text, e.g. an informative text would have a serious tone. The tone can also say something about the audience, e.g. a **serious** tone suggests a **mature** or **interested** audience.

Genre groups texts that have **Similar Features**

1) Similar types of text often seem to follow a **distinctive pattern**.

2) A group of texts with the same features is called a **genre**.

3) Knowing about genres means you can **classify** language. It allows readers to form **expectations** about the text based on their **experience** of the **genre**.

4) Examples of **written genres** include: letters, reports, poems, stories, advertisements, postcards, recipes, e-mails, cartoons, text-messages etc.

5) Each genre has a different **writing style** associated with it. For example:

> **Letters**
>
> **Formal convention:**
> 1) Sender's address at the top
> 2) Date and *Dear Sir/Madam*
> 3) Ends *Yours sincerely/faithfully*
> 4) Followed by a signature

Genres can be **Broken Down** into **Sub-genres**

As if that's not enough, you can divide genres into smaller groups of texts, called **sub-genres**:

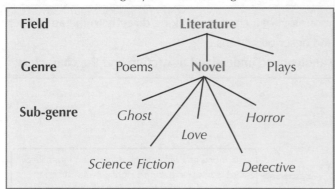

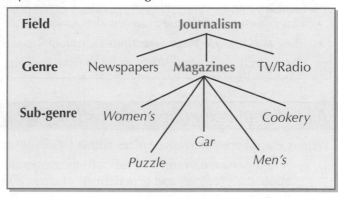

Each of these sub-genres has developed its own **specific lexis** that relates to that sub-genre in particular. For example, the word *autocue* is specific to the **sub-genre** of **TV presenting**, and *blog* relates to the **sub-genre** of **online publishing**.

Practice Questions

Q1 What is the purpose of a persuasive text?
Q2 What four things can help you identify the intended audience of a text?
Q3 Give six examples of written genres.

Essay Question

Q1 How would you expect the language used in a sales brochure for hot tubs to be different from the language used in a hot tub user manual?

Thanks for reading these pages — you've been a great audience...

The stuff in this section boils down to thinking about what you're reading. Why was it written? Who was it written for? What kind of language is used? What's the tone of the writing? Does it have zombies in it? Do the zombies solve crimes? Do the zombie-detectives fall in love? Do the love-struck zombie-detectives invent a time-machine? Do they?

Fiction

These pages are for OCR (Language of Popular Written Texts option). This is the kind of stuff you might expect to be reading if you were in an English Literature class — but from more of an English Language-y perspective.

Authors of Fictional Texts can be very Creative

Literary texts are part of the very broad entertainment field. People read literary texts because they can:

1) **Entertain** or **amuse** the reader.
2) Affect the reader's **emotions**, e.g. make them scared, excited or sympathetic.
3) Describe the **atmosphere** of a place or setting.
4) Examine the **personality** of a **character**.
5) Influence how the reader **looks at the world**.

His wife's shopping list evoked an atmosphere of mild panic.

There are Three Main Types of Fiction

The most common types of literary text are **prose** (like books), **poetry** (like poems), and **plays** (er... like plays).

PROSE

- For example, **novels** and **short stories**.
- It's structured as **running text**, and divided into paragraphs and chapters (for novels).
- There are often no subsections, charts, or lists, and **usually no illustrations**.
- It has a **beginning** and usually a **definite ending**.
- The narrative is told from a certain **point of view**.

POETRY

- Poems **vary** in content, structure, style and intention.
- Some present **narrative stories**, some are written to be **performed**, others explore **emotional issues**.
- Poems are organised into **stanzas** (verses) of varying sizes.
- **Line length** can vary considerably and the poem may or may not **rhyme**.
- There are some **traditional forms** poems can take, e.g. sonnet or limerick.
- There are also traditional **metres** (rhythms) e.g. pentameters.

PLAYS

- Plays consist of **dialogue** between characters, or (if it's a monologue) a character talking **directly** to the audience.
- They also include **stage directions** to instruct the actors and describe actions etc.
- The speech is very important, as it's the main way for the audience to **understand** the **action** and the **characters**.

All fictional texts use a Narrative Voice

Writers use different **narrative voices** within literary texts.

1) A **first-person narrator** in a text tells the reader directly about their **feelings and experiences**. The text is viewed through the character's eyes.

> The moment I woke up that morning I just knew that something wasn't right. I was utterly exhausted and Ryan wouldn't stop talking...

2) A **third-person narrator** tells the story from a detached viewpoint, as a voice separate from the characters.

3) A **third-person omniscient narrator** lets the reader see into the **minds** and **thoughts** of **all** the characters.

> Kit explained it to her as gently as he could, there was no point upsetting her even more. But still, poor Sarah was devastated. As soon as she got home she flung herself on the bed and was overcome with sorrow...

Fictional texts use lots of Figurative Language

Figurative language adds layers of meaning to texts.

1) **Imagery** creates a scene in the reader's mind e.g. *the sea was wild and stormy*.
2) A **simile** is when something is described in **comparison** to something else, e.g. *The sea is <u>like</u> a savage beast*.
3) A **metaphor** creates a **comparison**, like a simile, but it implies the subject and the thing it's being compared to are the **same**, e.g. *the sea <u>is</u> a savage beast*, rather than comparing them.
4) **Personification** is a kind of metaphor, in which the **attributes** of a person are given to abstract or non-human things, for example *the sea <u>shrieked</u> and <u>roared</u>*.
5) **Symbolism** is where a word or phrase **represents something else**, e.g. the colour *red* could represent danger.

Fiction

Rhetorical Language is used to provide Extra Effects or Meanings

There are **two categories** of rhetorical language.

Phonological — manipulates sound. Words or phrases might be used because they sound good.

1) **Rhyme** is particularly effective in poetry because it can contribute to the **musical quality** of a verse. It unifies the poem and can **add emphasis** to certain words. There are different kinds of rhyme, including **half rhyme** — where the vowel or consonant may vary (e.g. *roll* and *tell*) and **internal rhyme** — where rhymes occur within a line itself (e.g. *in mist or cloud, on mast or shroud*).

2) **Alliteration** is the **repetition** of the **same sound**, usually at the beginning of each word, over **two or more words together**, e.g. <u>s</u>ink <u>s</u>lowly into a <u>s</u>oothing <u>s</u>leep.

3) **Assonance** is a similar repetition, but of **vowel sounds** in the middle of words e.g. *a hoover manoeuvre*.

4) **Onomatopoeia** refers to words that sound like the noise they describe, e.g. *buzz, pop, bang*.

Structural — affects the overall meaning of a text by manipulating its structural features.

1) **Repetition** is often used to add **emphasis or persuasiveness** to a text. It can add **power** to a subject, or help a text lead to a **dramatic climax**.

2) **Parallelism** repeats **structural features**, like the construction of a **phrase**, e.g. *She jumped from the bed, and raced to the window,* which repeatedly uses the **past tense** form of the verb with a preposition and noun. An example of **non-parallelism** is something like *He loves films and to eat* — the construction of the phrases *loves film* and *to eat* are different and seem awkward to the reader.

3) **Antithesis** is when contrasting ideas or words are balanced against each other, e.g. *when there is need of silence, you speak, and when there is need of speech, you are silent.*

Dialogue can also be Very Effective

Dialogue is an especially effective device in **plays**.

1) Different characters may speak in **different ways** to influence the audience's opinions of them.

2) Dialogue helps to show the **relationships** between characters — whether they get on, or if there's **tension** between them. It also tells you about a character's **personality** through their **interactions** with other characters, e.g. if they're assertive, nervous, thoughtful, domineering, etc.

3) There are differences between dialogue in **literary texts** and **natural conversation**. In plays and novels, the dialogue tends to be **organised** and **fluent**, e.g. there is strict **turn-taking** and not much **interruption** or **hesitation**. In real-life conversations there are a lot of **non-fluency features** because the dialogue is **spontaneous**.

4) **Dramatic writing** relies on **dialogue** to create and develop **characters**.

Practice Questions

Q1 What's the difference between plays and prose?
Q2 What is a third-person omniscient narrator?
Q3 Explain the term 'personification'.
Q4 What are the two categories of rhetorical language?

Essay Question

Q1 Give five examples of rhetorical language used in fiction and explain the effects produced by each one.

In a flash she realised she was going to learn it all — every last detail...

No you haven't stumbled on an English Lit. page by accident — you need to know this stuff too. I guess one advantage is you can read "The Fabulous Five get Funky" again and claim it's all for revision purposes. Make sure you get to know this stuff on fiction first though — said Timmy quietly — as the fog settled on the hillside, grey and grim like a half-forgotten...

Non-Fiction

These pages are for WJEC and OCR (Language of Popular Written Texts option). *If arty farty poems about feelings make you want to be physically sick, then non-fiction is the thing for you. There'll be none of that fancy talk here.*

Non-fiction Texts are usually Factual

1) Non-fiction is basically any writing that **isn't literary** — so it's anything that isn't a story, play or poem.

2) This means that there are loads of **different types** of **non-fiction text**, with different **audiences**, **purposes** and **genres** (see p.64-65).

3) These pages cover a few specific types of non-fiction — **biography** and **autobiography**, **historical writing** and non-specialist writing about **science** and **technology**. Have a look at **section 5** for stuff on **newspapers**, **magazines**, **adverts** and **electronic texts**.

Autobiographies and Biographies are Accounts of a person's Life

Firstly, it's important that you know the difference between **autobiographies** and **biographies**:

- **Autobiographies** are written by the person they're about, so they're written in the **first person**.
- **Biographies** are accounts of someone's life written by **someone else**, so they're written in the **third person**.
- They tend to be written by and about **famous** or **notable** people.

1) Autobiographies and biographies tend to be written in the **past tense**. However, sometimes writers use the **historic present tense** to make the action seem more **relevant** or **urgent**, e.g. *so he calls me over and by now I'm feeling really nervous.*

2) The information is often presented **chronologically** (it starts at the beginning of the person's life and works through it). Texts don't always start with the person's birth though — they could start at any point during their life, e.g. when they became famous. Some autobiographies start with an exciting event, and then jump between different important periods in the person's life. The aim of this is to **subvert** the **genre** and to keep the reader **interested**.

3) Because autobiographies and biographies often contain **funny anecdotes** and **emotional stories**, writers use **literary techniques** to make them more effective, e.g. **figurative language**, **rhetorical devices** and **dialogue** (see p.66-67).

4) Autobiographies can be quite **informal** and **chatty**. Writers often use **colloquialisms** and **dialect words** to make themselves seem more **accessible** to readers. They might directly address the reader using the **second person pronoun** *you*, to make it seem like they're a **friend** telling you about their life.

5) **Biographies** tend to have a more **formal tone** because they're based on detailed research of things like the person's **family history** and **diaries**, while **autobiographies** can just be based on the person's **memories**.

Historical Writing is designed to Inform and Persuade

1) Historical writing **informs** readers about particular historical events. It has to include lots of **facts** like **names** and **dates**, e.g. *On 22nd January 1655 Oliver Cromwell dissolved the First Protectorate Parliament.* It also includes lexis from specific **semantic fields**, e.g. **war** or **medicine**, depending on the **subject** of the text.

2) The tone is usually quite **formal** — **Standard English** is used rather than slang or dialect.

3) **Historians** tend to write in the **third person**, and include **quotations** and **sources** to **support** their **arguments**. This makes them seem **distant** and **objective**.

4) However, the way an event is portrayed depends on the writer's **point of view**, so all texts are **subjective** to a certain extent. This means that they also have to **persuade** the reader that this interpretation is right. To do this, writers often use **rhetorical devices** and **figurative language**, e.g. *The sea of soldiers surged forward in a wave of desperation.* This also makes the text more **interesting** to read than a list of bare facts.

5) Historical writing has some **distinctive linguistic features**. For example, writers often use **personification** when they're referring to a place, and use the **third person female pronoun** to refer to countries, e.g. *Russia was struggling — she was no longer a global superpower.*

6) Historical texts have **changed** over time. This is partly because of the impact of **political correctness** (p.11). For example, a text from the 1940s might talk about *the habits of the Chinaman.* This sounds **old-fashioned** to modern-day readers, and makes it seem like people are only **defined** by their **nationality**. A modern text would be more likely to talk about *people from China.*

Non-Fiction

Some *Science* and *Technology* texts are written for *Non-specialists*

Non-fiction writing about **science** and **technology** for **non-specialists** can be designed to **instruct**, **inform** or **persuade**, depending on its **purpose** and **genre**.

Instructional texts

- Non-fiction texts on science and technology include things like lists of **instructions**, e.g. to tell people how to take medication or use gadgets.
- Instructions tend to include lots of **imperatives**, e.g. *take* two twice a day, *press* the start button.
- They usually contain **short sentences** and **simple syntax** with few subordinate clauses.
- They're often set out with **bullet points** or **numbered lists** so they're easy to follow.
- They might be written in the **second person** to make them more **user-friendly**. The reader is addressed directly, e.g. *your* camera is now ready to use.

Informative texts

- Texts to **inform** non-specialist audiences about scientific or technological breakthroughs tend to **explain** any **lexis** from a **specialist semantic field**.
- For example, a newspaper article about genetics would explain terms like *ribosomal RNA*. It might not explain specialist terms that have been used in non-specialist texts for a while, e.g. *DNA* or *chromosome*.

1. Remove from box.
2. Bend into desired shape.
3. Place on lilo.

Texts with a dual purpose

- Texts about science and technology can have a dual purpose — to **inform** and **persuade**.
- For example, a leaflet on healthy eating would be written to **inform** people about healthy food, and **persuade** them to eat it.
- To do this the text would probably have quite an **informal** tone and not use **specialist vocabulary**. It might also try to engage the reader by using the **second person pronoun** *you*.

Practice Questions

Q1   What's the difference between an autobiography and a biography?

Q2   Outline two features of autobiographies.

Q3   What are the two main purposes of historical writing?

Q4   Give a linguistic feature of historical writing.

Q5   Explain three linguistic features of science and technology texts for non-specialists.

Q6   Give an example of a dual purpose text.

Essay Question

Q1   Find an example of non-fiction writing. Analyse the specific linguistic features of the text, and discuss the impact of purpose and genre on the language.

My favourite autobiography has got to be Chitty Chitty Bang Bang...

You might think you're a dab hand at linguistic analysis, but now's the time to embark on a strict regime of eating, sleeping and breathing non-fiction. Start in the morning — rise early and take a pen down to breakfast. Study the back of the cereal box in detail, noting down any distinctive linguistic features. Do the same for jam and toast, and top marks could be yours...

Political Writing

WJEC and OCR (Language, Power and Identity option). These pages are mostly focused on transcripts of political speeches, so you need to look out for linguistic features that make the speech more interesting. Up the revolution...

Political Speeches *contain lots of* Rhetoric

The **purpose** of political language is to **persuade**. To do this, politicians use **rhetorical devices**, for example:

Three-part list	• This is where three elements are used in a list to give **emphasis** and build to a **climax**. • E.g. *Blood, sweat and tears* is a **list** of three **nouns**.
Repetition	• Words or phrases are repeated for **emphasis**. • E.g. *Those who **betray** their party **betray** themselves.*
Hyperbole	• Hyperbole means using **exaggeration** for **effect**. • E.g. *Plague would be a better option than the health policies proposed.*
Rhetorical questions	• A rhetorical question doesn't require an **answer**, because it's phrased in a way that **assumes** the answer is obvious. • E.g. *Is there any good reason for this development to go ahead?*
First person plural pronoun (*we*)	• Politicians use *we* to make listeners feel **included** and give them a sense of **responsibility**. • E.g. ***We** must all pull together in these difficult times.*
Alliteration	• Words that start with the **same sound** are used together to place **emphasis** on them. • E.g. *This <u>d</u>amage and <u>d</u>estruction is <u>d</u>estroying the land for our children.*
Figurative language	• Metaphors and similes are used to create **strong images**. • E.g. *We are planting a seed, from which a tree will grow, and branches will spread.*
Allusion	• Politicians might allude to **literary texts** or **other political speeches**. They might use a quotation to **support** their point, or to create a particular **impression**. • E.g. American politicians might use the line *ask not what your country can do for you — ask what you can do for your country.* This is from a speech by President Kennedy, so it would suggest that politicians who used it were comparing themselves to him.
Imperatives	• Imperatives address listeners and give the impression of **direct action**. • E.g. *Grasp the opportunity to do something for your local area.*

Political Language *is usually* Formal

1) The language used in political texts tends to be **formal**. For example, the writers of **white papers** (reports giving information on government policy) use **Standard English** and avoid colloquialisms. Using Standard English makes the writer appear **well-educated** and **knowledgeable**, so it makes them seem **authoritative**.

2) In speeches, politicians often **change** their language depending on the **audience** they're addressing and the impression they want to create. For example, politicians might use **everyday** language like **colloquialisms** and **simple syntax** when they're talking to young people.

3) Political language contains lots of **jargon**, e.g. *backbench, whip, Euroscepticism*. Politicians might use jargon to make themselves seem **knowledgeable** and **powerful** — it's harder to challenge someone if you don't understand what they're saying. However, they can be accused of not answering questions or trying to cover up the truth, especially by journalists and interviewers.

4) Politicians are also often accused of '**spin**' — using language to present information in a way that makes it look as **good** as possible. For example, *friendly fire* is a **euphemism** for accidental attacks from allied forces in wartime. The use of the word *friendly* and the alliteration **distract** people from the **true meaning** of the phrase, and the fact that a mistake has been made.

Language and Identity

This page is just for OCR (Language, Power and Identity option).

Texts are Shaped by different Identities

1) The **writer's background** and **experiences** affect what they write. This can be quite **obvious**, e.g. people wrote poetry about their experiences fighting in World War One. It can also be more **subtle**, e.g. a writer who'd had a bad relationship with his mother might present all female characters as cruel and manipulative.

2) The **assumed identity** of the reader also affects what's written. For example, journalists working for women's magazines assume that the reader is female and interested in fashion, celebrities and men. They write to **appeal** to this group, and the way they **represent** their audience fits in with this assumption. The text is then **reinterpreted** by the reader depending on their **identity** and **experiences**.

Texts Construct Identities in different ways

1) In **fiction** texts, look out for how the **characters** are represented. Some texts contain **stereotypical** characters, e.g. the **women** in traditional fairy stories or Mills and Boon books tend to be **passive** and subordinate to the male characters.

2) If you got a text like this in your exam, you could look at the **verbs** used to portray male and female action. For example, the **passive voice** might be used more for the female characters than the male ones, e.g. *she was swept up into his arms*.

3) You could also focus on **address terms** and how people are referred to in texts. For example, adults might be referred to as *girls* or *boys*, no matter how old they are.

4) You also need to bear in mind the **context** of the text. Women might be called *girls* in a women's magazine to create an informal, friendly tone and a sense of **positive identity**. But if women were referred to as *girls* in a political speech then it would suggest that women have **lower status** than men.

> See p. 40-43 for more on language and gender, and p. 34-35 for how identity affects language use.

5) In older American texts, you might find black men being addressed as *boy* by white people, even if they're older than the speaker. This represents them as having **low status** and suggests a sense of **white dominance** in society, which goes back to the time of slavery.

6) The way that **speech** is represented is also important. For example, a newspaper editorial writer might try to **undermine** a politician by spelling out their **regional accent** phonetically, e.g. *Jones says that "educashun staanderds are slippin"*. This representation of non-standard speech gives the impression that the speaker is **lower class** and **uneducated**, so it gives them **less authority**.

Some texts try to **subvert traditional representations**:
- Some writers have **updated** genres that usually rely on **stereotypes**, e.g. lots of children's stories now feature female characters who climb trees and have adventures, rather than just playing with dolls.
- Sometimes this is **satirical**, e.g. writers like James Finn Garner have mocked **political correctness** by rewriting fairy stories without stereotypes, to show that the traditional representation of characters is actually crucial to the story.

Practice Questions

Q1 Give three examples of rhetorical devices used by politicians and say what their effect might be.

Q2 What is 'spin'?

Q3 How might the writer's identity shape a text?

Q4 Outline two ways that a text can construct a character or reader's identity.

Essay Question

Q1 Discuss how different linguistic techniques can be used to create power and construct identity.

Oh, think of your own...

Don't you think I might have had enough of these by now? I'm not a machine you know. Considering this stuff is about language and identity, I reckon it's about time you used language to stamp your own identity on this book. If you can think of something amusing to say about these pages then you're clearly one of this country's great intellects, and I salute you...

Sources and Exam Questions

Here are some exam-style questions, with sources like the ones you'll get in the real paper.
The exact question style will vary depending on your exam board, but these will still be good practice.

Text A is from *The Adventures of Sherlock Holmes* by Sir Arthur Conan Doyle (1892).
Text B is from a short detective story written in 2009.

1. Analyse the linguistic devices used by the authors. You should also analyse and evaluate the effect
   of social and historical context on the language used.

   [30 marks]

Text A — From *The Adventures of Sherlock Holmes* (1892)

"This is indeed a mystery," I remarked. "What do you imagine that it means?"

"I have no data yet. It is a capital mistake to theorise before one has data. Insensibly one begins to twist facts to suit theories, instead of theories to suit facts. But the note itself. What do you deduce from it?"

I carefully examined the writing, and the paper upon which it was written.

"The man who wrote it was presumably well to do," I remarked, endeavouring to imitate my companion's processes. "Such paper could not be bought under half a crown a packet. It is peculiarly strong and stiff."

"Peculiar—that is the very word," said Holmes. "It is not an English paper at all. Hold it up to the light."

I did so, and saw a large "E" with a small "g," a "P," and a large "G" with a small "t" woven into the texture of the paper.

"What do you make of that?" asked Holmes.

"The name of the maker, no doubt; or his monogram, rather."

"Not at all. The 'G' with the small 't' stands for 'Gesellschaft,' which is the German for 'Company.' It is a customary contraction like our 'Co.' 'P,' of course, stands for 'Papier.' Now for the 'Eg.' Let us glance at our Continental Gazetteer." He took down a heavy brown volume from his shelves. "Eglow, Eglonitz—here we are, Egria. It is in a German-speaking country—in Bohemia, not far from Carlsbad. 'Remarkable as being the scene of the death of Wallenstein, and for its numerous glass-factories and paper-mills.' Ha, ha, my boy, what do you make of that?" His eyes sparkled, and he sent up a great blue triumphant cloud from his cigarette.

"The paper was made in Bohemia," I said.

"Precisely. And the man who wrote the note is a German. Do you note the peculiar construction of the sentence — 'This account of you we have from all quarters received.' A Frenchman or Russian could not have written that. It is the German who is so uncourteous to his verbs. It only remains, therefore, to discover what is wanted by this German who writes upon Bohemian paper and prefers wearing a mask to showing his face."

Text B — From a short story written in 2009

As soon as the Super let her go, Inspector Langham jumped into her battered Renault and drove to the lab at breakneck speed. She burst in on Dr Verne, who was hunched quietly over a bench, gently stroking his mousy little moustache. He didn't look up, even when the door slammed shut behind her. Ignoring people was one of his many infuriating habits, but Jo was too desperate to know what he'd found to start an argument now.

"What did the ESDA bring up?" she breathed urgently.

He made a little snorting noise and said, with some satisfaction, "Beats me."

"What?"

"Someone decided to check for latent fingerprints. They've been at the note with the Ninhydrin — the pen indentations have been altered and some of the ink's dissolved."

Jo was aghast, "But who would do that before the document analysis had been done? We'll never know if the signature was forged without electrostatic detection."

"Well," shrugged Dr Verne, "You want to tell your boys to keep their paws off your evidence."

"But it doesn't make sense. It must have been done in the lab — so it would have to have been somebody here."

"Look, we just follow your orders, Inspector," he said sarcastically. "If there's a problem then I suggest you take it up with your Superintendent." He turned back to his work with a sly smile. Jo stood in front of him for a moment, and then walked slowly back to her car. Her mind was racing. Someone must have had a reason for contaminating the evidence. Somebody *inside* the lab must want to jeopardise the inquiry.

Sources and Exam Questions

Text A is an extract from an entry in an online encyclopedia about an MP.
Text B is an extract from a speech given by the politician Liam Byrne in 2008.

2. Analyse the linguistic devices used by the authors. You should also analyse and evaluate the effect of contextual factors, like time and mode of production, on the language used. *[30 marks]*

Text A — From King Herman's entry in an online encyclopedia*

Career

Kingsley Herman Temmar (known as King Herman), born 27th November 1937, died 16th March 2005, was a British politician who became well known for his work in the area of immigration.

Between the years of 1969 and 1980 he worked for the Labour Party in Redisham, and between 1979 and 2001 he was Member of Parliament for Lewbridge.

King Herman was seen by many to have ultra left-wing views. During the Thatcher years he was a constant thorn in the side of the Conservatives, and was seen as something of a maverick even by members of his own party, often having to be brought to order by the Speaker of the House of Commons for refusing to observe parliamentary conventions.

Even after standing down as an MP, King Herman continued to work behind the scenes at his local branch of the Labour Party and was honoured there by constituents in a birthday party only a few months before his death.

Anti-racist

In 1999, King Herman was named by the anti-racist magazine 'Change' as one of the top ten figures in the fight against racism in the UK, and he also spoke at the annual 'Fight for the Future' rally at Hyde Park on seven occasions.

He met Nelson Mandela in Paris in 1998, and later said that the moment had been awe inspiring and moving.

During his lifetime he published several papers about public policy towards immigrants, many of which were taken on board by subsequent Labour governments.

Text B — From a political speech by Liam Byrne delivered in 2008

I want to talk about winning the debate on immigration today. It's a debate that many of you are marshalling in your communities and I want to outline the three key pieces of the argument that I see as vital in 2008.

First, the public needs to be satisfied that its demand for a different system has been heard, has been accepted and has been acted on. Today I tell you emphatically. The Government has got the message.

Last year I said that five foundation stones were needed – in strategy, press, technology, money and global alliances. Each we systematically put into place. On that foundation we will in 2008 deliver the biggest shake up of our border security and immigration system in its history.

My goal therefore is as ambitious as it is urgent. There are 4 themes to our work. Protection, prevention, accountability and compassion: To deliver a sweeping programme of border protection, learning from the world's most advanced nations like the US, we will;

· Check fingerprints before we issue a visa

· Screen all travellers against watch-lists before they land

· Introduce a single border force to guard our ports and airports

· Introduce police-like powers for frontline staff

· And crucially, we will reintroduce the checks to count foreign nationals in and out of the country

To prevent illegal immigration we will make changes too - change that is needed because prevention is always cheaper, and safer and fairer – than cure. And because we have obligations, not just to the British public, but to the potential victims of human trafficking and smuggling, the vulnerable victims of a global 21st century slave trade.

* Just in case you're confused, King Herman's not a real MP — we just invented him for this exam question.

Newspapers

AQA B, WJEC and OCR. What's black and white and read all over? Sorry, that doesn't really work written down, but the answer is... a newspaper. Boom boom. The language of newspapers can influence people's attitudes and values.

Journalese *is* Journalistic Language

Newspaper language can be quite **different** from other styles of written language. **Journalese** is an **occupational sociolect** (see p.34) that **journalists** use to make their writing more **exciting** and **appealing** to readers, and to **save space**. It's also used by **TV journalists**. It has some common **lexical**, **grammatical** and **phonological** features:

Lexis

- Journalese often makes use of **old-fashioned** or **unusual** words that don't tend to be used in other **contexts**. Some of the most **common** ones are *oust*, *boost*, *fury*, *slump*, *horror* and *probe*. They're used a lot because they're **short**, so they have more **impact** and take up **less space** in **headlines**.
- It also contains **unusual phrases**, e.g. *the driver escaped injury*. A phrase like this sounds very **familiar** because it's used so often in journalese, but it's **hardly ever used** in other types of language.

Grammar

- **Modifier + headword** constructions are very common in **journalese**. They're used to communicate **facts** without taking up lots of space e.g. *experienced* manager, *Dublin-born* criminal. They're also often used for **sensational effect**, e.g. **emotive modifiers** like *tragic* hero, *heartbroken* midfielder, *chilling* image.
- **Headlines** usually feature **ellipsis** (missed out words) because it **saves space**, e.g. *Sex Beast Caged* rather than *A Sex Beast Has Been Caged*.

Phonology

- Headlines often contain **alliteration** and **rhyme**, e.g. *Cash Cow Row*.
- They can also include **phonetic spelling**, e.g. *No Bovver Says Becks*.
- **Puns** are also very common in headlines, e.g. *Santa's Grotty*.

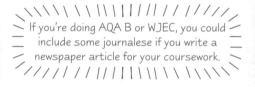

If you're doing AQA B or WJEC, you could include some journalese if you write a newspaper article for your coursework.

Tabloid Newspapers *use* Different *language from* Broadsheets

Every newspaper takes a slightly **different political viewpoint**, so their purpose is to **persuade** as well as to **inform**. Newspapers are in **competition** with each other, so they also need to **entertain** readers to keep them interested.

1) **Tabloid newspapers** are ones like *The Sun* and *The News of the World*. They tend to be written in an **informal register** and make their viewpoint on a story very clear. They use quite **straightforward language**, which often contains features of **spoken English** like **slang** and **contractions**.

2) **Broadsheets** are newspapers such as *The Guardian* and *The Daily Telegraph*. They're aimed at a **professional**, mostly **middle class readership**, so the **register** is more **formal**.

3) **Tabloids** tend to contain **more journalese** than **broadsheets**. Tabloids have **less space**, so writers need to get the story across in as **few words** as **possible**. They also rely more on **grabbing** the reader's **attention** and **entertaining** them.

Features of tabloid newspapers	Features of broadsheet newspapers
Short paragraphs	**Longer** paragraphs
Large font, spread out	**Smaller font**, compact
Large print, sensational headlines (*May Day Massacre*)	**Smaller print**, factual headlines (*PM Defeat at Polls*)
Lots of **large photographs**	Fewer, **smaller photographs**
Short, Anglo-Saxon words (*think, dead*)	**Long, Latinate** words (*cogitate, deceased*)
Simple sentences with few clauses	**Complex sentences** with more **subordinate** clauses
Simple punctuation, exclamation marks	**Complex punctuation**, few exclamation marks
First names or **nicknames** (*Gordon, Macca*)	**Full names** or **surnames** (*Gordon Brown, McCartney*)
Sensationalised news stories, **one-sided** point of view	**Fact-based** news stories, often more **objective** stance
Emotive vocabulary (*Monster rapist gets off with five years*)	**Neutral** vocabulary (*Rapist gets five year sentence*)
Personal tone	**Impersonal** tone
Informal vocabulary (*pal, kids*)	More **formal** vocabulary (*friend, children*)

Newspapers

Newspapers are made up of Different Styles and Genres

The **same newspaper** will contain **different types** of **writing** because the **purpose** of the article will **vary**.
The **mode** and **register** of the article will also **vary** depending on its **purpose**. For example:

Reviews

1) Newspapers often include **reviews** of **books**, **films**, **theatre productions** and **music**.

2) They're often highly **descriptive**, because they have to **explain** something that the reader **hasn't seen** before. They might include **cross-references**, and the **language** can be **unusual** and **abstract**. This is especially true of **music** reviews, as it's difficult to describe **sound** accurately, e.g. *a sexy fusion of shimmering guitar riffs and African beats*.

3) The good and bad points of what's being reviewed are often **exaggerated** because the **purpose** of the article is to **entertain** as well as **inform**.

4) The **register** tends to be quite **informal**, so reviews are often **multi-modal** because they contain **elements** of **written** and **spoken** language.

Obituaries

1) These are **accounts** of **notable** people's **lives**, printed after they die.

2) They're a combination of **factual information** like date of birth and cause of death, and **descriptive writing** that outlines their career, achievements and early life.

3) The **register** is usually **formal**, which means that the **mode** is **written** rather than multi-modal.

Newspapers can be Biased

Bias is the tendency to **take sides** and view things **subjectively**, e.g. newspapers show political bias when they show preference for one political party over another.

1) **Newspaper reports** show bias through the writer's **word choices**. The **purpose** of particular word choices is to **shape** the reader's **perceptions** of an event.

2) Bias is shown in **different ways**. For example, **coverage** of a particular **news item** may be:

- **selective** — e.g. only focus on the positive aspect of a new law.
- present only **one viewpoint** — e.g. always present negative judgements of a particular political party.
- use **loaded** and **emotive** language to present **factual information**, e.g. adjectives like *outrageous*, *tragic*.

Newspapers can show Prejudice towards Social Groups

1) **Prejudice** is a **preconceived** opinion of a person or a group, that isn't based on **experience** or **reason**.

2) It often includes **negative judgements** about different **ethnic**, **religious**, **gender** or **ability** groups.

3) The **language** used by the media can **create** and **reinforce** these negative opinions.

4) For example, if a newspaper consistently runs headlines about **asylum seekers** *scrounging from the taxpayer*, then it shows **prejudice** against this particular group. The **effect** of these headlines might be that readers start to **associate** asylum seekers with being dishonest or lazy.

Practice Questions

Q1 What is journalese?

Q2 Outline four ways in which tabloid newspapers are different from broadsheets.

Q3 How might a newspaper show bias?

Essay Question

Q1 Compare and contrast the language used in these two headlines:
Gentle Giant Savaged By Yobs   Man Attacked By Teenage Gang

A-LEVEL STUDENT FACES PAINFUL EXAMINER PROBE...

Here's a creepy fact about obituaries — the ones for really famous people are written long before they die, kept on file and added to every time they make another film or are involved in another sex scandal. So when a paper finds out that they've snuffed it, it can print a nice up-to-date account of their life within a few hours. There, I bet you were dying to know that...

Magazines

AQA B, WJEC and OCR. There are loads of different magazines to choose from. I always used to think they were a real waste of money, but that was until I realised that they're full of words and pictures and everything. Now I'm hooked.

Magazines have their own *Conventions* and *Style* of *Language*

1) People read magazines to be **entertained**, to get **lifestyle advice**, or to find out about a **specific hobby** or **pastime**. This means that magazines have to **give** readers what they want, and **tell** them what they want at the same time.

2) The language of magazines can be quite similar to the language of **tabloid newspapers**. It's often **informal** and uses **phonological devices**, **puns**, and **familiar phrases** in headings, e.g. *Girls Just Wanna Have Sun* for an article on the dangers of sunbathing. This is designed to grab the reader's attention. It also aims to create a strong **identity** that readers can feel part of, so they'll be persuaded to buy the magazine again.

3) Most magazines make money by selling **advertising space**. This means they're **never** completely **objective**. They need to **persuade** people to buy things, so that companies will keep wanting to buy advertising space. This means magazines often contain **advice** on products, e.g. *this watch is guaranteed to turn heads*.

The *Type* of language used *Depends* on the *Purpose* and *Audience*

There are loads of **different types** of magazine, so here are some general points on how some of them differ.

1) **Lifestyle** magazines are **aspirational** — people read them for advice, mostly about what to **buy**. They contain lots of features on *must-have* items, *wish lists* and things you *can't live without*.

2) Magazines aimed particularly at **men** or **women** often **reinforce gender stereotypes**. Women's magazines can reinforce the idea that women need to **impress** and **please** men, e.g. *Embrace a hot new look and you can be sure he won't stray*. Men's magazines tend to contain more **innuendo** and **swear words**, which might suggest an assumption that men are only interested in sex.

3) Magazines often attract readers by using the language of their **target audience**, e.g. magazines for teenage girls sometimes use **text speak** and **phonetic spellings**, e.g. *BF* for best friend and *nailz* instead of nails.

4) Magazines for younger children are often more **educational**, so the language **mimics** what they hear at **school**, e.g. *Can you count the number of birds in the picture?*

5) Specialist magazines contain a **specific lexical field** that only people interested in the subject will **appreciate**, e.g. you'd find words like *molecules* and *dilution* in a **science** magazine, but not in a fashion magazine.

The type of **feature** in the magazine also affects the type of **language** used. Articles could be written to:

- **Entertain** — e.g. real-life stories like *My kidnap hell*. They tend to be set out like **newspaper articles**, with **quotes** from the person involved and **sensational language**, e.g. *horrific ordeal*.

- **Inform** — e.g. *Online banking in 10 simple steps*. Articles to inform often use **graphological** features like **bullet points** and **lists**. The language is quite **neutral**, e.g. *it's important to have a safe password*.

- **Advise** — e.g. *From work to flirt in 10 minutes*. Articles to advise use lots of **imperatives**, e.g. *blast your hair for 2 minutes before styling*. They also **assume** that the reader **agrees** with what's being said, e.g. *No one wants to be the girl with her skirt tucked into the back of her tights*.

Magazines use *Persuasive Language*

To be **persuasive** a writer has to be **confident** and **authoritative** e.g. *If you see just one film this year, it has to be 'Pig Wars'.* Magazines use a number of **linguistic devices** to do this, for example:

- **Addressing the reader** — magazines use the second person pronoun (*you*) to **directly address** the reader. This grabs people's attention and makes them feel included.

- **Lists** — lists are used to get **lots** of **information** across **quickly**, e.g. *Top 10 Holiday Spots for Surf Lovers*.

- **Imperatives** — commands are used to make the reader feel like the magazine knows best, e.g. *Don't leave the house without one...*

- **Rhetorical questions** — rhetorical questions can **flatter** readers by addressing them as **experts**. They can also make readers feel like they're missing out on something really important, e.g. *Who hasn't looked at the latest super-lightweight bike and wanted one?*

Magazines

How the magazine *Looks* is *Important*

1) There are lots of magazines for readers to choose from, so they need to be **eye-catching** if they're going to sell.

2) The **appearance** of a magazine lets readers know what to **expect** from it, e.g. you'd expect a magazine made with high-quality paper to be upmarket and expensive.

3) Most magazines have the same basic **layout** — an eye-catching front cover, headings, articles and pictures. However, the **purpose** of the magazine determines its overall **look**, e.g. nature magazines have more photos than magazines about creative writing.

4) All of the **components** of the magazine need to work together to create a **consistent** look that readers instantly **recognise**. This is part of the magazine's **identity**.

Ted wondered what more he could do to get on this month's cover of 'Extreme Dentistry'.

Photos

- Photos on the front cover have to **present** the whole magazine's **image**. The photos inside the magazine need to **maintain** this **look**, e.g. if you saw a glossy photo of a celebrity on the cover, you'd expect to see glossy photos inside the magazine too.

- The kind of photos included depend on the **purpose** and **audience** of the magazine. For example, **lads'** magazines appeal to the **stereotypical image** of **male interests**, with photos of cars and attractive women. The photos tend to be **big** and in **colour**, so they **dominate** the page.

Colour

- **Colour schemes** are important for creating a consistent **brand image**.

- The colours used depend on the **purpose** and **audience** of the magazine. For example, **children's magazines** tend to use lots of **bright primary colours**, which might **clash**. In contrast, **interior design** magazines often use **subtle** colours, to make the magazine appear more **stylish** and **upmarket**.

Typeface

- Magazines use the same **distinctive typefaces** for consistency, as this helps with **brand recognition**.

- The typeface sends a message about the magazine's **purpose**. For example, a magazine about new technology might use a **modern typeface** to make it seem **cutting edge**, e.g. **technophile**.

Headings and subheadings

- **Headings** are usually **short** with **big letters** to grab the reader's attention. Sometimes headings are written entirely with **lower case** letters to seem **fashionable** and **modern**, e.g. **the camera phone revolution**.

- **Subheadings** are used to **break up** the page and **direct attention** to important features.

Practice Questions

Q1 How is the language used by some magazines similar to that of tabloid newspapers?

Q2 Outline two linguistic devices used to persuade magazine readers.

Q3 Describe the basic layout of most magazines.

Essay Question

Q1 Write the heading and first paragraph of a magazine article about the pros and cons of eating nothing but chips and cheese for a month.

Write a version aimed at 13-year-old chip enthusiasts, then rewrite it for 35-year-old fitness fanatics.

Spotted! A-level student losing will to live...

If you ask me magazines are more trouble than they're worth. Just recently I had a run in with 'Tea Drinker's Monthly' over their views on bags vs. leaves. Fortunately I've still got my subscription to 'You and Your Blisters' to keep me going. Last month they had a special feature on lancing boils, AND it came with a complimentary dressing. You can't say fairer than that.

Broadcasting

AQA B, WJEC and OCR. Ever walked into a room and walked straight out again because whatever's on the telly 'looked rubbish'? Ever wondered how you knew without even watching it? Nope, me neither, but you're about to find out.

TV and Radio shows have lots of Familiar Conventions

You probably already know loads of different **programme types**. Here are a few, with some of their **distinctive features**.

Sketch Shows

1) On TV and radio, sketch shows follow similar conventions — **brief**, **scripted scenes** build up to a **punchline**, usually something surprising and often involving **wordplay**.

> **For example** — two well-spoken ladies having a conversation in a **serious tone** of voice could say something **outrageous** even though their **delivery** remains **normal**. The **contrast** and **incongruity** between what the audience **expects** from the scene and what **actually happens** creates **humour**.

2) The laughter of a **studio audience** is used to make the viewer or listener feel **involved**.

3) Sketch shows on TV also have **visuals** to help them. On the radio, **prosody** (things like stressing certain sentences, phrases or words, and changing pace and volume) is even more important.

Soap Operas

1) Soaps have their own conventions — they're made up of **swift scene changes** and **chop** between storylines. Regular viewers are **familiar** with this so it doesn't seem confusing, and the **characters** are **easy to recognise**.

2) Characters often have **regional accents** and use the **dialect** of the area where the soap's set.

News

1) TV and **radio** news programmes **share** some **conventions**:

- They start with some **high-powered music** and an **introduction** by the main newsreader.
- There's a summary of the **headlines** followed by the reports in **more detail**.
- They sometimes finish with a **light-hearted story** — an '*and finally*'.

2) The news tends to be **scripted** in **formal language**, and read in an **authoritative** and **serious tone**.

3) Newsreaders speak in **Standard English**, but they may have a **regional accent**.

4) Despite common features, channels or stations often put **their own stamp** on the news format. For example, BBC Radio One's *Newsbeat* has background music while the newsreader speaks, doesn't contain much in-depth analysis and includes some celebrity gossip.

Some shows require Input from the Audience

In some shows, such as radio talk shows, the audience is invited to **email**, **text** or **call in**. In radio phone-ins, it's up to the presenter to use **pragmatic** techniques to keep the conversation running, e.g. by inviting speakers to talk:

> **Presenter**: good morning Mike (.) from North London (.) now Mike you've called to ask us what exactly
>
> **Listener**: well Brian I've been growing runner beans for years now (1) but this year they've really drooped
>
> **Presenter**: ok so you're hoping our gardening expert Doug can help (.) Doug
>
> **Expert**: yes well this seems to have been a problem across the country this year really
>
> **Presenter**: right (.) so is there anything you can recommend to pick them up a bit

TV and Radio Reflect the World Around Us

1) TV and radio programmes **reflect** the world and society around us, creating something that **seems like** reality. This is called **verisimilitude** — it seems like reality, but it's not.

2) Characters in soap operas have regional accents, sometimes use **dialect** and make use of all the conventions of conversations such as **turn-taking**, **pauses**, **fillers** and **hedging** — but it's all **scripted** to make them seem **realistic**.

3) Talk shows and interviews are also often carefully scripted with **discourse markers** so they seem natural and real. Even live shows are produced or managed **behind the scenes**, so what you hear and see is created to convey a **certain meaning**. Some people reckon that even if you think your response to a programme is your own, the chances are it isn't — you've been **manipulated** to think in a certain way about the content.

Broadcasting

Radio Language is Different from TV Language

1) **TV language** has the support of **pictures**, **gestures** and **facial expressions**, and sometimes **text**.

2) On the **radio** there aren't any visual clues, so listeners have to rely on **what** speakers say and **how** they say it.

3) This affects the **type** of language used in each medium. For example:

> **Radio commentary of a football match**
> *here's Burton making space along the left hand side (1) Peters in support to his right (1) cross hit hard and low (.) Oliver picks it up on the far right side by the corner flag (.) cuts inside (.) passes to Hilton*
> **Linguistic features**
> • Lots of information.
> • Mainly full sentences.
> • Lots of adjectives (e.g. *hard*, *low*).
> • Short pauses.

The numbers in brackets indicate the length of pauses in seconds. This symbol (.) indicates a shorter pause.

> **TV commentary of a football match**
> *here's Burton (3) Burton's cross (2) Oliver (3)*
> **Linguistic features**
> • Minimal information.
> • Incomplete sentences.
> • Long pauses.

You have to know the Conventions of the Genre you write for

If you decide to use broadcast media as part of your **coursework**, here are a few final things to look out for:

1) If you're writing for **TV**, think about things like **camera angles**, the effect of **lighting** and other **visual effects**.

2) You should be confident about the effect of any **accents** or **dialects** you've chosen, and the language you're using — think about the formality, tone, style, register, syntax, grammar and pragmatics of the discourse.

3) This is even more **important** if you're writing for the **radio**.

> Writers use familiar TV and radio conventions to manipulate their audiences, by **fulfilling their expectations** of a particular type of show. However, these expectations can also be **subverted**:
>
> • A famous instance of this happened in 1938, when the director Orson Welles terrified many American listeners into believing that the country was being **invaded by Martians**.
>
> • He interrupted a seemingly normal broadcast with **spoof newsflashes**, delivered in **authoritative language** and **tone**, and including **consultation** with "experts".
>
> • It wasn't the content but the **use of conventions** that made the broadcast so **realistic**.

Practice Questions

Q1 What sort of conventions would you expect in a sketch show?

Q2 Apart from what is said, what conventions or techniques could a radio show use to convey ideas to its audience?

Q3 What is verisimilitude?

Q4 List some conventions of a television news broadcast.

Q5 List some of the things you need to consider if you're writing for TV or radio.

Essay Question

Q1 Compare and contrast the linguistic devices used on TV and radio breakfast news.

We interrupt this revision session for a newsflash...

All porcupines can float. That is genuinely true... Imagine the plumpest porcupine you've ever seen. Yeah? Well, it floats. Like a ping-pong ball. Unless it's a porcupine witch, in which case it sinks like a stone. Now, Welles's spoof newsflashes were a bit more believable than that, but by following conventions, I bet I had you going there. No? Fine then.

Adverts

Just for AQA B and OCR. Do YOU need help analysing adverts? Would you like to consolidate your advert revision into one manageable double-page spread? Well look no further — pages 80-81 are the ONLY pages to be seen with this year.

Adverts are designed to Persuade

There are a few basic things you need to think about when you're looking at any advert:

1) **Subject matter** — the advert will focus on a **product**, **service**, or **cause**.

2) **Purpose** — adverts are designed to **persuade** the audience — usually to **buy** a **product** or **service**, **support** a **charity**, or join a **campaign**. They use different approaches to do this, e.g. they might show attractive people with luxurious lifestyles using a product to persuade the audience to buy it.

3) **Form** — written adverts come in different forms, e.g. in newspapers and magazines, appeal letters that come through your door, leaflets, posters and emails (spam). There are also the scripts for TV and radio adverts.

4) The **target audience** is the group the advert is aimed at. This could be very **broad** (food shoppers, drivers) or more **specific** (boys who like snowboarding).

5) The **hook** is the device advertisers use to get the audience's attention — it could be **verbal**, **visual** or **musical**.

6) In paper-based adverts the **text** is referred to as **copy**. People who **write** adverts are sometimes called **copywriters**.

Adverts use Language in Specific Ways to Achieve their Purpose

1) Lexis

- The lexis of an advert is designed to be **persuasive**. Copywriters use comparatives (*better, larger*) and superlatives (*best, largest*) to make their product or service seem better than their competitors'.
- Adverts often use **hi-tech jargon** to make a product seem **state-of-the-art**, e.g. *CBC* (cornering brake control).
- **Compound words** are common in lots of adverts, e.g. *farm-fresh*.

2) Grammar

- Adverts use different **sentence functions** as **hooks** — e.g. **exclamatives** (*it's your life!*), **declaratives** (*it's all you'll ever need*), **imperatives** (*come in from the cold*) and **interrogatives** (*why not have what you've always wanted?*).
- **Imperatives** without **subjects** are common **hooks** because they're short and snappy, e.g. *unite, create, enjoy*.
- The **syntax** of most adverts is quite **simple**, with few subordinate clauses. Sentences are often **disjunctive** (they set up contrasts, e.g. *elegant but sturdy*), rather than **discursive**. This ensures the message is very **clear**.

3) Graphology

- Often the first thing that attracts you to an advert is the **immediate visual impression** it makes, e.g. **colour**, **visual images**, and the **size**, **type** and **colour** of the **typeface**.
- **Larger** text tends to be more **persuasive**. **Smaller** text tends to focus on **giving information** about the product or service.
- **Unconventional spelling** is sometimes used to make a product stand out or seem hi-tech, e.g. *frooty, pix, FX*.

4) Phonology

Phonetic features of language (what it **sounds** like) are often used to keep the audience interested:

- **alliteration**, e.g. *local, live and loud*
- **onomatopoeia**, e.g. *crash! bang!*
- **rhyme**, e.g. *try before you buy*

5) Pragmatics

- The **tone** of an advert varies, depending on **subject matter**, **audience** and **purpose**.
- Adverts often try to **engage** with the consumer by **addressing** them **directly**, e.g. by using the **second person pronoun** (you), **imperatives** (orders) and **interrogatives** (questions).

6) Discourse

Adverts have a discourse structure. This is made up of different elements:

- the **hook** (e.g. *Together We Can End Hunger*)
- further **persuasion** and/or **information** (e.g. *a child dies from starvation every 5 seconds*).
- **instruction** on what the reader should do next (e.g. *Simply donate £2 a month...*)

Adverts

Adverts need to Engage the Audience

Creative language is more likely to grab the audience's **attention**, and stick in their minds. For example:

- **Semantic puns**, e.g. *Fly with us, the sky's the limit.*
- **Phonetic puns**, e.g. *Hair today, gone tomorrow.*
- **Figurative language**, e.g. *Is there a black hole in your pocket? Start saving now!*

Adverts can Create and Reinforce Stereotypes

1) Adverts are usually very **short**, so they have a **limited** amount of **space** and **time** to get their message across.

2) Because of this, adverts often show **simplified** images of people and events — **stereotypes**.

3) For example, adverts can show **gender stereotypes** by casting men and women in **traditional social** and **occupational** roles. They might show men going out to work and women looking after children, or men working as plumbers and women as secretaries.

4) **TV** adverts often show a **woman** using a product, then have a **male** voiceover **explaining** how the product works. This **reinforces traditional gender roles** by implying that a man **invented** the product, **understands** how it works, and has more **authority** to explain it.

5) Some adverts **parody** the **stereotypes** of traditional adverts, often for **humorous** effect.

Intertextuality is the Relationship between Different Texts

Adverts often **make references** to other texts to create a particular effect.

1) References to well-known texts are **accessible** to lots of people, and will be **easily remembered**. For example, a **hook** for a mattress advert might be *and on the seventh day he rested*. This echoes words from the Bible, so a lot of people will recognise it.

2) Other adverts aim to appeal to a more **specific** audience. They reference lesser-known texts to '**stroke**' the audience by assuming that they're knowledgeable. This suggests that the product will only appeal to an **elite few**. For example, a **hook** for a luxury travel company advertising city breaks in London and Paris — *A Tale of Two Cities*. This references the title of a Charles Dickens novel, which not everyone would be familiar with.

Practice Questions

Q1 Name the six language frameworks you should use when you're analysing adverts.
Q2 Why do adverts often contain hi-tech jargon?
Q3 How might an advert directly address the audience?
Q4 Why do adverts often contain stereotypes?
Q5 Why might an advert reference another text?

Essay Question

Q1 a) Write an advert for whatever you're sitting on at the moment. The advert will appear in a magazine and should be between 50 and 100 words. The target audience is 16-25 year olds.

b) Analyse your advert using the language frameworks on p.80.

This is not just revision — this is CGP revision...

I'm finding it pretty difficult to muster up a huge amount of excitement over the language of adverts. It seems to me that in their quest to grab your attention and froth you up into such a frenzy that you go out and spend without thinking, they forget that sometimes all you actually want is to watch a TV programme without it being interrupted every 15 minutes. Humph.

Electronic Texts

For AQA B and OCR. Electronic devices have had a huge effect on written language. Electronic communication can be almost as fast as spoken conversation, so there's no time for all the usual spelling, punctuation and grammar. The rules of Standard English often get thrown out of the window. And then run over by a bus. That's progress for you...

New Technology has Created New Words and Meanings

Every piece of new technology needs **new words** to describe it. This can involve giving **existing** words **new meanings**, or **inventing** completely new terms.

Way of forming new words	Example
acronyms — the initial letters from a group of words form a new word	**r**adar (**r**adio **d**etection **a**nd **r**anging)
affixation — adding a prefix or suffix to an existing word	**hyper**text
compounding — combining separate words	spyware
clipping — a shortened word becomes a word in its own right	fax (from facsimile)
blending — parts of two words are combined	netizen (internet + citizen)
conversion — an existing word changes its grammatical function	**the text** (noun) becomes **to text** (verb)

Text Messages have created Shorter and Quicker forms of language

Text messaging from mobile phones is often quicker and cheaper than a spoken phone call. However, typing complete words into a phone keypad is time-consuming, so a **shorthand** form of language called **text speak** has evolved.

Text messaging is **creative** — it's not **standardised**, so everyone uses it slightly differently. It's a **mixed mode** of communication, because it's a **written** language that contains many features of **spoken** language (see p.50-51).

Feature	Example
acronyms	*LOL* (Laugh Out Loud)
numbers for words	*2* (to)
numbers for phonemes (sounds)	*gr8* (great)
symbols for words	*@* (at)
phonetic spelling	*coz* (because)
incomplete clauses	*home safe. speak soon*
no punctuation	*how u doin wana go out 2nite*
simple sentences	*went to the zoo. it was good.*
smileys / emoticons	*:-)*

Roger hadn't quite got the hang of this texting lark.

The Internet has had a Big Impact on Language

The internet and mobile phones gained popularity at roughly the same time. As a result, the language used by internet users has many features in common with text speak. **Emails** are one of the most common types of internet texts, allowing messages to be sent and received almost immediately.

1) Emails are a **mixed mode**, containing **spoken** and **written** features. The mode that dominates depends on how **formal** the email is. The language used in an email is dependent on **context**.

2) An email from one business to another business might be set out like a **formal letter** and use **Standard English**. **Less formal emails** are often written **quickly** between friends and family. They can contain time-saving devices such as **abbreviations**, **missing punctuation**, non-standard use of **lower-case letters** (e.g. 'monday', 'rebecca'), or any of the features of text speak.

3) Emails are usually typed on a full-sized keyboard, and they have no word limit, so they don't have to be as brief as text messages. There are **no set conventions**, so the style of language is decided by the individual writer.

4) Emails can be written and replied to **spontaneously**, as if they were part of a spoken conversation. As a result, the language used is often more **direct** and **vivid** than the language in letters written on paper.

Sandra liked to explore the darker side of e-mailing.

Electronic Texts

Different Types of Websites use Different Language

Weblogs

A **weblog** (or **blog** for short) is a website which allows internet users to **publish** their writing online. These sites are usually **unregulated**, so the content is decided by the writer. Blogs can take a lot of **different forms**.

- Many blogs take the form of **diaries** or **editorials**, where the writer shares their experiences and opinions with their internet audience. These blogs can be written **anonymously**, allowing writers to express views that they might otherwise keep to themselves. The language used can be forthright and confrontational.
- As with email, there are no standard language **conventions** for blogs. They can use **any or none** of the abbreviations used in other electronic texts. More professional blogs use Standard English to mimic newspaper editorials and make them **accessible** to a wide audience. However, blogs can be written by anyone, and many bloggers write for internet-literate friends, using the **slang** and **shorthand** they'd use in a text message or email.

Chat rooms

Chat rooms are websites where groups of people can have 'live' online conversations.
Messages are often exchanged **extremely quickly** in chat rooms, so people use **abbreviations** to save time.

- Chat room language is strongly based on **conversational** language, and many chat room acronyms stand in for **conversational clichés**. Examples include BTW (by the way) and OMG (oh my God).
- Some abbreviations reflect the **practical problems** of typing at a computer. Gaps in the conversation can be explained by BRB (be right back), AFK (away from keyboard) and D/C (disconnected).
- Many chatroom users are teenagers who share a computer with their parents. They use terms such as PW (parents watching) and MOS (Mum over shoulder) so **adults can't understand** what they're saying.

Online Video Games

Many PC and video games now feature **online modes**, allowing groups of players to **communicate** while they play. Regular gamers often use a dialect called **Leetspeak** (a semi-phonetic spelling of 'elite'). It's also used in chatrooms and other internet forums to show **enthusiasm** or **surprise**. It has some distinctive features, for example:

- Letters are often **replaced** by similar-looking **numbers**, e.g. *Leetspeak* might be written *13375p34k*.
- Some features are based on **typing errors**. For example, *the* is often written as *teh*, and exclamation marks are deliberately replaced by the digit *1*, because the two symbols are on the **same key**.
- Leetspeak has evolved its own **unconventional grammar** based on **American slang**, e.g. *this rocks!* might become *teh r0xx0r!!1!*.
- There are lots of ways to write the same thing in Leetspeak, so it's a **flexible** variety of English. It's unusual because it can't be **spoken** or **handwritten** — you need a **keyboard** and an **electronic display**.

Practice Questions

Q1   List six characteristics of text speak.

Q2   What does 'mixed mode' mean?

Q3   What kind of language is usually used in informal emails?

Q4   What is leetspeak?

Essay Question

Q1   Discuss how internet communication has influenced language.

Breaking down the language barrier — or just breaking the rules...

Mobile phones and the internet have made everyone remember how to write again — texts and emails are quick and easy, and nobody's going to grade you on your spelling and grammar. Some people think these new forms of language encourage creativity, while others worry that the rules of Standard English are being forgotten. It's a bit of both, IMHO.

Film and the Visual Arts

This is for AQA B and OCR. Films and plays have been around for quite a while, establishing a few conventions of their own. Read on, because these pages are gold if you need to start a conversation with someone posh at dinner.

Film and Theatre Language is **Carefully Constructed**

In a film or play, no matter how believable the performances, every word the actor speaks has usually been **scripted** to achieve a certain effect. What's more, someone will also have directed **how** the words are spoken too.

LEXIS

A film or play will have a **specific lexis** depending on the **subject matter** and **genre** — for example, a **science-fiction action film** about an alien invasion may have words like *extra-terrestrial*, *intergalactic* and *humanoid*. They're all words that relate to the genre, but they're also quite **dramatic** (compared to *alien*, *space* and *robot*, for example).

ACCENT AND DIALECT

The way a character speaks can reveal a lot about them, for example, they might have a **strong regional accent** and use **dialect** words to make them appear uneducated or lower class. Or this might be a **technique** used by the director to give a production more **realism**. The important thing to bear in mind is that the way the characters speak is **intentional** and is used to create a particular effect.

PROSODY

Pauses, **stress**, **pace** and **intonation** all influence the audience's **interpretation** of a character's words. Prosodic features might be included in the **stage directions**, or they might be added according to the **director** and **actor's interpretation**. Prosody plays an important part in **creating meaning**, for example, whether a character said *I love you* sincerely or sarcastically could have a huge impact on the rest of the story.

ACTIONS

OK, it's not technically language, but gestures and facial expressions are used to **emphasise** what's being said. They also **vary** depending on the **genre**, for example, **theatre** actors tend to use much more **exaggerated** actions than **film** actors because they're **easier to see** from a distance.

Film and Theatre language is **More** than **Just Conversation**

When you're reading a book, the author can go off on a **tangent** to explain a **character's motivations**, or the **atmosphere** of a particular scene, etc. This sort of explanation isn't possible in films or on stage.

1) In the absence of detailed character histories or a narrator, the dialogue has to tell the story. An audience can **infer** things about the characters from the way that language is used in a script, and how it is **delivered**. For example, a film about gangsters in the east end of London will have actors speaking with a **Cockney accent** and using dialect features like **rhyming slang**.

"Speak up Dennis, I can't hear a word you're saying down here."

2) Dialogue can also provide **information** about **characters** who **aren't** in the scene, e.g. Shakespeare put **clues** in his dialogue to suggest a character's **traits**. In ***King Lear***, a father describes his son as a *knave* and a *whoreson* — this kind of lexis means the audience can guess what he might be like without seeing him.

3) The language in plays or films can represent **political anxieties** too. For example, a writer who thinks that people in power **shouldn't be trusted** may write a script that tells the story of their **downfall**. This will be supported by the linguistic devices given to the character, e.g. an **insincere tone**, **disrespect** for conversational rules, or a vocabulary full of **hyperbole** and **clichés**.

4) Language is only a small part of the **sound** you hear when you watch a film. The **soundtrack** and **sound effects** can **enhance** or **direct** meaning. For example, a scene with two lovers **fighting** could have **loud** background music with a **strong beat**, which would suggest **passion** and **violence**. Or it could be accompanied by **slow**, **soft** piano music, which would suggest the **sadness** of a relationship ending. **Fast**, **comic** music would **undermine** what was being seen, and create a sense of **irony**.

Film and the Visual Arts

Scripts are Written In a Unique Way

All film and play scripts are set out in a **similar way** — and if you're writing one you have to know the **conventions** too.

1) There isn't usually a **narrative voice** in a film or play, so things like *he said* and *she was a nice girl but she was caught up in something she didn't understand* **don't exist**.

2) Instead, everything that isn't directly stated in the dialogue has to be shown through the **stage directions** and **prosodic features** (how the lines are delivered), for example:

> **James**: Why don't you tell me what "Sad Panda" means to you, Naomi?
>
> *Fear flickers across Naomi's face; she avoids looking at James by staring at the floor.*
>
> **Naomi**: Noth- [*her voice wavers, she steadies herself against the desk*]. Nothing. I've never heard that before.
>
> *James stares intently at her then advances across the room.*
>
> **James**: [*quietly*] You're lying. [*shouting*] TELL ME WHAT I NEED TO KNOW!

3) Film and play scripts use **jargon** in their stage directions to tell a director about the author's ideas and how they would like them to be **communicated** to the audience. **Detailed directions** tell the **director** what the **writer** had in mind for the play and help to set the scene:

> It is August, early evening. The scene is a gentlemen's club in London. The ceiling is high. All the walls are covered in heavy maroon paper. Back wall has a tall rectangular Georgian window centre. Up (L) there is an ornate bar with expensive liquor bottles arranged on a shelf behind it. At (curtain up,) Fred and Sam are sitting in two shabby armchairs (down) R, drinking brandy and in obvious disagreement about something...

The letters L and R mean left and right — but from the actors' point of view, not the audience's.

Up is the back of the stage, and down is the front of the stage — this is all jargon the director will understand.

The directions also specify what should be happening when the curtain is raised and the audience sees the stage for the first time.

4) Jargon in a film script might be **more technical** than in a play script. For example, a film script may include **camera angles** and **movements**, and film-making terms like *close-up*, *fade*, *dissolve*, *pan shot*, and so on.

Practice Questions

Q1 How might a character's accent and dialect reveal something about them?

Q2 How is prosody important in films and plays?

Q3 How can music be used to affect an audience's interpretation of a scene?

Q4 Where would you find jargon in a script and why?

Q5 What differences might there be between stage directions in a film and a play?

Essay Question

Q1 Discuss the different ways that scriptwriters use language in film and theatre.

Well film me up with knowledge and call me a textbook...

It's a pretty nifty little section this one. You can bet your bottom dollar that at some point, somewhere on this course, some kind of media text will spring from stage left (or right) and force you to analyse it, or something equally horrible. You might even decide to produce one voluntarily, in which case make sure you're fully fluent in all the conventions we've discussed.

Sources and Exam Questions

These questions aren't exactly like ones you'll get in the exam, because for most boards you'll focus on media texts for your coursework. You could still get a media text to analyse in the exam though, so doing these questions will be good practice.

1. Text A is an advertisement for a holiday company. Analyse the use of persuasive devices in this text.

Voyages Du Monde

Are you looking for a company that has seen the world and wants to share it with you?
Are you a discerning and demanding traveller who will settle for nothing less than the best?
If you are one of these special people, you have reached your perfect destination for
exploring the wonders and mysteries our planet offers — Voyages Du Monde.

We can arrange experiences and trips of a lifetime to suit any style and budget of travel.
Perhaps you are a maverick explorer who wishes to see the world alone, but with the back-up
of a highly respected and experienced team arranging the day to day practicalities of your journey.
Or perhaps you are a single traveller looking to journey with a select group of like-minded individuals
with the expertise of a hand-picked, specialist tour guide. Whatever your requirements, Voyages Du Monde *is here to*
transport you on a holiday you won't forget.

Based in the UK, with 25 years of experience in the travel industry, you can rest assured that travelling with us will
be smooth, straightforward and suited to your individual needs – leaving you relaxed and focused on the enjoyment
of your holiday. Our team of dedicated Voyages Du Monde *call handlers, based in our purpose-built office in the New*
Forest, are here to take you through our wide range of travel options.

In addition to our UK team, we have strong local contacts in all of our partner countries – so wherever your journey
takes you, you know Voyages Du Monde *is never far away. And it may interest you to know that the people who work*
for us around the world are paid a fair wage and supported in their local community – we take our responsibilities to
others extremely seriously – and that includes everyone who joins our family.
So pack up your bags today and let Voyages Du Monde *take care of everything else.*

Visit our website at www.voydum.com for a comprehensive list of our exclusive destinations at highly competitive prices, or call us on 09876 234156 to speak to one of our team.

Voyages Du Monde We look forward to your holiday as much as you do

2. Text B is a transcript of an item on the local television news. Analyse the language in terms of the conventions of television news.

NEWSREADER: figures released today show a rise in the amount of people returning to work following the recent slump in the jobs' market (1) industry experts have welcomed the figures (.) which were issued by the financial think tank Fiscal Britain (1) a statement from the Department of Trade and Industry said that they were now cautiously optimistic (.) that measures put in place to secure Britain's future in the global markets were starting to show success (1) the recent downturn was linked to a global recession (.) and sectors such as the car industry were particularly hard hit (.) but in recent days (.) several companies have begun increasing their output to levels closer to those seen last year (.) when sales were much higher (1) our economics expert Damian Briggs has been looking into the importance of the figures for our region (1) Damian

DAMIAN: thank you Jane (.) well (.) as we all know (.) this year has been one of the worst on record for the car industry (.) but recently we have had reason to believe that things are looking up (1) two companies in the north east re-introduced production lines that had been stopped earlier last month (.) and issued statements saying they expected sales to show a partial recovery into the back end of the year (.) all this comes as a huge relief to workers who were faced with losing their jobs if the factories failed to increase their output (1) earlier today I visited one site in Sunderland to speak to workers there

Sources and Exam Questions

3. Text C is a transcript from a radio talk show. Analyse the language in terms of the conventions of radio language. Speaker A is the host, speakers B and D are callers and speaker C is an 'expert'.

A: okay so with us today in the studio we have a specialist in the field of journalism (.) Professor Pat Spinks (.) Professor Spinks is the head of the school of journalism at London's West University (.) thank you for joining us today Professor (1) now we're a bit rushed but we're also taking your calls so if you have something to add to the debate about celebrities in the press then give us a call on (.) on (.) the (.) usual (.) number (1) okay so <u>pressing</u> on we're crossing now to line one (.) we'll hear from Brenda (.) Brenda are you there

B: yes (.) hello (.) er sorry

A: // what would you like to say Brenda

B: well really I just think it's well it's a bit <u>unfair</u> you know that you get these young girls photographed wherever they go and really (.) er (.) why is it when they're not even really what I would call er <u>famous</u>

A: so you think it's not fair on them that they're followed about then

B: well yes (.) but I mean in my day you had to <u>do</u> something really good you know to become erm famous

A: ah right yes (.) and would you agree with that Professor Spinks

C: well <u>yes</u> and <u>no</u> in reality (.) I think Brenda makes a good point that <u>perceptions</u> about what makes someone famous probably have changed (.) but also if you think about the <u>technology</u> we have available nowadays in comparison with say the sixties (.) it's just that nowadays people have more opportunity to photograph and distribute pictures of good looking women (1) not that I would argue they make particularly good <u>news</u> stories (1) I think you have to consider the whole issue in the context of changing standards in the media industry as well as changing demands from the public

A: so you're saying that the whole issue is quite a complex one

C: yes exactly

A: okay (.) thank you for your question Brenda (2) Brenda (1) okay looks like we've lost you there (.) well let's hear what someone else has to say (.) line two (.) is that have we got <u>Brian</u> from Leeds

D: yes (.) hello there Simon (.) how are you

A: oh er yes good thanks good thank you (.) now Brian (.) what have you got to say to us

D: well (.) erm (.) I think I don't really <u>agree</u> with your previous caller (.) because I think these celebrities <u>deliberately</u> put themselves out to get in the papers and (.) really if you're in the public eye then well that's up to you isn't it

A: okay (.) but would you say that's true of people like (.) say the wives and girlfriends of the Royal Family Brian

D: er (.) erm well they're not the same (.) no (.) but then if you want to join the Royal Family then we need to know who you <u>are</u> don't we

Transcription Key		
(.) *Micropause*	**//**	*Interruptions / overlapping speech*
(1) *Pause in seconds*	**<u>underlining</u>**	*Indicates stress / increased volume*

4. Text D is an extract from a film review in *FilmStar* magazine. Analyse the language in terms of the conventions of journalism.

An Owl Hunting (15)

Director: Molly Turner   Running time: 118 mins

Cast: Dylan Edgestone, Jim Nelson, Emily Hayes

It's been this year's most hotly awaited sequel, and since its release, the most talked about film of the year. An Owl Hunting is the follow up to Molly Turner's spectacular directorial debut The Fishing Hut. A film of great complexity, it was last year's surprise hit at the London Film Festival, and it went on to win several awards at the star-studded New Film event in Los Angeles. An Owl Hunting follows Turner's original characters, Sid and Jack, as they continue their long march through the cold plains of Siberia. Joined by an extensive array of colourful characters, played by both local people and world famous actors, the story of Sid and Jack is undeniably captivating. The dialogue is as precise as we have been led to expect from The Fishing Hut and Turner's magic touch makes the film as stunning as any of the road movies that have gone before it. Beautifully shot in breathtaking locations, the cinematography is, if anything, a step up from the sweeping views we were treated to in The Fishing Hut.

Sources and Exam Questions

5. Text A is an extract from an article taken from an online music news page.

   Text B is an article taken from the entertainment page of a newspaper.

   Analyse the similarities and differences between these texts in terms of the language of the media.

Text A — from an interview in an online music news page

The talent at this year's FreshRock festival was as outstanding as we've come to expect over the last few years, and the winning duo were no exception. We hot-footed it over to the hospitality tent to ask Bootclass's Nadine and Paula a few questions before the night grew too long.

FreshRock: Fantastic news there — congratulations! So, how does it feel?

Nadine: We're really just so stunned, we couldn't believe it, could we?

Paula: No, we'd had such a blast just doing the whole festival that we'd just accepted we weren't ever gonna win, just didn't even give it a moment's thought and then...

Tell us a bit about the build up, the preparation for the festival.

Nadine: Well obviously we had the auditions back in January, it was our music teacher who suggested we went, 'cos we were gonna wait 'til next year...

Paula: Yeah it was definitely something we wanted to do, but we never thought we'd be ready this year, but she just said go for it, you're ready.

And she was clearly right. How did you choose your set?

Nadine: Well, we have a few favourites that we were never gonna not play, and then we knew really that we ought to be pushing ourselves a bit more and we'd been writing a bit of stuff so we just thought what the hell let's put that in too.

Paula: Yeah, we'd done a bit for our teacher and she thought it was OK but it's hard to tell as she's always totally 100% behind us whatever we do, so we thought she was just being kind...

Nadine: Although we'd done that gig in The Ship and it'd gone down OK, hadn't it...

Paula: Yeah, it's a pub near us where you can go and play a few tunes, anyone can go, and it's quite popular. Well, it's always been there I think 'cos my dad used to play there too...

Nadine: ...and if you play something rubbish, someone'll always tell you so we thought what we had must be OK.

Paula: But we still never thought we'd win.

So what is your background? Aren't you both still at school?

Paula: Yeah we are, we're still doing our A-Levels...

Nadine: ...so we've known each other for ever because our parents were in a band together and we used to have to go and sit in a corner and watch. Or worse they would have us on stage playing with them or something, so in the end we just had to give in and start playing seriously. And now we're both going to the same college which will be brilliant actually cos we love playing and writing music together...well, I do anyway... (laughs)

Paula:...yeah, speak for yourself... no, I mean we've grown up together, we've got a similar sort of background in terms of what we've listened to and been exposed to so we do have a pretty good understanding of each other's music. But it's also been great over the last couple of years to have an amazing music teacher in school who's been able to broaden our influences and she's taught us a couple of new instruments each so that we're a bit more versatile.

You make it all sound so easy – how do you pick up a couple of new instruments just like that? And then start writing too – it's a pretty big step to take.

Paula: Well I guess we've just been lucky really, there's always been instruments around at home and music about us so it's never seemed a big deal to learn something new. I mean, we've had to practise loads but...

Nadine: ...it's never really seemed like hard work cos everyone around us was doing it, it just seemed normal. And also you hear all this amazing music you know at festivals and stuff and it just really makes you want to be that good and write stuff of your own too.

Sources and Exam Questions

Text B — an article from the entertainment page of a newspaper

Starry starry Knight

Edinburgh soul singer sets out for success in the big smoke

Andrew Conway
Culture Editor

She was working as a waitress in a cocktail bar... yes, she really was. But now it looks like Anneka Knight will be saying a fond farewell to Screwdrivers, Rusty Nails and Sex on the Beaches, and saying hello to a new life where people will be mixing the drinks for her.

The 20-year-old former cocktail waitress is already lined up to perform alongside the legendary DJs Dom Williams and Lex Cole in London early next year, and she's not even released her first single yet.

So how did this Edinburgh-born unknown make her rapid ascent to the top? It's an almost unbelievable tale of chance discovery — one that Anneka herself is still unable to take in.

"I was singing at a private party in the bar," says the petite blonde, "my manager knew I'd been having some lessons and was desperate to embarrass me. But I love singing, so I belted out a couple of songs. Later a bloke who'd actually been turned away from the door rang the bar to say he'd heard a little of me and wanted to hear more. It was a producer from the Music Scene show."

It was the start of what turned out to be an audition for a slot on the show. She passed without any difficulty, and even got the chance to sing some of her own compositions to a studio audience when she travelled down to record a test piece in London.

She's been described by her champions as having a soulful voice well beyond her years, and the proof is there in her performances. She's rapidly gathering a following on the live circuit in London, and it's her straightforward, no-nonsense style the audiences like.

She mixes up old classics, in a voice that could have been handed straight down from Bessie Smith, with her own songs — about everything from her former life in a bar to the day she said goodbye to her best friend after she set off for fame. In fact she's made such a name for herself that it seems there's no return to Edinburgh planned in the near future — she's booked up nearly every evening in the weeks ahead and it's now her plan to get herself a big gig in a big place.

"I'm writing all the time I'm not singing, and I feel like I've got to keep my pace going in case I wake up from this dream and find out I'm actually due behind the bar for the late shift again. What I really want is to get my album out there and then play somewhere big. I've never been scared of crowds and I'm ready to show them my soul".

Anneka's already been signed by False Modesty, who manage some of the biggest singers around, and she's got a single due for release at the end of this month. This will be followed by an album in the new year, as well as the gig alongside Williams and Cole. Not bad for someone who never really considered a life in the music business. Despite being told by many people as a young teenager that she should be singing professionally, she turned down a place at the famous Scottish Performance School because she didn't want to be different from her friends. Now she admits that she wishes she'd taken the chance, but if her current upward rise continues, it's not going to be something she'll need to regret much longer.

Early Language Development

This section is for AQA B and Edexcel — if you're doing WJEC you might need this if you're doing your coursework on language acquisition. Language development is a long process, so get cracking, else you'll never get those first words out

Language Development *may* Begin *in the* Womb

There is some evidence that suggests language development starts **before** birth.

1) **DeCasper and Spence (1986)** found that babies sucked on their dummies more when their mothers read them the **same story** that they'd also read aloud during the last six months of the pregnancy.

2) **Mehler et al (1988)** found that four-day-old French babies increased their sucking rate on a dummy, showing interest or recognition, when they heard French as opposed to Italian or English. This suggested that they had acquired some awareness of the **sounds** of **French** before they were born.

3) **Fitzpatrick (2002)** found that the heart rate of an unborn baby **slowed** when it heard its **mother's voice**.

> All this suggests that even in the womb, babies become familiar with the **sounds**, **rhythms** and **intonations** of language.

Babies start to use their **Vocal Chords Straight Away**

1) The period between birth and the first word being spoken is known as the **pre-verbal** or **pre-language** stage.

2) **Crying** is the first main vocal expression a baby makes. It makes the **caregiver** (e.g. parents, sibling, or baby-sitter) aware that the baby needs something. Crying can indicate **hunger**, **discomfort** or **pain**.

3) This isn't really a **conscious act** on the baby's part. It's more an **instinctive response** to how it feels.

Babies then start to **Form Sounds** — the **Cooing Stage**

1) At the **cooing** stage (which starts when they're **six to eight weeks old**), babies start making a **small range** of sounds — they get used to moving their lips and tongue.

2) This starts with **vowels** like /u/ and /a/. Then they start linking these to produce **extended vowel combinations** like *ooo* and *aaah*. They start to use **velar consonants** (ones made using the back part of the tongue) like /k/ and /g/ to form sounds like *coo* and *ga*.

3) These sounds don't carry any **meaning** — the baby is just **experimenting** with sounds.

4) Gradually these sounds become more **defined** and are strung together. This **vocal play** is the start of babbling.

Babbling *is the next significant stage*

1) Babies usually start to babble when they're about **six months** old.

2) At this stage, they start producing repeated consonant / vowel combinations like *ma-ma-ma, ba-ba-ba, ga-ga-ga*. These sounds are common in babies from many different nationalities. Repeating sounds like this is known as **reduplicated** or **canonical babbling**.

3) Sometimes these sounds are not repeated, e.g. *goo-gi-goo-ga* or *da-di-da*. This is called **variegated babbling**.

4) The **consonants** that you usually get in **reduplicated** or **variegated** babbling are: *h, w, j, p, b, m, t, d, n, k, g*.

5) Research has shown that **deaf** babies who've had some exposure to **sign language** will **babble** with their **hands** — producing consonant and vowel combinations in sign language. This suggests that babbling is an **innate activity**, which is **preprogrammed** to happen in the process of language development.

6) Most people argue that babbling is a **continuation** of the baby's experimentation with **sound creation** (cooing) rather than the production of sounds which carry **meaning**. For example, the infant may produce *dadadada* but they're not actually saying anything referring to *Dad* or *Daddy* at this stage.

7) Some people argue that babbling is the **beginning of speech**:

> **Petitto and Holowka (2002)** videoed infants and noted that most babbling came more from the **right side** of the mouth, which is controlled by the **left side** of the brain. This side of the brain is **responsible for speech production**. Their findings suggest that babbling is a form of **preliminary speech**.

Early Language Development

The *Babbling Stage* can be divided into *Two Parts*

1) When babies start to babble, the number of different **phonemes** (see p.58) they produce **increases**.
2) This is called **phonemic expansion**.
3) Later in the babbling stage, they **reduce** the number of phonemes they use (**phonemic contraction**).
4) This is the period when the baby starts to concentrate on **reproducing** the phonemes it hears in its **native language**. It **stops using** the sounds that it doesn't hear from its carers.
5) It's at this stage (about **ten months old**) that children of **different nationalities** start to sound different.

> A study at **Bristol University** in **2008** showed that babies who are exposed to different languages in the first nine months of their life are more able to pick out the sounds of these languages as they get older. This is because **phonemic contraction** has occurred less than it would if the baby had been exposed to one language only.

Infants start to show *Intonation Patterns* at the babbling stage

1) Even in the early stages of babbling (at six months) some babies will use **rhythms** that resemble the **speech patterns of adults**. There will be recognisable **intonation** in the strings of phonemes they put together.
2) For example, at the end of a babbling sequence the intonation may **rise**, mirroring the kind of intonation adults use when **asking a question**. Babies can also accompany these sounds with **gestures**, like pointing.

Babbling leads to the production of a *Child's First Words*

1) Eventually, certain **combinations** of **consonants** and **vowels** start to carry meaning. For example, a child might say *Mmm* to show that they want some more food. This is not a word in itself but it **functions** like one. These are called **proto-words**, and sometimes they're accompanied by **gestures** as well.

"AUDREY! Get this checked monstrosity off of me!"

2) Another example of a proto-word is when a child refers to a cat as /da/. This is still just a **sound** rather than a recognisable word, but it **refers** to an **object** and is not just a random utterance. At around **9 months** children start to sound like they're speaking their own **made-up language**. This is called **jargon**.
3) In the later stages of babbling, sound and meaning start to **come together**. At this stage, *ma-ma* does indicate *Mum* and *ka-ka* does mean *car*. This usually happens by the time the baby is **ten months old**.

Practice Questions

Q1 Outline a piece of research that suggests language development begins in the womb.
Q2 When does the cooing stage usually start?
Q3 What's it called when babies produce repeated consonant / vowel combinations?
Q4 What evidence is there to suggest that babbling is the beginning of speech?
Q5 Outline what happens in the two parts of the babbling stage.
Q6 What are proto-words?

Essay Question

Q1 With reference to research, outline the different stages that babies go through up to and including the babbling stage.

All this revision is making me go a bit ga-ga...

I don't know how babies get their tiny little heads around proto-words and extended vowel combinations. They must be smarter than they look. It's hard enough learning about them learning about this learning about... but don't mind me and my canonical babbling. Get learning all the important information on this page and you can be as clever as a baby.

Phonological and Pragmatic Development

These pages are for AQA B and Edexcel. *Once babies have moved on from the babbling stage, they start trying to pronounce words. They might not always get them right first time but they can still make themselves understood.*

Phonological Development depends on the Individual

1) Children learn **vowels** and **consonants** at different speeds. They learn to use some **phonemes** earlier than others.

2) Most children will be able to use all the **vowels** in English by the time they're two-and-a-half years old.

3) They might not use all the **consonants** confidently until they're **six** or **seven** years old. The earliest consonants that they master tend to be /m/ and /n/ (known as **nasals**), and /p/, /t/, and /k/ (known as **voiceless plosives**). The last ones tend to be the /th/ sounds in words like *thought* (the /θ/ **phoneme**) and *this* (the /ð/ **phoneme**), and other sounds known as **fricatives** like /v/, /tʃ/ and /dʒ/ as in <u>v</u>ery, <u>ch</u>urch and <u>j</u>ack.

4) Children find using consonants at the **beginning** of words (**word-initial**) easier than consonants at the end of words (**word-final**). For example, they'll find it easier to say the /t/ in *teddy* than the one at the end of *sit*.

Simplification helps children Communicate

1) Learning to **pronounce** things properly is difficult, but children can still **communicate** — if they can't pronounce a word as adults do, they use a simpler version. Simplification mainly applies to **consonants**.

2) There are three main kinds of phonological simplification — **deletion**, **substitution**, and **cluster reduction**:

> **Deletion** Sometimes a child **drops** a consonant altogether, particularly at the **end** of a word. For example, they might say *ca* rather than *cat*.

> **Substitution** Instead of dropping a consonant, a child might **replace it** with one that's easier to say. For example, they might say *wegs* rather than *legs*, or *tup* rather than *cup*.

> **Cluster Reduction** Where there are **consonant clusters** (two or more consonants together in a word), a child may **drop one** of the consonants. For example, the child will say *geen* rather than *green*.

> **Berko and Brown (1960)** reported what they referred to as the *fis phenomenon*. A child referred to his plastic fish as a *fis*. When an adult asked *Is this your fis?*, the child said no, stating instead that it was his *fis*. When the adult then asked *Is this your fish?*, the child replied *Yes, my fis*.
> This suggests that children can **recognise** and **understand** a **wider range** of phonemes than they can **produce**.

Other Features are common in phonological development

1) **Addition** is when a vowel is added to the end of a word, e.g. *dog* is pronounced *dogu*.

2) **Assimilation** is when one consonant in a word is changed because of the influence of another in the same word, e.g. *tub* becomes *bub* because of the influence of the final /b/.

3) **Reduplication** is when a phoneme is repeated, like *moo-moo* (for *cow*), or *bik-bik* (for *biscuit*).

4) **Voicing** is when voiceless consonants like *p, t, f, s* (sounds produced without using the vocal chords) are replaced by their voiced equivalents *b, d, v, z*, so instead of saying *sock*, a child might say *zok*.

5) **De-voicing** is when voiced consonants (sounds produced using the vocal chords as well as the mouth / tongue / lips), are replaced by their voiceless equivalents, so instead of saying *bag* a child might say *pag*.

It takes longer to Develop Intonation

1) Even at the babbling stage, babies begin to demonstrate **intonation** patterns. When they start to put words together, it becomes even more obvious, e.g. they put stress on certain words, e.g. *that's <u>mine</u>.*

2) It takes a long time for children to understand the complexities of intonation and stress. For example, **Cruttenden (1985)** found that ten-year-olds had difficulty distinguishing between:

> a) *She <u>dressed</u>, and fed the <u>baby</u>* (she dressed *herself*, and fed the *baby*), **and**
>
> b) *She dressed and fed the <u>baby</u>* (she dressed the *baby* and fed it too).

Phonological and Pragmatic Development

Children's Language has a range of Different Functions

1) At first, a child can get responses or reactions by using **proto-words**. After a while they start to use **recognisable** words, which have **different functions** depending on their context. For example, the word *dummy* could be an order (*get my dummy*), or a question (*where's my dummy?*).

2) **Halliday (1975)** states that the early language of children has **seven functions**:

Instrumental	to get something (e.g. 'go toily' meaning 'I want to go to the toilet').	These four are about the child satisfying their social, emotional and physical needs.
Regulatory	to make requests or give orders (e.g. 'Not your teddy' meaning 'Leave my teddy alone').	
Interactional	to relate to others (e.g. 'Nice Mummy').	
Personal	to convey a sense of personal identity and to express views and feelings (e.g. 'naughty doggy').	
Heuristic	to find out about the immediate environment (e.g. 'What boy doing?').	These two are about the child coming to terms with their environment and their place within it.
Imaginative	to be creative through language that relates to imaginative play, storytelling, rhymes and humour (e.g. 'One day my Daddy came home and he said...').	
Representational	to convey information (e.g. 'I'm three').	

Children quickly learn to Interact With Others

1) Babies learn about **social conventions** even before they can speak. For example, the game of "peek-a-boo" familiarises the baby with **turn-taking** and is an early form of social interaction.

2) Even at the babbling stage, a child's carer might respond to their babbling as if they were having a **conversation** — so there's some basic **interaction** between child and caregiver.

3) As children develop they can interact in more **sophisticated** ways. They will **start conversations**, use a full range of **speech functions** and show **politeness features**. They start to use more adult forms of interaction like **turn-taking**, **adjacency pairs**, and **opening and closing sequences**. There's more on this on p.54.

4) **Non-verbal communication** (like hand gestures and facial expressions) and **non-verbal aspects of speech** (like pitch, volume, intonation and pace) also become increasingly **sophisticated** as children grow up.

Practice Questions

Q1 Which phonemes do children usually learn to pronounce last?
Q2 Outline the three different kinds of simplification.
Q3 What is the *fis phenomenon* and what does it suggest about how children acquire language?
Q4 What is meant by assimilation in the context of language acquisition?
Q5 According to Halliday, what are the seven functions of early language? Give examples.

Essay Question

Q1 Explain the phonological features that are found in the speech of young children who haven't yet learned to pronounce all the phonemes correctly.

Phonological development — babies are always looking at their mobiles...

Ah, if only life was as simple as it used to be when you were little. Remember the good old days on the farm playing in the mud and digging for worms. Sadly life's a bit more complicated these days what with revision and exams. Don't worry though, everything you ever wanted to know about phonological development is right here on these pages. Phew.

Lexis, Grammar and Semantics

AQA B and Edexcel need to know these pages. Children start off by using one or two words to express themselves. As their range of vocabulary grows, they start to use several words together in basic grammatical relationships.

Children acquire vocabulary *Very Quickly*

1) This table gives you an idea of how your **vocabulary grows** as you get older:

Age	Number of Words Used
18 months	50 +
2 years	300
5 years	approx. 3000
7 years	approx. 4000

A child's ability to **understand words** will always develop quicker than their ability to **use** them. At 18 months old, a child can **actively** use 50 words, but can **understand** around 250.

The **increase** in vocabulary between age 2 to 7 is so big that these figures can only ever be an **estimation**.

2) Children's first words relate to their **immediate surroundings**. They're connected to things that children can see, hear, taste, smell and touch, or that have a **social function**. Words that express concepts and more abstract ideas start to appear as the child becomes more **self-aware** and **experiences** more of the world.

First Words *can be put into* Categories

Nelson (1973) studied the first fifty words produced by eighteen children and grouped them into **five categories**:

1) **Classes of Objects** — *dog, shoe, ball, car*
2) **Specific Objects** — *Mummy, Daddy*
3) **Actions / Events** — *give, stop, go, up, where*
4) **Modifying things** — *dirty, nice, allgone*
5) **Personal / Social** — *hi, bye-bye, yes, no*

Classes of **objects** formed the largest group — it's easier for children to identify things that they can actually **touch**.

*Don't tell me... don't tell me...
Dog... No? Table?*

Children soon learn to *Use Words Creatively*

When they're between 12 and 18 months old children will **improvise** if they don't know the word for something. This takes **two** main forms — **underextension** and **overextension**:

1) **Underextension** is when a child uses a word in a very **restricted way**. For example, when a child says *hat*, but means only the hat that she wears rather than any hat.
2) **Overextension** is when a child uses a word to refer to several **different** but **related** things. For example, she might use the word *cat* to refer to anything with four legs, like foxes, dogs, etc.

Rescorla (1980) said there were two types of overextension — **categorical** and **analogical**:

- **Categorical** is when a word is used to refer to things in a similar category, e.g. the word *car* is used to refer to buses, trucks and other forms of four-wheeled vehicle. This kind of overextension is most common.
- **Analogical** is when a word is used to refer to things that aren't clearly in the same category but have some **physical** or **functional relation** to each other, e.g. the word *hat* is used for anything near or connected with the head.

Aitchison (1987) *suggested three other* Development Processes

1) **Labelling** is when a child links a **sound** to an **object** — they are able to call something by its **correct name**.
2) **Packaging** is when a child begins to understand the **range of meaning** a word might have. They recognise that the word *bottle* can cover different shapes and sizes, but that they all have a similar **function**.
3) **Network building** is when a child starts to make **connections** between words, e.g. they understand that words have **opposites** like *big* and *small*, or know that *little* and *small* are **synonyms**.

Lexis, Grammar and Semantics

Most first words function as Holophrases

1) The stage where a child says their first words is known as the **holophrastic** or **one-word stage**. **Holophrases** are **single words** that express a **complete idea** — an individual word performs the same function as a sentence would.

2) For example, when a child says *teddy*, the **meaning** of this utterance isn't obvious straight away. It could be *here's my teddy* (like a **declarative** sentence), *where's my teddy?* (an **interrogative**), *get my teddy* (**imperative**), or *here's my teddy, excellent!* (**exclamative**).

3) Caregivers often need **contextual clues** (e.g. being able to see the objects surrounding the child, intonation and stress) and the child's **non-verbal communication** to interpret holophrases.

The two-word stage is the Beginning of Syntax

At around **eighteen months** children start to use **two words** in **conjunction**. When they do this they automatically begin to create **grammatical relationships** between words — the start of **syntax**.

There are some common combinations:

baby crying	**subject + verb**
catch ball	**verb + object**
daddy dinner (*daddy is cooking dinner*)	**subject + object**
dolly dirty	**subject + complement**

- These combinations show **similar patterns** to more complex grammatical constructions.
- The phrases use the **basic blocks of meaning** needed for sentences (subject, verb, object and complement).

complement — gives more information about the subject or object.

The Telegraphic Stage combines three or more words

At around **two years old**, children start to use three or four word combinations — the **telegraphic stage**.

These utterances are also formed according to grammatical rules:

doggy is naughty	**subject + verb + complement**
Jodie want cup	**subject + verb + object**
give mummy spoon	**verb + object + object**

- Children still focus on the words that carry **most meaning**.
- They **omit functional words** e.g. prepositions (*from, to*), auxiliary verbs (*has, is*) and determiners (*a, the*).

By **age five**, children will be able to use a **range** of **grammatical constructions** which include:

1) **Coordinating conjunctions** (like *and* and *but*) to link separate utterances.
2) **Negatives** involving the auxiliary *do* (e.g. *don't like it*).
3) **Questions** formed with *Who, Where* and *What*.
4) **Inflections** like *-ed* for past tense, *-ing* for present participles and *-s* for plurals.

Practice Questions

Q1 What five categories did Nelson put first words into?

Q2 What is overextension? Outline the two types that Rescorla identified.

Q3 What are holophrases?

Q4 Write down three common grammatical combinations that you find in the two-word stage.

Q5 What happens in the telegraphic stage?

Essay Question

Q1 Discuss children's early language acquisition with reference to the research of Nelson, Rescorla and Aitchison.

Holophrases — words with lots of ho les in the mid dle...

Wouldn't it be great if babies could speak English fluently from the moment they were born? It would certainly make your life a lot easier. But then this section would just be a load of blank pages in the middle of a book and you'd probably feel a bit ripped off. So learn the wonderful facts on these pages and then at least you've got your money's worth.

More Grammar Acquisition

This bit is for AQA B and Edexcel again. Ah, good old grammar — it always pops in to cheer you up when you're feeling a bit jaded. Have a look at p.110 if you need a reminder of any of the technical terms, then just sit back and enjoy...

Inflections seem to be Acquired in a Set Order

1) Children start to **add inflections** to their words as early as **20 months old**.

2) Studies have shown that inflections are acquired in a certain order. A study by **Brown (1973)** of children aged between 20 and 36 months suggested that the **order** in which children learn inflections is as follows:

If you're a little rusty on inflections and affixation, have a look at p.123 in Section 7.

	Inflections	A Child Will Say (e.g.)
1	present participle *-ing*	*I going* (although *am* will still be missing)
2	plural *-s*	*cups*
3	possessive *'s*	*Teddy's chair*
4	articles (*a, the*)	*get the ball*
5	past tense *-ed*	*I kicked it*
6	third person singular verb ending *-s*	*She loves me*
7	auxiliary *be*	*It is raining* (or, more likely, *It's raining*)

3) **Katamba (1996)** found that there was **little connection** between the **frequency** with which these inflections are used by parents and the **order** in which children acquire them.

4) *A* and *the* are used **most frequently**, and *-ed* **least frequently**, but they're fourth and fifth in terms of acquisition. This suggests that **imitation** doesn't have a strong influence on how children acquire inflections.

5) The *-ing* inflection is acquired the **earliest** — probably because it represents the **present tense**, and the child will relate more to things happening 'now', than in the past or the future.

Inflections are Learnt in Three Stages

Cruttenden (1979) identified **three stages** in the acquisition of inflections:

Stage 1 — Inconsistent Usage
A child will use an inflection correctly **some of the time**, but this is because they've learnt the **word**, not the **grammatical rule**, e.g. they might say *I play outside* one day and *I played outside* the next.

Stage 2 — Consistent Usage but sometimes misapplied
For example, applying the regular past tense inflection *-ed* to irregular verbs. A child will say something like *I drinked it*, rather than *I drank it*. This is called an **overgeneralisation** or a '**virtuous error**' — they understand how past tense verbs are formed but **mistakenly apply** the construction to an irregular verb.

Stage 3 — Consistent Usage
This is when children are able to cope with **irregular forms successfully**, e.g. they say *mice* rather than *mouses* and *ran* rather than *runned*.

Children use grammatical rules Without Being Taught Them

1) Children seem to acquire the grammatical rules of language just by being in an environment where language is spoken and where they can **interact with others**:

Berko's (1958) 'Wug' Test
Children were shown a picture of a strange creature and told it was a *Wug*. They were then shown a drawing of **two of the creatures** and told 'Now there is another one. There are two of them — there are two...', encouraging the children to complete the sentence. Three-to-four-year-old children said there were **two Wugs**.

2) The test showed that children hadn't used the *-s* because they were **imitating someone**, as they'd **never heard** of a *Wug* before. They'd **automatically** used the **rule** that states *-s* is added to a noun to form a plural.

3) This is called **internalisation** — they'd heard the rule so often that it was second nature to **apply** it to make a plural.

More Grammar Acquisition

Learning to Ask Questions is a three-stage process

In the first **three** years, children develop the ability to construct **questions**.

> **Stage 1 — around 18 months**
>
> During the two-word stage, children start to use **rising intonation** to indicate a question, e.g. *Sit me?*, or *Go walk?*

> **Stage 2 — between the ages of two and three**
>
> In telegraphic talk, children continue to use rising intonation but now **include *Wh-* words** in the utterances, e.g. *Where tractor?* or *What Mummy doing?* As they continue to develop, they use a wider range of **interrogative pronouns**, such as *why*, *when*, and *how*.

> **Stage 3 — From the age of three upwards**
>
> Children will use what's called a **subject-verb inversion**, e.g. *Can I see it?*, or *Did she break it?*, instead of constructions like *I can see it?* They also use **auxiliary verbs** for the first time, e.g. *What is Mummy doing?*

Oscar the Grouch was never that intimidating before he went into make-up.

Negatives follow a Similar Pattern

At the same time as they start using **interrogatives** (questions), children learn to use **negatives**.

> **Stage 1 — around eighteen months**
>
> Children use *no* or *not* to make things negative, normally at the **beginning of the phrase** rather than at the end, e.g. *no juice*, *not baby's bed*.

> **Stage 2 — between two and three years**
>
> Children start to use *no* and *not* in front of **verbs** too, like *I no want juice* and *I not like teddy's bed*. They also develop the use of **contracted negatives** like *can't* and *don't*, e.g. *I can't drink it* and *I don't like it*. These two forms can sometimes get **mixed up**, e.g. *I can't like it*.

> **Stage 3 — from three years upwards**
>
> Children stop using *no* and *not* in the way they did in stage 1. They **standardise** their use of *can't* and *don't*, and start using other **negative contractions** like *didn't* and *won't*, e.g. *she didn't catch it* and *he won't build it*. The use of *isn't* develops **slightly later** (e.g. *Mummy isn't here*).

Practice Questions

Q1 Outline the order in which inflections are acquired. Give examples.

Q2 List Cruttenden's (1979) three stages in the acquisition of inflections.

Q3 What evidence is there to suggest that children use grammatical rules without being taught them?

Q4 What is subject-verb inversion and when do children start to use it?

Q5 At what age do children start to use contracted negatives?

Essay Question

Q1 Describe how children acquire the grammatical rules of English, with reference to appropriate research.

The examiner won't let you get away with a virtuous error...

Goodness me, they're so demanding — they want the right answers and they want them now. Well, in the exam anyway. But it's better if you get to grips with these pages sooner rather than later. That way, you can get on with the important things in life, like continuing to marvel at the thrilling twists and turns that English Language Acquisition throws at you.

Theories of Language Development

These pages are just for AQA B. Get your fountain pen out and prime your serious face, cos here's a bit of highly intellectual, slightly dry theory. It's quite dull, but get these pages learnt and you'll be on the way to tons of lovely marks.

Behaviourists argue that Language is Acquired by Imitation

Imitation Theory

1) **Skinner (1957)** suggested that language is acquired through **imitation** and **reinforcement**:
   - Children **repeat** what they hear (imitation).
   - Caregivers **reward** a child's efforts with **praise**.
   - They also reinforce what the child says by **repeating** words and phrases back and **correcting mistakes**.

2) This approach says that children learn all the **specific pronunciations** of individual words by copying an adult — therefore in theory it explains an important part of their **phonological development**.

Problems with Imitation

There are some problems with imitation theory:

- Children can construct new sentences they've **never heard before**, so they aren't always directly **imitating**.

- They don't **memorise** thousands of sentences to use later, so their development can't be **exclusively based** on repeating what they've heard their parents or other people saying.

- Imitation can't explain **overgeneralisations**, like *he runned away* (see p.96). Children **can't copy** these errors because adults don't make them.

- Imitation theory also **can't explain** things like the *fis* phenomenon (see p.92) — the fact that children can **recognise** a much larger range of words than they are actually able to **use**.

Other people argue that Language Acquisition is Innate

1) **Chomsky (1965)** argued that a child's ability to acquire language was **inbuilt**. He said that language isn't taught, but it's a **natural development** that occurs when children are **exposed to language**.

2) He suggested that each child has a **Language Acquisition Device (LAD)**, which allows them to take in and **use** the grammatical rules of the language that's spoken where they live.

3) Chomsky's approach seems to explain **how** children end up making overgeneralisations and **why** they acquire inflections in a **certain order** — it's as if the brain is **preprogrammed** to make this happen.

4) Therefore children might learn language quickly because they are **predisposed** to learn it.

5) More evidence for Chomsky's theory is that **all children** pass through the same early stages of language acquisition, before **refining** their range of sounds to their native language (see p.90-91).

6) There are some **common features** of language known as **linguistic universals**, e.g. every language uses a combination of regular and irregular verbs. This suggests that all speakers acquire language in a similar way, so it supports the idea that children have an **LAD**.

7) One criticism of Chomsky's theory is that the innate approach **underestimates** the **significance** of Skinner's argument that **interaction**, **imitation** and **reinforcement** are important in language development.

Piaget developed the Cognitive Approach

The **cognitive approach** focuses on the importance of **mental processes**. **Piaget (1896-1980)** stated that a child needs to have developed certain **mental abilities** before he or she can acquire particular aspects of language:

1) At first a child can't mentally process the concept that something can exist **outside** their **immediate surroundings**. This is called being **egocentric**.

2) By the time they're 18 months old, children realise that things have **object permanence** — they can exist all the time, even if the child can't see them. This coincides with a big increase in vocabulary (see p.94).

3) The child is then mentally better equipped to understand **abstract** concepts like **past**, **present** and **future**.

4) One **criticism** of this approach is that it doesn't explain how some people with **learning difficulties** are still **linguistically fluent**. This suggests that **cognitive** development and **language** development aren't as **closely connected** as the cognitive approach suggests.

Theories of Language Development

Language Development needs Input from Others

The **input approach** argues that in order for language to develop there has to be **linguistic interaction** with **caregivers**.

1) **Bruner (1983)** suggests that there is a **Language Acquisition Support System (LASS)** — a system where caregivers **support** their child's linguistic development in **social situations**.

2) There are clear **patterns** of **interaction** between child and caregiver in **everyday social situations**, like meal times, bath-time and when playing. The caregiver talks to the child and encourages them to talk back by pointing things out and asking questions, e.g. *what's that there, is it a doggy?* As a result of this **linguistic support** the child gradually learns to play a more **active part** in social situations, e.g. asking the caregiver questions.

3) Children who are **deprived** of language early on don't seem able to acquire it easily later. **Lenneberg (1967)** proposed the **Critical Period Hypothesis**, which states that without linguistic interaction **before** ages 5-6, language development is **severely limited**.

4) This view is supported by some rare cases where children **without** any exposure to language in the first five years of life (e.g. cases of extreme **child abuse**) subsequently fail to develop **normal speech**.

Vygotsky presented a Socio-cultural Theory of Language Development

This theory suggests that **social interaction** and experiencing different **social and cultural contexts** are very important for language development. **Vygotsky (1978)** identified two significant factors that contribute to language development — **private speech** and the **Zone of Proximal Development (ZPD)**.

1) **Private Speech** — when a child **talks aloud** to itself. Vygotsky saw this as a major step forward in a child's mental development — this is evidence the child is **thinking for itself**.

2) **The ZPD** — when a child needs a caregiver's help in order to **interact**, e.g. if a doctor asks *Where does it hurt?*, the child might not answer. The caregiver either responds for the child or tries to encourage a response. This gives the child a **model** to apply to **similar situations** in the future when it might respond without help.

This kind of support is known as **scaffolding**. Children require it less and less once they become more able to deal with different social and cultural situations on their own.

Language Acquisition can't be explained by Just One Theory

Unfortunately, there isn't one model of language acquisition that can **fully explain** how a child learns to speak.

1) Theories of **innate acquisition** and **cognitive developments** do not take into account the role of **interaction** in the development of a child's language.

2) Theories of **imitation** and **reinforcement** can't explain the fact that some features of language apply to **everyone**, and that all babies show similar cooing and babbling features, **regardless** of their native language.

3) The most likely explanation is that language development involves **all** of these different influences to some degree.

Practice Questions

Q1 Outline the behaviourist theory of language acquisition.
Q2 What evidence is there to suggest that all children have an LAD?
Q3 What is object permanence?
Q4 Outline Bruner's theory of the LASS.
Q5 Outline Vygotsky's socio-cultural theory of language development.

Essay Question

Q1 "Children acquire language through imitation and reinforcement." How far do you agree with this statement? Your answer should refer to the benefits and drawbacks of specific linguistic theories.

Surely only boys have LADs...

Welcome, child. Many brave souls have hacked through the Forbidden Forest to reach the mystical land of Kwebegon. And many brave souls have been taken. For it is written in the stars that only one will conquer the dreaded Borsidone Beast and reach the Zone of Proximal Development. Open your mind, and prepare to enter. Just watch your head on the scaffolding...

Social Interaction

AQA B and Edexcel here. You may think that kids aren't very skilled in the delicate art of social interaction, but actually, tantrums in supermarkets are just their way of interacting with the general public. Well, they've got to practise somewhere.

Caregivers Talk to children in a Particular Way

1)   This kind of language is referred to as **child-directed speech** (CDS), **caretaker speech**, or even **motherese**.

2)   The language features of CDS are often **simplified** or **exaggerated** and often have the purpose of **encouraging** a child to **interact** as they're easier to understand.

Child-directed Speech has Distinctive Linguistic Features

Phonology and Prosody

1)   **Intonation** is exaggerated and words are **stressed** more strongly than they are in adult conversation, e.g. stress on *good* in *What a good girl you are, Annie*. The **pitch** is usually **higher**.

2)   Words and phrases are **repeated**, e.g. *Get the ball, Annie, get the ball.*

3)   The **pace** is often much **slower**, with **longer pauses** than in adult speech.

Lexis

1)   **Vocabulary** is often **simplified**, so instead of saying e.g. *banana*, a parent might say *nana* instead.

2)   Caregivers use **reduplication** (see p.90) — constructions like *choo-choo, din-din*, or *moo-moo.*

3)   They also use **diminutives** — like *birdie, doggie* or *fishy.*

4)   A high proportion of words will refer to objects that the child can **see** and **touch** e.g. *Look at the pussy-cat, Annie, it's playing with the ball.*

Grammar

1)   **Sentence structures** are simplified, and **function words** (e.g. auxiliary verbs) are often **omitted**. E.g. instead of saying *Annie, shall we go for a walk?*, a caregiver might say *Annie go for walk?*

2)   **Proper nouns** (including frequent **repetition** of the child's name) are often used instead of pronouns, e.g. instead of *Are you making a sandcastle?* a parent will say *Is Annie making a sandcastle?* A higher proportion of nouns will be **concrete nouns** (e.g. *cup, apple, bottle*).

3)   The **present tense** will be used more than the past tense. The caregiver will talk more about what's **happening 'now'** e.g. *Are you singing?* rather than in the past e.g. *Were you singing yesterday?*

Caregivers use Techniques to Encourage Language Development

1)   They **repeat** certain **structures**, e.g. *Annie get the tractor, Annie wash the baby, Annie find the bottle.*

2)   They ask lots of **questions**, e.g. *Annie, where's doggie gone?, Have you got a poorly hand?, Is Sally crying, Annie?* This **encourages** the child to **respond**.

3)   They use lots of **imperatives**, e.g. *pick up dolly, eat din-dins, drink milk.*

4) Caregivers often **recast** what a child has said, re-presenting information in a **different way**:

Mother:	*What you doing, Annie?*
Child:	*Playing with my car.*
Mother:	*Yes, that's your car, isn't it?*

5) Caregivers also **expand** on what children say:

Mother:	*What you doing, Annie?*
Child:	*Playing.*
Mother:	*Yes, you're playing with your car.*

No one really knows if CDS has any Impact on Development

1)   Child-directed speech isn't used by parents in **every culture**, but speakers of all cultures grow up to be **fluent**.

2)   There's **nothing conclusive** to suggest that CDS does or doesn't work — research has produced conflicting results.

3)   It could be that CDS is more about **building a relationship** than about language development in particular.

Social Interaction

Children learn how to **Interact** with their **Caregivers**...

Care-givers use **CDS** to **encourage** children to **respond** and teach them about how **dialogue** works.

1) The **early** conversations that children have (at around **age two**) are usually **initiated** and **maintained** by **adults**.

2) They tend to be made up of **short statements** by the child that the **adult** responds to — the child **doesn't** really **respond** to what the adult says. For example:

> **Father:** *Look at the ducks, Annie, can you see the ducks?*
> **Child:** *Quack quack.*
> **Father:** *That's right the ducks go quack quack don't they?*
> **Child:** *In the water.*

3) Children **develop** a lot between the ages of **two** and **four**. They start to understand **turn-taking** and take part in **dialogues**. They start to **understand** the **needs** of the **listener** — they learn to give appropriate **answers** to questions and to **respond** in a way that can **initiate** a **further response** from the other speaker.

4) They also develop more **awareness** of **social factors** in conversations, e.g. they begin to understand when to use **politeness forms** like *please* and *thank you*.

5) They become better at getting someone's **attention**, e.g. they use **adverbs** like *well* to show that they have something to say. They also start to use **people's names** to get their attention.

6) **Starting school** or **nursery** has a big **impact** on **social interaction skills**, as children meet **more people**. They develop more awareness of what **kind** of **language** is **appropriate** in certain **contexts**, e.g. they start to use more **formal** language in the **classroom** compared to the **playground**.

...and with **Other Children**

At around the age of **two** children also start to have **conversations** with **each other**.

1) These **early conversations** are **limited** because at this age the children only have a **lexis** of about **300 words**.

2) They're known as **closed conversations** because there's no **progression** in them. The speakers don't have the **skills** to make **meaningful responses**, so they can't keep the conversation going. The conversations are made up of **short statements**:

> **Child A:** *I got sweeties.*
> **Child B:** *Nice sweeties.*
> **Child A:** *I got big bag.*

As they get **older**, children's use of **lexis** and **grammar** increases, so they're able to have more **complex** conversations.

1) They develop **pragmatic skills** — they learn to use language to **form relationships** with each other, and to try and **get** what they **want**. This can involve **repetition**, e.g. *Can I have the pen now? Can I have the pen now?* and **persuasive tactics**, e.g. *If you don't give me it then I won't be your friend.*

2) They also **imitate** adult speech and develop more **awareness** of the **type** of **language** that's **appropriate** for different **audiences**, e.g. **older** children often use **CDS** when they're talking to **younger** children.

Practice Questions

Q1 List three grammatical features of child-directed speech.

Q2 How do conversations between children and their caregivers change as children get older?

Q3 Why are most two year olds only able to have closed conversations with each other?

Essay Question

Q1 "The main aim of CDS is to encourage the child to respond." To what extent do you agree with this statement?

Does ikkle babba think CDS is annoying? Oo yes he do, yes he do...

When I was at primary school most of our assemblies seemed to be about the story of Louis Braille (the man who invented Braille...). After one such assembly the head asked if anyone had any questions, and Ashley Ross in Year One stuck his hand up and said "My mummy bakes pizzas". Aww, see — knowing the right thing to say in a situation isn't as easy as it sounds...

Learning to Read

Just AQA B and Edexcel. If you're reading this now then I can pretty much guarantee that you must have been taught how to read at school. And it's a good thing too, cos now you get to read about how you learnt to read. Yay.

There are **Different Approaches** to Teaching Children to **Read**

There are **three** major **approaches** to the teaching of **reading**:

1) The phonics approach

- This approach involves looking at **letters** and **letter combinations** in terms of **sounds** (reading '**by ear**'), e.g. *cow* is separated into the phonemes /c/ and /ow/. It means that children can **sound out** unfamiliar words.
- It's **useful** for words like *latch* that are **pronounced** as they're written, but is **less useful** for words like *through*.
- The approach has also been **criticised** because it just **focuses** on **sounds** and **letters**, rather than on the **meanings** of the words.

2) The "look and say" approach

- This is also known as the **whole word** approach. It involves **recognising** whole words by **sight** alone, **rather** than **breaking** them down into **separate phonemes** (reading '**by eye**').
- It focuses on the **meaning** of words, and teaches children to recognise **common** words like *and*, *see*, *went* etc.
- However, relying on this method requires children to **memorise** a **large number** of words, and **doesn't** give them the **skills** to **work out** the **sound** or **meaning** of **unfamiliar** words.

3) The psycholinguistics approach

- This approach sees reading as a **natural development** that comes from being in an **environment** where books are **read**, **valued** and **available**.
- It's an **active approach** to reading — the **reader** is given **responsibility** for **working out** what a word **means**, rather than just being **told** the meaning.
- When children come across a word they **can't** read, they're encouraged to **work out** the **meaning** by looking at the **rest** of the **sentence** and other **clues** like **illustrations**.
- The idea is to encourage children to **focus** on **meaning**, rather than just working out **symbols**. It's also designed to make them aware of the **importance** of **context**.
- However, the approach has been **criticised** because it leaves a lot to **chance**.

Teachers tend to use a **Combination** of **Approaches**

Over the past **sixty years**, there's been a lot of **debate** about which method for teaching reading is **best**.

1) Schools tend to use a **combination** of **approaches** rather than just rely on one. This is because some children **respond** better to one method than another.

2) It also ensures that children develop a **range** of **skills**. The **phonics approach** teaches them to recognise **symbols**, while the **look and say** and **psycholinguistics approaches** teach the importance of **meaning** and **context**.

3) It's also really **important** that children **practise** reading **outside** of **school** — some researchers see this as the **most important** factor in **improving** a child's reading ability.

Techniques for **Developing Reading Skills** depend on the **Child's Age**

1) Up to age **five**, caregivers may **read** stories and nursery rhymes to children, and help children enjoy the **physical experience** of books, e.g. turning pages, pointing to letters and saying the sounds out loud.

2) Between **five** and **six**, caregivers / teachers will read them fiction and non-fiction, get them to **break down** words into individual sounds (**phonemes**), and get them to **match sounds** to **letters**.

3) Between six and seven, they'll get children to **read aloud**, set classroom tasks involving speaking, interacting and reading, and encourage them to **talk** about what they've read.

4) Between seven and eight, they may introduce children to **different genres** and provide them with the chance to **discuss** different aspects of what they've read.

Or, here's an idea. How about you TURN YOUR OWN PAGE AND STOP BEING SO LAZY.

Learning to Read

Reading **Develops** in **Stages** as you go through school

Obviously, everyone progresses at different rates, but there are some **general stages** that **most children** pass through.

Pre-school (up to age 5)	• Kids take part in activities that **prepare** them for reading e.g. playing with bricks, jigsaws, and matching pictures. This helps them distinguish between **different sizes**, **shapes** and **patterns**. In turn this prepares them for identifying **letters** and **combinations of letters**. • They can turn pages in books themselves and verbally **create** their own **stories**. • They begin to identify some **individual letters**, such as the first letter of their name, and also begin to match some **sounds** to letters.
Between five and six years old	• They **increase** the number of **letter-sound** matches that they know. • They realise that in English, letters on a page move from **left** to **right** and **top** to **bottom**. • They begin to **recognise** frequently used words.
Between six and seven years old	• They can read stories they're **familiar** with. • They use a range of **reading strategies** — when they're stuck on a word they may use the context to guess what it is, or sound it out **phonetically**. • They recognise more and more words just **by sight**. • They **break down** words into individual **sounds** to read an unfamiliar word. • They start to read with some **fluency**.
Between seven and eight years old	• They read more **fluently**, and their **vocabulary** continues to increase. • They use reading strategies **accurately** (such as **predicting** what words might come next). • They're better at working through **individual sounds** to read unfamiliar words.

Reading **Skills** carry on **Developing After** you've learnt to read

The learning process **continues** for a long time **after** children are first able to read **fluently**. Up until about the age of **18**, their reading continues to **improve** and their **vocabulary** grows:

- They become **familiar** with a **wider range** of texts.
- They **read to learn** — their reading improves enough that they can use texts to find out **information**.
- They're able to use more **complex** and **varied** texts to find out information **without help**.
- They read in **different ways** for **different reasons**, e.g. for work and for pleasure.

1) Some children's progress stops here — they're able to read fluently, but they never reach a stage where they can **interpret** what they're reading **critically**.

2) This is often because they **stop reading** apart from when they **have** to.

3) Other children's reading **continues** to **improve**, until they're able to **analyse** and **criticise** what they're reading. This means they can **select** the most **important** points from a text and **develop** their own **opinions** about them.

Practice Questions

Q1   Outline one criticism of the "look and say" approach.
Q2   What does the psycholinguistics approach to teaching reading involve?
Q3   Outline what most children are able to do in terms of reading at a pre-school age.
Q4   How do a child's reading skills continue to improve after the age of 8?

Essay Question

Q1   With reference to the three main approaches to teaching reading, explain why it's often thought to be best to teach a combination of approaches.

Psycholinguistics — not something you'd think would be encouraged...

Seeing the whole process of learning to read set out in a big table like that has made me realise just how much work goes into it. It's amazing to think that at one point I was a little pipsqueak who struggled with the alphabet, and now I'm a fully fledged reader who can understand all the letters and some whole words. My parents are very proud, but they hide it well...

Learning to Write

This is for AQA B and Edexcel. As if learning to read wasn't enough, children have to learn to write too, even though they'd probably much rather be having a nice little nap. It's really not fair, but it does come in handy I suppose.

Writing develops in Stages

1) Children go through **stages** of **development** before they can write and spell entire words. Although they need to be able to **recognise** letters and words before they can write, they seem to learn to write **alongside** learning to read.

2) When young children do **drawings** they're actually starting to learn the **motor skills** (coordination) they'll need for **writing**.

3) As their **motor skills** develop, children are able to learn the **conventions** of written language, e.g. **spelling**, **punctuation** and **layout**.

4) How **quickly** a child learns to write depends on how much **practice** they have, e.g. whether they're given crayons to use before they start school. It also depends on the child's **intelligence**, and how much they've been exposed to **role models** who write.

5) Theorists have **different ideas** about how many stages are involved in learning to write, and how old children are when they go through them.

After eating 74 crayons Gabi's writing had started to suffer.

Barclay (1996) outlined 7 Stages of Writing Development

Stage 1 **Scribbling**	Kids make random marks on the page, which **aren't related** to letters or words. They're **learning the skill** of keeping hold of a pencil or crayon, which prepares them for writing. They often **talk** about what they're scribbling.	
Stage 2 **Mock Handwriting**	Children practise drawing **shapes** on paper, although it's still not usually possible to work out what the drawing represents. Letter-like forms (**pseudo-letters**) begin to appear in or with drawings as the first sign of **emergent writing** — an attempt to write letters.	
Stage 3 **Mock Letters**	Children produce **random letters**, but there's still no awareness of spacing or of matching **sounds** with **symbols**.	
Stage 4 **Conventional Letters**	Children start matching **sounds** with **symbols** — writing down letters that match the sounds being heard or spoken. Words are unlikely to be spaced out. Children start using **initial consonants** to **represent words**, e.g. *h* for *horse*. The initial letter might be read out as if the **full word** is there on the page.	
Stage 5 **Invented Spelling**	Most words are spelled **phonetically**, though some simple and familiar words are spelled correctly.	
Stage 6 **Appropriate Spelling**	Sentences become more **complex** as the child becomes more aware of standard spelling patterns. Writing becomes more **legible**.	
Stage 7 **Correct Spelling**	Most words are spelled **correctly**.	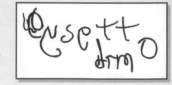

Learning to Write

Kroll (1981) outlined **4 Stages** of **Writing Development**

1 The Preparatory Stage — from 18 months

- Children develop the **motor skills** needed for writing.
- They begin to learn the basics of the **spelling system**.

James's motor skills were developing, and yet his writing was still appalling.

2 The Consolidation Stage — 6-8 years

- Children **write** in the same way as they **speak**.
- They use lots of **colloquialisms**.
- They use **short declarative statements** and **familiar conjunctions** like "and".
- They won't yet be sure how to **finish** off a sentence.
- They begin to express ideas in the form of **sentences**, though without much punctuation.

3 The Differentiation Stage — age 8 to mid-teens

- Children become aware of the **difference** between the **conventions** of **spoken** and **written** language.
- They begin to understand that there are **different genres**, for example letters and stories.
- They begin to **structure** their work using writing **guides** and **frameworks**.
- They use **more complex grammar** and **sentence structures**.
- **Punctuation** becomes more **accurate** and **consistent**.

Every child develops at a different rate, so this is just a rough outline of how old they are at each stage.

4 The Integration Stage — mid-teens upwards

- Writing becomes more **accurate**, with a **wider vocabulary** and more **accurate spelling**.
- Children understand that **style** can **change** according to **audience** and **purpose**.
- **Narrative** and **descriptive** skills improve. They write expanded stories, with **developed characters**, a **plot** and a **setting**.
- They develop a **personal writing style**. This continues to develop throughout **adulthood**.

Practice Questions

Q1 How do scribbling and drawing help prepare young children for writing?

Q2 Name two factors that can affect how quickly a child learns to write.

Q3 What is emergent writing?

Q4 According to Barclay (1996), what happens in stage 6 of learning to write?

Q5 According to Kroll (1981), what happens in the consolidation stage?

Q6 According to Kroll (1981), what skills do children develop in the differentiation stage?

Q7 According to Kroll (1981), in which stage do children develop a personal writing style?

Essay Question

Q1 Children go through different stages of development when they learn to write. Outline what happens with reference to one theorist in particular.

One day I woke up and I decided to revise and it was very nice...

There's another stage — the 'learning to write about learning to write' stage. And you reach that stage at the exact age you are today. What a happy coincidence. Anyway, it's the end of the section — hurrah. To celebrate, why not go back to your childhood by getting the squirty cream out the fridge and squirting it straight into your mouth until it inflates like a big toad.

Sources and Exam Questions

Now have a go at these practice exam questions. **This is an AQA B style exam question.**

Text A is a transcript of a conversation between a two-and-a-half-year-old and her mother. They are looking at a picture storybook. In text B they are talking about the story later.

1. With reference to the texts and knowledge from your study of language acquisition, analyse how Ellie is being helped to understand and remember what happens in the story.   *[48 marks]*

Text A — Conversation between Ellie (aged 2 years 6 months) and her mother

Ellie:	they're in bed (.) aren't they
Mum:	no (.) they're getting out of bed
Ellie:	(2) why
Mum:	they've heard a noise outside (.) outside in the darkness
Ellie:	// ooh
Mum:	and they're going to find out what it was
Ellie:	getting out of (.) out of bed
Mum:	and they're going out through the window
Ellie:	ooh (3) naughty
Mum:	yes very naughty
Ellie:	very naughty
Mum:	that little boy see (1) he's holding a torch
Ellie:	// and they're getting (.) out of the window
Mum:	and they're climbing down
Ellie:	// down
Mum:	and then they hear another noise (1) it's an owl (.) look
Ellie:	an owl
Mum:	an owl (.) hooting in the darkness (2) so what do they do
Ellie:	(3) they run away
Mum:	that's right they run away (.) and climb back up to the window (.) and go back to bed
Ellie:	naughty
Mum:	and soon (2) they're back in bed again (.) fast asleep
Ellie:	[laughs] moon
Mum:	that's right the moon

Text B — Conversation between Ellie (aged 2 years 6 months) and her mother

Mum:	what can you remember about the story Ellie
Ellie:	the story
Mum:	the one we were looking at earlier (.) can you remember anything about it
Ellie:	the children (.) they were naughty
Mum:	what did they do that was naughty
Ellie:	(2) they got (.) out of their beds at night time (3) and went (.) went out of the window
Mum:	that's right (.) and what happened next

Sources and Exam Questions

(Text B contd.)

Ellie: they (2) heard a noise and came back again

Mum: they were frightened weren't they

Ellie: yeah frightened (2) and they came back again

Mum: you wouldn't do a naughty thing like that Ellie would you

Ellie: no (.) naughty

Transcription Key

(.)   *Micropause*

(2)   *Pause in seconds*

//   *Interruption / overlap*

This is an Edexcel style exam question.

2. Study texts A, B and C below. Using text A as your starting point, comment on the ways in which David's writing has developed during this period, as shown by these three pieces.

   Text A is a transcript of a piece of story writing by David, aged 6.

   Text B is a transcript of part of a longer story that David produced, aged 7.

   Text C is a transcript of part of a story that David produced at the age of 9.   *[40 marks]*

Text A — a piece entitled 'The Magic Box'

In the morning I went down stairs and opound one of my pesents I saw a box I Jumped in the box I found myself In the forest some foxes were chasing me I lepeped on a tree I Jumped on to the next branche I found myself in the launge it was stele 9 o'clock I said no one well notes then I went back to bed

Text B — from a piece entitled 'David and the Beanstalk'

One day my mum told me to sell our cow at the market. On the way I met an old man.
He said can you swop cow for these magic beans. Yes I said so David went off with the magic beans. When I got home my mum said where's the money. I told my mum about the story.
She was furiuse so she frew the magic beans out the window. She sent David up to his bedroom without any supper. In the morning David looked out of his window there was a beanstalk.
David climed out of his window. He jumped onto the beanstalk and started to clime.

Text C — from a piece entitled 'At the Seaside'

One night I was at the beache with my friends Marc and Ben. We were climbing rocks and I slipped. I fell and hit my head on a trap door handle. Marc and Ben said "cool a trap door lets go inside." We opened the trap door and there was a big hole. We jumped in when we got to the bottom we were inside a cave. Suddenly Ben heard a noise it sounded like a roar. Me and Marc said "it's just your hearing." Then Ben heard it again and this time me and Marc heard it too.

Language Frameworks

This section is for everyone. You should be familiar with this stuff from AS, but for A2 you need to be really confident that you understand technical terms and can use them in your analysis. So it's probably worth a quick recap I'd say...

You should aim to **Analyse** all **Texts** in a **Similar** way

If you have to analyse a piece of language or discourse, there are several things to think about:

1) **Genre** — **what kind** of language it is. Written discourses could be **instruction booklets** or **adverts**, and spoken discourses could be **formal speeches** to an audience or **casual conversations** between friends.

2) **Register** — a type of language that's appropriate for a particular audience or situation, e.g. the language of a political party or the language of the justice system. Register also includes the level of **formality** in a discourse.

3) **Audience** — the **listener** or **reader**. When you're analysing language, think about how the audience is **addressed**. It might be **formal** or **informal**, **direct** or **indirect**. For example, in advertising the audience is often directly addressed as *you*.

4) **Subject** — what the discourse is **about**. This will be reflected in the **lexical choices**, e.g. a discussion about healthy eating may contain words like *low-fat*, *diet*, and *nutrition*.

5) **Purpose** — what the speaker or writer is trying to **achieve** through language (e.g. to persuade, instruct, etc.).

6) **Mode** — whether the language is **written or spoken**. You can also get **mixed modes** — e.g. in text messages, where the language is written, but contains many of the informal features of spoken language.

There are **Seven Main Language Frameworks**

This table is an **overview** of what makes up each language framework (also called **linguistic frameworks**, or **toolkits**) and how they can be used. You should use this every time you **analyse** a text.

Lexis	• **Lexis** means the **vocabulary** of a language — the total stock of words. • When you're analysing spoken and written language you'll notice words that share a **similar topic** or **focus**. For example, in an advert for mobile phones you'd find words such as *SMS*, *text-messaging*, and *battery life*. Words that are linked together in this way are known as a **lexical field**.
Semantics	• **Semantics** is the study of how **meaning** is created through words and phrases. Sometimes this meaning is **explicit**, but sometimes it's **implicit**. A word will have a **literal** meaning but it can also be **associated** with other meanings. • For example, the word *red* refers to a **colour**, but it can also be associated with **danger**.
Grammar	• **Grammar** is the system of **rules** that governs how words and sentences are **constructed**. There are three parts to this: 1) A system that **groups** words into classes according to their **function** (e.g. nouns or verbs). 2) A system of **rules** about how these types of words function in relation to each other (**syntax**). 3) The individual units that make up whole words (**morphology**).
Phonology	• **Phonology** is the study of **sounds** in English — how they're **produced** and how they're **combined** to make words. • This framework includes **Non-Verbal Aspects of Speech** (NVAS) or **prosody** — features of spoken language such as pace, stress, rhythm and intonation.
Pragmatics	• **Pragmatics** is sometimes called **language in use**. It's about how social conventions, context, personality and relationships influence the **choices** people make about their language. • For example, how you address other people shows **levels of formality** and **social conventions** — a student might address a teacher as *Miss Rogers* or *Lizzie* depending on what the college or school expects, and what the teacher finds acceptable.
Graphology	• **Graphology** is the study of the **appearance** of the writing and the effect this has on a text. • When you discuss a text's graphology you describe and analyse features like the **typeface**, the **positioning** of text on a page and the relationships between **text** and **images**.
Discourse	• **Discourse** is an **extended** piece of spoken or written language, made up of more than one **utterance** (in spoken language), or more than one **sentence** (in written language).

Language Frameworks

Discourse has a Structure

The way language is organised is called its **discourse structure**. You need to look out for different features, depending on whether the discourse is written or spoken.

1) In **written discourse**, look at how a text is **put together**. It may have an **opening** section which leads the reader into the text. The following sections may develop a **theme or argument**. The final section may make some kind of **conclusion**.

2) In **spoken discourse** the structure can be less organised. For example, **conversations** are often **unpredictable** and speakers often **digress** (go off the subject). This is because conversations are usually **spontaneous**.

3) Even spontaneous conversations have some structure, though.

There'll often be an **opening sequence**, e.g.

> Speaker 1: *Hi, how you doing?*
> Speaker 2: *Fine thanks. How about you?*

This is often followed by **turn-taking** as the speakers talk about a topic (or topics). There's often a **closing sequence** too, e.g.

> Speaker 1: *Well, nice seeing you...*
> Speaker 2: *You too.*
> Speaker 1: *Catch you later.*

4) You can also look at how the discourse **fits together** — **cohesion**. There are **two types** of cohesion — **lexical** and **grammatical**. One example of grammatical cohesion is using **adverbs** like *furthermore* and *similarly* at the beginning of a sentence or paragraph to link it to the previous one. Lexical cohesion is when the words in the discourse **relate** to each other throughout, e.g.

> There was no sign of **the car** — **her lift** was obviously stuck in **traffic**.
> Was it really worth it, just for a **ride** in a **Porsche**?

There are Three Main Steps to Discourse Analysis

1) The **first step** in **discourse analysis** is to think about **what kind** of discourse you are looking at. To do this you need to think about genre, register, audience, subject, purpose and mode.

2) The **next step** is to look at how each of the **language frameworks** contributes to the discourse. You might not need to use all of the language frameworks, or you might need to give more emphasis to one than another. It depends on the discourse.

3) And finally, don't forget to discuss **discourse structure** (how the text has been organised) and **cohesion** (the devices used to knit the text together).

Dr. B. Godwin
Harvard's leading
phonologist

Practice Questions

Q1 Name six things you should consider when analysing a piece of language.
Q2 What seven items can be found in a linguistic toolkit?
Q3 Define the term discourse.
Q4 Explain the key features in the structure of written and spoken discourse.
Q5 What is grammatical cohesion?
Q6 Outline the three main steps to discourse analysis.

My bike's fallen apart — I don't think the frame works...

This nuts and bolts stuff really isn't anything to get freaked out about. If you think about it, it's much easier to learn than all that other wishy washy waffly stuff, and the more you know the better you'll look in the exam. These pages are basically spewing potential marks left right and centre, so you just need to drink up as much as possible. Sorry, that was gross...

Introduction to Grammar

You might not believe this, but some people think that grammar is really dull and boring, when actually... erm...

Grammar controls how Language is Constructed

1) Grammar is the set of **structural rules** that controls the way language works.

2) There are **three aspects** of grammar that you need to focus on — word classes, syntax and morphology.

3) **Word classes** define the **roles** that each word can play in a sentence. **Syntax** is the set of **rules** that control where each word class can appear in a sentence. **Morphology** describes the **construction** of individual words.

There are Eight Main Word Classes

Words are **categorised** by the **function** they have in a sentence.
There are eight main **word classes** — also called **parts of speech**.

Word Class	Function	Example
Nouns	'naming' words	*London, book, romance*
Adjectives	describe nouns (and sometimes pronouns)	*large, sunny, featureless*
Verbs	'doing' words	*jump, read, return*
Adverbs	describe verbs (and sometimes adjectives and other adverbs too)	*steadily, incredibly, sadly*
Pronouns	take the place of nouns	*you, they, him, me, it*
Conjunctions	'connecting' words	*and, or, but, because*
Prepositions	define relationships between words in terms of time, space and direction	*before, underneath, through*
Determiners	give specific kinds of information about a noun (e.g. quantity or possession)	*a, the, two, his, few, those*

Word Classes are Controlled by Rules

Word classes can take **different positions** in a sentence, but there are **grammatical rules** about how they work with each other (**syntax**). In the following sentence you can see all the word classes working together:

She	*saw*	*the*	*new*	*manager*	*and*	*his*	*assistant*
pronoun	**verb**	**determiner**	**adjective**	**noun**	**conjunction**	**determiner**	**noun**

at	*the*	*store*	*yesterday.*
preposition	**determiner**	**noun**	**adverb**

1) People **instinctively** know the rules for connecting words together. For example, you know that words in this order — *doctor she the yesterday saw* — are wrong, and you can **rearrange** them into something that makes sense straight away — *she saw the doctor yesterday*.

2) You also intuitively know **less obvious rules** about word order — you'd always say *the big brown bear* rather than *the brown big bear*, because you know that adjectives of size **come before** those of colour.

3) Sometimes there are **fewer restrictions** — some sentences mean the same thing wherever a word is placed, particularly with **adverbs**, e.g. *I **completely** disagree* or *I disagree **completely***.

4) Sometimes the **meaning** of a sentence changes depending on the position of a word:
   *He **quickly** told me to leave* (he said it fast)   **or**   *He told me to leave **quickly*** (he wanted me to leave fast)

Grammatical rules Affect Word Formation

Grammar affects word formation (morphology) because extra bits have to be added to words to **change** things like number or tense. The extra bits are called **inflections**. Here are a couple of examples.

- *-s* is added to *cup* to change a **singular** noun into a **plural** — *cups* (see p.112).

- *-ed* is added to *remember* to change the **present** tense verb into the **past** tense *remember**ed*** (see p.114).

Introduction to Grammar

Grammar Choices can Influence the reader or listener

You can influence your **audience** in different ways by **changing** the **grammar** of a word or sentence.

Tense

1) Events that happened in the past are usually described in the past tense. Sometimes however, in both spoken and written discourse, past events are described using **present tense forms**.

- *So she **went** up to the customer and **gave** him a good telling off.* ← past tense
- *So she **goes** up to the customer and **gives** him a good telling off.* ← present tense

2) The first example sentence is in the past tense. There is a clear sense that some **time has passed** since the event actually happened. In the second, although the action happened in the past, the present tense creates a more **immediate** and **dramatic** impact. You'll see this technique used a lot in **newspaper headlines**:

| **New evidence casts doubt on verdict** | **Pop star admits to private hell** | **Cop raid closes nightclub** |

Plurals

1) As well as telling you that there's more than one of something, plurals can **increase** the scale of a **scene**.

- *There was a **mass** of fans outside the hotel.* ← singular
- *There were **masses** of fans outside the hotel.* ← plural

2) Using the singular form *mass* creates the impression of a **specific** body of people. Adding the **-es inflection** to form the plural *masses* creates the image of a **big crowd** of people across a **wider area**.

Adjectives

1) Adjectives are a great way to **influence** your **audience** — compare the following two examples:

- *If you're looking for the holiday of a lifetime, simply treat yourself to a **great** resort in Sri Lanka. Relax in **fine** accommodation.* ← simple adjectives
- *Looking for the holiday of a lifetime? Simply treat yourself to the **greatest** resort in Sri Lanka. Relax in the **finest** accommodation.* ← superlative adjectives

2) These are similar **advertising discourses**, but the second example is much more **persuasive** than the first. The writer uses **superlative** adjectives (see p.113) (*greatest* and *finest*) rather than the simple adjectives in the first example (*great* and *fine*).

3) There are some **other grammatical features** that influence the reader in these examples.

- The second example begins with a **question**. This makes the reader feel **involved immediately**.
- The first example uses the **indefinite article** *a* before the adjective *great*, but the second uses the **definite article** *the* before *greatest* (see p.116). This makes the reference very **specific** in the second example (it is **the** greatest resort), but the first could be referring to any one of **several** resorts.

Practice Questions

Q1 Define the terms word class, syntax and morphology.
Q2 What function do conjunctions have in a sentence?
Q3 What function do prepositions have in a sentence?
Q4 Identify each word according to word class in the following sentence:
There were few talented actors in town, but the agent from Paris skillfully located the star he needed.
Q5 Give two examples of an inflection.
Q6 What effect can the use of superlative adjectives create?

My grammar's brilliant — she always gives me 20 quid at Christmas...

Grammar was clearly invented by authoritarian loons — look how many times you see the words 'rules' and 'control'. If you don't like being put in a box and held back by 'the man', then it's time to go and live in a commune in Holland and rename yourself Sage. If, however, you want to pass your Eng Lang exam, then you'll have to put up with it for a teensy bit longer.

Nouns and Adjectives

*Noun pay attention (ho ho ho), because **noun's** the time (tee hee hee) to learn about... err... nouns. And also adjectives..*
The first thing you need to remember is that nouns are naming words, and adjectives are describing words.

Nouns can be **Divided** into **Categories**

There are different **types** of nouns. They can refer to unique **people** or **places** (**proper nouns**), or identify more general **objects**, **states** or **groups** (**common nouns**). See below for some examples.

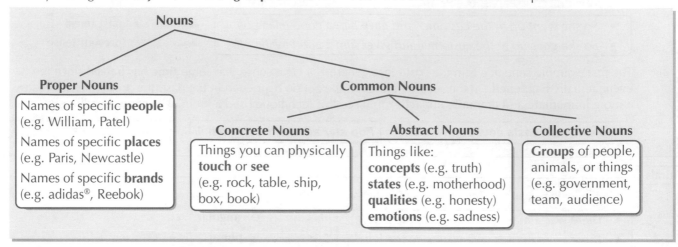

Nouns can be either **Singular** or **Plural**

1) To form the **plural** of a noun you usually add an *-s* or *-es* so that you get, for example, *birds,* or *buses*.

2) Where a noun ends in a consonant and then *-y*, the *-y* is replaced with *-ies* e.g. *lady* ⟶ *ladies*.

3) Word endings that include an *f* like *knife* and *dwarf* often replace the *f* with *-ves* ⟶ *knives* and *dwarves*.

4) Some nouns form **irregular plurals**, different from the **standard** pattern, e.g.
woman ⟶ *women*   *foot* ⟶ *feet*   *mouse* ⟶ *mice*

5) There are some nouns that **don't change their form** at all, whether they are singular or plural, e.g.
deer and *sheep* stay the same even when you are referring to more than one.

Nouns can be classified as **Count Nouns** or **Mass Nouns**

1) **Count nouns** (a bit obviously) can be **counted** — like *brick*. You can have *one brick, two bricks, three bricks*, and so on. Nouns that form irregular plurals can be count nouns too — *one mouse, two mice*, etc.

2) **Mass nouns** can't be counted. Nouns like these **don't** have a **plural**, e.g. you talk about *information* rather than *informations*.

3) Some nouns can function as **both** count and mass nouns, depending on the **context**. For example, in the phrase *war is evil*, *war* is a **mass noun** — it refers to war in general. However, *war* becomes a **count noun** when you use a determiner — e.g. *the war is evil*. This time *war* refers to a **specific** war rather than war in general.

Nouns can be **Modified** to give **More Information**

Nouns **don't usually stand alone**. They're often accompanied by words that **modify** them or that tell you **more** about them. There are two types of modifier — **pre-modifiers** and **post-modifiers**.

- **Pre-modifiers** — these come **before** the noun, e.g. a sign that reads <u>*Dangerous*</u> *Animal*. The adjective *dangerous* premodifies *animal* and tells you something about it. You can also have **more than one** pre-modifier, e.g. *very dangerous animal* — *very* and *dangerous* are both pre-modifiers.

- **Post-modifiers** — these come after the noun, e.g. *Examination* <u>*in progress*</u>. The noun *examination* is postmodified by *in progress* — it tells the reader something about the examination.

In **noun phrases**, the noun is called the **head word** — the most important word of the phrase. The other words **modify** it.

determiner	pre-modifier	head word	post-modifier
the	*largest*	*whale*	*in the world*

Nouns and Adjectives

Adjectives Describe Nouns

Adjectives are classified according to their **position** — **before** or **after** the noun.

1)   **Attributive** adjectives are **premodifying**, e.g. *the **sudden** noise*, or *the **red** balloon*.

2)   **Predicative** adjectives are **postmodifying**. They're usually **linked** to the noun they are modifying by a form of the verb *be*:

> **Examples of predicative adjectives**
>
> - *Revision is **brilliant*** — the adjective is **linked** to the noun by a form of the verb *be*.
> - *The food looked **amazing*** — although forms of *be* are the most common links, **other verbs** can link the adjective to the noun (e.g. *looked, seemed, felt*).

Adjectives also make Comparisons

Adjectives are **gradable** — they can show **how much** of a certain property a noun displays.

1)   **Comparative adjectives** are generally formed by adding an *-er* **inflection**. For example, the simple adjective *long* becomes the comparative adjective *long**er***.

2)   **Superlative adjectives** are generally formed by adding *-est*. For example, *long* becomes the superlative *long**est***.

> Look back at p.111 to see the effects of gradable adjectives in the holiday advertisement texts. Gradable adjectives make you interpret the sentences and the type of accommodation they advertise differently:
>
>       
>
> | *fine* accommodation | *finer* accommodation | *finest* accommodation |
> |:---:|:---:|:---:|
> | **simple adjective** | **comparative adjective** | **superlative adjective** |

3)   Some adjectives are **irregular** in the way they form comparatives and superlatives:

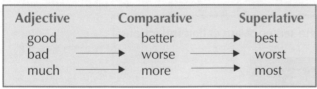

Adjective	Comparative	Superlative
good	better	best
bad	worse	worst
much	more	most

4)   Some adjectives need *more* and *most* to form comparisons. For example, you can't say *significant**er*** or *significant**est***. You use ***more** significant* or ***most** significant* to make the comparison.

Practice Questions

Q1   Name the three types of common nouns and give an example of each.

Q2   What's the difference between mass nouns and count nouns?

Q3   What is a post-modifier of a noun?

Q4   What's the difference between attributive and predicative adjectives?

Q5   Give the comparative and superlative forms of the following adjectives:
          big, pretty, convincing, bad, colourful, clean.

Road, pavement, car park — all concrete nouns...

I think it's disgraceful that in the 21st century we're still calling some nouns 'common'. How exactly are they expected to ever have equal chances in life if they're stuck with this negative label? Especially when the 'proper' nouns have always looked down on them. It's discrimination at its worst — I really thought that an English Language book would have known better...

Verbs and Adverbs

Ok, try to get your head round this first — verbs are doing words, adverbs tell you how the doing is being done. Hmmm, no I'm none the wiser either. Read the rest of the page and see if it makes it any clearer, I'm off for a lie down...

Verbs tell you exactly **What Happens**

The base form of a verb is called the **infinitive** — it normally follows 'to', e.g. to *be*, to *laugh*, or to *think*.
You can describe verbs in two ways:

1) **Main Verbs** (lexical verbs) identify the action of the sentence — e.g. *she sings like a hyena, he gave me his shoe*. The **verbs** *sing* and *gave* tell you what **action** is taking place.

2) **Auxiliary Verbs** go **before** the main verb in a sentence. They give **extra information** about the main verb and can affect the **meaning** of the sentence. There are **two** types of auxiliary verb:

Primary auxiliaries	Modal auxiliaries
There are three primary auxiliaries — *do, have,* and *be*. • I **do** like you • I **am** leaving tomorrow Primary auxiliaries can also be **main verbs**: • I **have** a surprise for you	Modal auxiliaries can **only** occur with reference to a main verb. For example : **can could will would must** **may might shall should** • I **can** play the drums • I **must** do something

Verbs can **Change** their endings depending on **Who** is **Doing** the **Action**

The **endings** of verbs can alter depending on **who** is doing the action — the **first**, **second** or **third person**.

Person	Singular Pronoun	Verb	Plural Pronoun	Verb
First	I	play	We	play
Second	You	play	You	play
Third	She/He/It	play(s)	They	play

Only the verb in the third person singular changes its ending — you add an -s to get plays. This rule applies to most of the verbs in English.

Changes to the ends of words that affect the grammar of the sentence are called **inflections**.

Verbs can tell you **When** something happens

Verbs change depending on whether something is happening in the **past**, **present** or **future**.

1) **Present tense** tells you about 'now' and uses the **base form** of the verb, e.g. *I write* or *they dance* — unless it's the third person singular (see above), when you need to add the *-s* **inflection**, e.g. *she/he/it talks*.

2) **Past tense** tells you about the past (obviously), e.g. *I danced yesterday*, or *He missed the bus*. For most verbs, you form the past tense by **adding -ed** on the end — another **inflection**.

3) **Future tense** — some people say that there's no future tense in English. This is because there **isn't** anything specific (like *-s*, or *-ed*) that you can **add** to a verb to show that the action will happen in the future. The future is expressed in **other ways** — often by using **modal auxiliary** verbs like **will** or **shall**.
   e.g.   *I **shall** see you tomorrow.*   *I **will** pick you up at eight.*

4) You can also use the **present tense** to talk about **future events** — e.g. *Rachel is **playing** hockey on Saturday*.

Verbs **Don't** always change in the **Same Way**

1) Most verbs are **regular** — they follow the same patterns outlined above.

2) Some verbs are **irregular** — they don't change like you'd expect, e.g. *I drink* becomes *I **drank***, not *I **drinked***. Other verbs with irregular past tenses include ***run***, ***sing***, ***write***, and ***speak***.

3) The verb *be* is very irregular — the forms it can take are the infinitive *to be*, plus *am*, *are*, *is*, *was*, and *were*. It changes more than any other verb according to **person** (first, second or third), **number** and **tense**.

Verbs and Adverbs

Verbs can create an **Active** or **Passive** voice

Sentences that involve an **action** can focus on either the **subject** or the **object** (see p.118 for more on this).

Active Voice

The **active voice** is when the **subject** is the focus and **performs** the action described by the verb, e.g:

- *Ahmed **kicked** the ball.*

The subject, *Ahmed*, acts **directly** upon the object — *the ball*. The object **receives** the action of the verb.

Passive Voice

The **passive voice** is less direct. It focuses on the **object**. The **order changes** so that the object comes first, followed by the subject, e.g:

- *The ball **was kicked** by Ahmed.*

The passive voice makes sentences seem more **formal**.

Verbs can change depending on the **Aspect**

Aspect shows whether the action described by the verb has **finished**, or is still **being performed**.

PROGRESSIVE ASPECT

1) The **progressive** (or **continuous**) aspect refers to actions that don't have a definite end.
2) It's made up of one of the auxiliary forms of *be* and the **present participle** of a verb, which is the **base form** + *-ing*.
3) For example, in the sentence *They **are doing** well*, *are* is an auxiliary form of *be* and *doing* is the present participle of *do*.

PERFECT ASPECT

1) The **perfect aspect** tells you about an action that has a definite end.
2) It's made up of one of the present forms of *have* (has/have) and the past tense form of the verb, e.g. *They **have bought** a car.*
3) The **past perfect** aspect is formed in the same way but with the past tense of *have* (had), e.g. *I **had missed** it.*

Adverbs are used to **Modify** verbs

Adverbs are mostly used to modify verbs, but they can modify nouns and adjectives too. Most people recognise adverbs as '**-ly** words' but many have different endings. Here are a **few ways** that adverbs **modify meaning**:

- Adverbs of **manner** — how something is done — e.g. *He talks **incessantly**.*
- Adverbs of **place** — where something is happening — e.g. *The book is **here**.*
- Adverbs of **time** — when something is happening — e.g. *The exam is **tomorrow**.*
- Adverbs of **duration** — how long something happens for — e.g. *The journey took **forever**.*
- Adverbs of **frequency** — how often something takes place — e.g. *Mandy visits **sometimes**.*
- Adverbs of **degree** — the extent to which something is done — e.g. *We **completely** understand.*

Some adverbs **express feelings** or opinions — ***Hopefully**, we'll find out where the garage is.*

Adverbs can also **link** sentences together — *The man was a great athlete. **However**, he didn't have a clue about adverbs.*

Practice Questions

Q1 Name three primary auxiliary verbs.
Q2 What are inflections?
Q3 Give three examples of verbs with irregular past tenses.
Q4 What's the difference between the active voice and the passive voice? Give examples.
Q5 What's the difference between the progressive aspect and the perfect aspect? Give examples.
Q6 What is the function of adverbs?

All these verbs are making me feel a bit tense...

Verbs might seem dull, but they're actually really important. I mean, just think where we'd be without them — we wouldn't really be able to communicate at all. Or should I say, we not really at all. See what I mean? Anyway, everything on this page probably seems quite familiar, but make sure you go over it properly and learn the correct terms for everything.

Pronouns and Determiners

Pronouns, determiners, prepositions and conjunctions are little words, but that doesn't mean you can just ignore them. For a start that would be size discrimination, and anyway, they're pretty important, so it's probably best to learn them.

Pronouns **Take** the **Place** of **Nouns**

Pronouns are a **sub-class** of **nouns**. They can identify subjects and objects, just like nouns do.

1) **Personal** pronouns can replace people or things who are the **subject** of a sentence. They're classified in terms of **person** and are either **singular** or **plural**:

	Singular	Plural
First Person	I	we
Second Person	you	you
Third Person	he, she, it	they

e.g.   Sarah thanked Sanjay
↓
She thanked Sanjay
(3rd person singular subject pronoun)

2) Pronouns can also be used to replace the person or thing who is the **object** of the sentence:

	Singular	Plural
First Person	me	us
Second Person	you	you
Third Person	him, her, it	them

e.g.   Graham thanked Adam
↓
Graham thanked **him**
(3rd person singular object pronoun)

Pronouns are used in **Other Ways** too

1) **Interrogative** pronouns are used to **ask questions**. They are *which, what, who, and whose*. As with other pronouns, they help you **simplify** your sentences by **replacing nouns**, e.g:

- *Give me the name of **the person** you're looking for.* ⟹ **Who** *are you looking for?*
- *Tell me **the thing** you are going to do.* ⟹ **What** *are you going to do?*

2) These aren't the only words you use at the start of questions. *Why, where, how* and *when* are also interrogatives, but they are **adverbs**. Interrogative pronouns and adverbs are usually **classed together** as *wh-words*.

3) **Demonstrative** pronouns like *this, that, these* and *those* can **replace** people and things in a sentence where there's some **shared understanding** of what's being referred to, for example:

- If you're in the kitchen, you might ask *is this my coffee?* — only people who are also in the kitchen will be able to tell you.
- You use different demonstratives depending on the **distance** of the object from the speaker — *this* and *these* are objects **near** the speaker. You use *that* or *those* for objects **further away**.

Determiners show what the noun is **Referring To**

There are several determiners, which all **go before** the noun and show what it's referring to.

1) The **definite article** *the* and the **indefinite article** *a* refer to nouns. The definite article indicates something **specific**. The indefinite article indicates something more **general**, for example:

*Is that **the** frog? (we are looking for, specifically)*   **or**   *Is that **a** frog? (or is it a toad?)*

2) **Numerals** such as *one, two* and *three* (cardinal numbers) and *first, second* etc. (ordinal numbers) are determiners.
3) **Possessive determiners** like *my, your, his, her, its, our* and *their* are **possessive pronouns** used as determiners. They're used before a noun to show **possession**, e.g. **my** car, **his** friend, **their** problem.
4) **Quantifiers** are determiners that show **quantity**, like *few, many* and *enough*.
5) **Demonstrative adjectives**, e.g. *this, that, these,* and *those* are also determiners. They **look the same** as demonstrative pronouns but there is a **significant difference** between them. They refer to specific objects or people that the participants are close to, rather than replacing them like pronouns do:

*I like **those***   **or**   *I like **those** shoes*
*(those **replaces** the noun — pronoun).*   *(those **precedes** the noun — adjective / determiner).*

Prepositions and Conjunctions

Prepositions show Relationships between things

Prepositions show the **relationship** between things in terms of **space**, **time** or **direction**. The preposition usually goes before the determiner and noun.

- *The books are **underneath** the bed* (spatial)
- *He moved **towards** the door* (directional)
- *She left **before** the end* (time)

Sometimes there's no determiner e.g. ⟹
- *See you **at** breaktime.*
- *We'll talk more about it **on** Friday.*

Conjunctions are Linking Words

There are **two types** of conjunction — **coordinating** conjunctions and **subordinating** conjunctions.

1) **Coordinating conjunctions** are words like *and*, *but* and *or*. They **connect** single words or longer units of language (phrases and clauses) that have **equal status**:

| *Robert **and** Bethany* | *A white shirt **or** a pink shirt* | *He kissed her on the cheek **and** she ran away* |

The **coordinating conjunction** *and* connects the two names — neither is given more importance.

The **coordinating conjunction** *or* links **two phrases**.

The coordinating conjunction *and* links two **equal statements**.

2) **Subordinating conjunctions** are words like *since, although, because, unless, whether* and *whereas*. They link a main clause to one that's **less important** to the subject of the sentence:

*Some people find Maths really difficult, **whereas** others find it easy.*

There's more about clauses on p.118-119.

The main clause is *Some people find Maths really difficult*. This is the main point of the sentence. The **subordinating conjunction** *whereas* introduces a less important clause *others find it easy*.

Other subordinating conjunctions give **different meanings**.
Some, like *after, before* and *until* are to do with **time**. Others, like *where* and *wherever* are about **place**.

1) Conjunctions are an important **cohesive device** — they help a discourse to flow smoothly.
2) A discourse **without** conjunctions seems very **disjointed** — e.g. *Last night I went out. I bumped into my friend Hayley. We talked for a while. She had to leave early. She was babysitting for her auntie.*
3) If you add **conjunctions**, the discourse is much more **fluent** — e.g. *Last night I went out **and** I bumped into my friend Hayley. We talked for a while **but** she had to leave early **because** she was babysitting for her auntie.*

Practice Questions

Q1 What is the function of pronouns?
Q2 What's the difference between the pronouns *we* and *us*?
Q3 Name five types of determiners and give an example of each.
Q4 What do prepositions show? Give an example.
Q5 What are coordinating conjunctions? Give an example.
Q6 What are subordinating conjunctions? Give an example.

If pronouns take the place of nouns, what do protractors do?

Phew, there's lots to learn on these pages, but it's all useful stuff. The problem with all this is there are just so many terms to learn, but I'm afraid you're just going to have to keep reading these pages and testing yourself on them until you're sure you know your numerals from your quantifiers and your possessive pronouns from your demonstrative adjectives. Lucky you.

Phrases and Clauses

Sadly, this isn't a page full of useful phrases for when you go on holiday. So if you need to know how to ask the way to the bus station in Greek, or how to reserve a table in Japanese, I'm afraid you'll have to buy a different book.

Phrases are **Units** of **Language** that have a **Head Word**

Phrases are units of language built around a **head word** that identifies the type of phrase, e.g. in the noun phrase *the empty house*, the noun *house* is the head word. Basic sentences are created from a combination of phrases.

1) The simplest noun phrase (NP) possible is just a **noun itself**.
   It can be accompanied by a **pre-modifier**, a **post-modifier**, or both.

Pre-modifiers come before the noun. They're often a determiner, followed by an adjective.

Pre-modifiers		Head Word	Post-modifiers	
determiner	adjective	noun	preposition	noun
the	*new*	*mayor*	*of*	*Bradford*

Post-modifiers come after the noun.

2) A very simple verb phrase (VP) has **one verb**, but you can also make up a verb phrase from the head word (a main verb) and one or more **auxiliary** verbs.

Auxiliary	Auxiliary	Head Word
should	*have*	*passed*

A **Clause** is a **Unit** of a **Sentence**

1) Sentences are made up of **clauses** — the **simplest meaningful units** of the sentence.

2) A **sentence** can be made up of **one clause** — e.g. *Katherine likes going walking*.

3) Or it can be made up of **more than one** clause. When there's more than one clause in a sentence, the clauses are usually separated by **conjunctions** — e.g. *Katherine likes going walking **but** she doesn't like running*.

4) **Clauses** can be made up of a **subject**, **verb**, **object**, **complement** and **adverbial**.

E.g. ***Harry chased the squirrel***

The **subject** is the person or thing that **does something** in the clause. *Harry* is the subject because he's **doing** the chasing. The subject can also be *it*, as in *it is snowing*, or *it is eight o'clock*.

The **verb** (or verb phrase) tells you what the subject is doing. Here the subject *Harry* is followed by the verb *chased*.

The **object receives** the **action**. In this clause *the squirrel* is the object because it's having the action done to it — it's being chased by the subject.

A **complement** gives more **information about** the **subject** or **object**. It **completes** the **meaning** of the sentence it appears in, for example:

- In *Harry is a great guitarist*, the noun phrase (NP) *Harry* is the subject. The second NP in the sentence, *a great guitarist* is a **subject complement**. It **completes** the meaning of the sentence by giving information about the subject.

- In *Harry found the film appalling*, *Harry* is still the subject. But the adjective *appalling* refers to *the film*, which is the object, so *appalling* is the **object complement**.

An **adverbial** is a word or group of words that **refers back** to the **verb**. The simplest adverbial is just an adverb e.g. *Harry kicked the ball **quickly***. In *Harry is playing on Sunday*, the adverbial is *on Sunday* as it relates to the specific time that Harry will play. Adverbials usually describe **time**, **place** or **manner**.

5) The verb, complements and adverbials of a clause or sentence are sometimes also called the **predicate**. The term 'predicate' refers to any part of the clause that is **not the subject**, but that **modifies** it in some way. The verb is sometimes referred to as the **predicator**.

Phrases and Clauses

There are **Seven** Common Types of **Clause**

These are created by **different combinations** of subject (**S**), verb (**V**), object (**O**), complement (**C**) and adverbial (**A**):

S + V	Harry + played
S + V + O	Harry + played + a game
S + V + C	Harry + was + great
S + V + A	Harry + played + on Tuesday
S + V + O + O	Harry + gave + him + a drink
S + V + O + C	Harry + thought + his performance + disappointing
S + V + O + A	Harry + passed + the ball + quickly

Harry + was + great,
and boy did he know it.

Clauses are defined by **Status**

The **status** of a clause depends on its **constituents** and whether it can **stand alone** as a meaningful unit of language.

1) **Main clauses (independent clauses)** can stand alone and still make sense:

> Harry played.

2) **Coordinate clauses** occur in sentences where there are **two or more** independent clauses.
   - They're joined together by a **coordinating conjunction** like *and* or *but*. For example:

   > The band played for two hours **but** I had to leave early.

   - The clauses could **stand alone** and still **make sense** — *The band played for two hours. I had to leave early.*

3) **Subordinate clauses** can't stand alone. They have to be with a **main clause**.
   - A subordinate clause gives **extra information** about the main clause.
   - In most cases, a subordinate clause is led by a **subordinating conjunction** (like *since, although, because, unless, if, whether, while, whereas* etc.). This links it to the main clause. For example:

   main clause → *Will you pop in to see me **while** you're here tomorrow?* ← subordinate clause (the clause can't stand alone in a meaningful way)

   subordinating conjunction

4) **Combining clauses** — you can combine coordinate and subordinate clauses in the same sentence:

   > He went to London **and** she went to Manchester **because** of a terrible row.

   coordinate clause | coordinating conjunction | coordinate clause | subordinating conjunction | subordinate clause

Practice Questions

Q1 What is a head word?
Q2 What's the difference between a clause and a sentence?
Q3 What's the difference between a coordinate clause and a subordinate clause?
Q4 Identify the main clause and the subordinate clause in the following sentence:
   Can you get me some bread when you go to the shop?

Out of all the clauses, I'd say my favourite's Santa...

It's easy to get confused between phrases, clauses and sentences, but keep going over the differences between them until you feel like they could be your specialist subject on Mastermind (or at least in your A level English exam). Don't forget that a sentence can just be one clause, or a few clauses joined together with conjunctions.

Sentences

Sentences are pretty straightforward, but that doesn't mean that there's nothing to learn. In fact, there are loads of different types of sentence, and that means — yep, you've guessed it — loads more terms for you to learn. Hurray.

Sentences can be anything from very Simple to really Complex

There are **five** types of sentence — **minor**, **simple**, **compound**, **complex** and **compound-complex**.

1) **Minor sentences** are complete and meaningful statements that **don't have** a subject and verb combination. Lots of everyday sayings are minor sentences, e.g. *Be quiet. Goodbye. Sounds good.*

2) A **simple sentence** must have a **subject** and a **verb**. It should express a **complete thought**, e.g. *The snow falls.* *Snow* is the **subject**, *falls* is the **verb**.

3) A **compound sentence** is an independent clause linked to another independent clause by a **coordinating conjunction**. Either one could be a main clause in a different sentence.

independent ⟹   *I went to Manchester **and** I went to Liverpool.* ⟸ independent
clause   clause

coordinating conjunction

One too many clauses
for Mr. Barrett.

4) A **complex sentence** consists of a main clause and a subordinate clause (or subordinating clauses). A **subordinating conjunction** connects the clauses together:

main clause ⟹   *The workers left the building **when** they heard.* ⟸ subordinate clause

subordinating conjunction

5) A **compound-complex sentence** is made up of at least two **coordinate clauses** connected by a **coordinating conjunction**, and **at least one** subordinate clause.

*Some of the children went home early **but** the others remained **because** they had no transport.*

first coordinate clause   second coordinate clause   subordinate clause
coordinating conjunction   subordinating conjunction

The Structure of Sentences tells you about the Target Audience

1) The length and complexity of sentences can be varied according to the **content** and **audience** of a text.

2) A good example of contrasting sentence structures is the difference between **broadsheet** and **tabloid** newspapers.

BROADSHEET NEWSPAPER	TABLOID NEWSPAPER
The scientific community is under the microscope as it nears hybrid embryo creation. (Complex sentence: main clause + subordinate clause)	Mad scientists are on the verge of creating monsters. (Simple sentence)
This is a serious ethical issue since it questions the very nature of what it is to be human. (Complex sentence: main clause + subordinate clause)	They will take the sperm and eggs of humans and animals and mix them up. (Compound sentence: coordinate clause + coordinate clause)
The intention to find new ways of treating diseases that have so far proved untreatable is clearly laudable, but the magnitude of the moral issue can't be ignored, as the procedure will involve destroying live embryos after fourteen days. (Compound-complex sentence: main clause + main clause + subordinate clause)	Living embryos will be trashed after fourteen days. (Simple sentence)

3) The writers create a different **mood** and **tone** depending on the types of sentences they use. They're intended to appeal to different **audiences**.

4) The first example is more complex — it has a **measured** and **serious tone**. The second, relatively simple set of sentences is more **emotive** and **subjective**.

Sentences

You can **Classify Sentences** by their **Function**

Sentences have **four** functions.

1) DECLARATIVES

- **Declarative** sentences are statements that **give information**, e.g. ⟶

> *This summer was the hottest on record.*
> *I don't like cheese.*

2) IMPERATIVES

- **Imperative** sentences **give orders**, **instructions**, **advice** and **directions**.
- They **start** with a **main verb** and **don't** have a **subject**, e.g. ⟶

> *Go left and it's first on your right.*
> *Answer one question from each section.*

3) INTERROGATIVES

Interrogative sentences ask **questions**.

- Some questions are formed by **inverting** (swapping round) the **verb** and the **subject** of a sentence.

E.g.

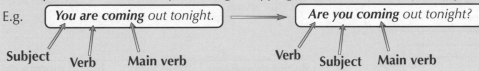

- Interrogatives can start with *wh-* words, e.g. ⟶

> *Where are you going?*
> *When will you be back?*

- They can also be added to the **end of a statement**. These are called **tag questions**, e.g. ⟶

> *It's cold, isn't it?*
> *She said she was on her way, didn't she?*

- In **spoken discourse** you can turn **declarative statements** into questions using **stress** and **intonation**. This is called a **rising inflection**, e.g. ⟶

> *He will get better?*

4) EXCLAMATIVES

- **Exclamative** sentences have an **expressive function** — they convey the force of a statement, and end with an **exclamation mark**, e.g. ⟶

> *I will not do this any more!*
> *That was fantastic!*

Practice Questions

Q1   What does a simple sentence have to contain?

Q2   Give an example of a compound-complex sentence, and label the different types of clauses and conjunctions.

Q3   Describe the differences between sentence structures typically used in broadsheet and tabloid newspapers.

Q4   What are imperative sentences?

Q5   What is a tag question?

Q6   Give an example of an exclamative sentence.

What's the longest sentence in the English language? A levels...

Who would have thought that learning about sentences would turn out to be so interesting? Try comparing a few tabloid and broadsheet newspapers and you'll really be able to see the difference in the sentence structures they use. And while you're at it, look for some examples of minor, simple, compound, complex and compound-complex sentences too.

Morphology

Here's a nice treat for you — a couple of pages all about how prefixes and suffixes are used to create new words.
In fact, I think these are my two favourite pages in the whole section, so I hope you like them too. Enjoy.

Morphemes are the Basic Units that make up words

1) **Morphology** is the study of **word formation**. It looks at how the **form** of a word **changes** because of **grammar**, and how the **meaning** of a word can **change** by adding an **affix** — a **unit** of a word like *un-* or *-ness*.

2) The separate units that make up words are called **morphemes**.

- Simple words are **morphemes** in their own right, such as *man, dog, ignore* and *journey*. They **can't** be **broken down** any further into meaningful units, e.g. *ig+nore*. They're called **free morphemes**, or **base**, **root** or **stem** forms.

- **Bound morphemes** are morphemes that are **not** words on their **own**. They're things like *-ful, -s, -ness* and *-est*, which can be added to **free** morphemes to create words like *thankful, cups, darkness* and *largest*.

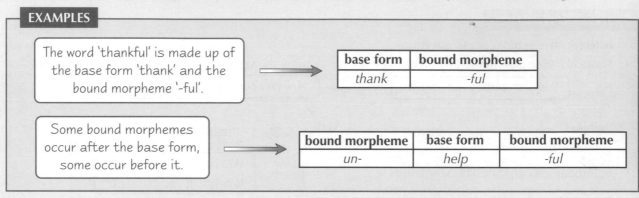

EXAMPLES

The word 'thankful' is made up of the base form 'thank' and the bound morpheme '-ful'.

base form	bound morpheme
thank	-ful

Some bound morphemes occur after the base form, some occur before it.

bound morpheme	base form	bound morpheme
un-	help	-ful

Prefixes can create New Words in the same Word Class

Prefixes are **morphemes** added to the start of a word. They change the **meaning** of nouns, verbs, adjectives and adverbs.

prefix	noun	new word
dis- →	parity →	disparity

prefix	verb	new word
inter- →	act →	interact

prefix	adjective	new word
ir- →	relevant →	irrelevant

prefix	adverb	new word
super- →	naturally →	supernaturally

Suffixes can change a word's Class and Meaning

Suffixes are **morphemes** added to the **end** of a word.

Suffixes and prefixes are both types of affix.

The tables below show how you form different words and word classes by adding **different suffixes** to the **base form**.

1) Base form is a **noun**:

noun	adjective	verb	adverb
type	typical	typify	typically

2) Base form is an **adjective**:

adjective	noun	verb	adverb
legal	legality	legalise	legally

3) Base form is a **verb**:

verb	noun	adjective	adverb
explode	explosion	explosive	explosively

Marjorie put a brave face on it, but she really didn't like the objects affixed to her head.

Morphology

Adding Morphemes to existing words is called Affixation

Affixes are **bound morphemes** that are added to words. There are **two** kinds of affixation — **inflectional** and **derivational**.

Inflectional affixation

1) **Inflectional affixation** changes the **grammar** of the word — e.g. its **number** or tense.

2) Inflectional affixes are always **suffixes** (they go after the base).
For example, *pushed*. The bound morpheme *-ed* attaches to the verb *push* to change the action from the **present tense** to the **past tense**.

3) Here are some common kinds of inflectional affixation:

Plural *-s* (also *-ies*, *-oes*)	*dogs, ladies, tomatoes*	Past participle *-ed*	*He has recovered*
Possessive *-'s*	*Bernie's car*	Present participle *-ing*	*He is recovering*
Third person singular *-s*	*She says*	Comparative *-er*	*Quicker*
Past tense *-ed*	*He recovered*	Superlative *-est*	*Quickest*

Derivational affixation

1) Derivational affixation has a **semantic function** — it changes the **meaning** of a word.

2) The **noun** *player* is formed by adding the **suffix** *-er* to the **verb** *play*. The word changes from being an **action** to the **performer** of the action.

3) **Prefixes precede** (go before) the **base form**, **suffixes** come at the end — both can **change** the meaning of a word:

Prefix	Meaning	Example	Suffix	Meaning	Example
auto-	self	*autobiography*	*-archy*	leadership	*hierarchy*
inter-	between	*interactive*	*-less*	absence of	*shameless*
un-	not, opposite	*unnecessary*	*-phobia*	fear	*claustrophobia*

Morphology and Coining Words

Coining is the general term for creating words. Many new words are formed through **derivational affixation** (see p. 8-9 for more on this). There are **four main ways** that new words are coined:

1) **Clipping** — sometimes prefixes or suffixes are **dropped**. For example, *the gymnasium* is now usually referred to as *the gym*, and you're more likely to say *phone* than *telephone*.

2) **Compounds** — new words are created by **combining** two free morphemes, e.g. *mankind, blackbird* and *sleepwalk*.

3) **Back-formation** — this involves a free morpheme that **looks like** it has a suffix, like *editor*, being adapted to create a word like *edit*. **Historically** the word *editor* is a **free morpheme**, but the verb *edit* has been created **from** it. This is also true of *writer* (historically a free morpheme) producing the verb *write*.

4) **Blends** — new words are also created by **fusing** two words into one. These words are referred to as **blends**. For example, *alcoholic* has been fused with *chocolate* to form *chocoholic*, and with *shopping* to form *shopaholic*.

Practice Questions

Q1 What is a morpheme?
Q2 Give three examples of words that have been formed using prefixes.
Q3 Explain how suffixes can change the class of a word.
Q4 What's the difference between inflectional and derivational affixation?
Q5 Explain the four main ways of coining new words.

Aren't clipping and back-formation something hairdressers do?...

See, I told you these pages were going to be good. I don't know about you, but that mention of blending has put me in the mood for a nice refreshing milkshake. So once you're sure you've learned everything on these pages, why not have a break and go and make yourself one — if it's banoffee, you're blending words too, so it's even better.

Register and Mode

*These pages are for everyone, but **OCR** people should have a particularly good look. It's really all stuff that you already know just from being aware of different types of language, and generally being alive. So go forth and state the obvious...*

Register is the Type of Language used in different Situations

Registers are the different **varieties** of language used in different **situations**. Deciding which register is **appropriate** to use depends on several factors.

Audience
- This is to do with the **relationship** between the speaker or writer and the audience.
- For example, if the speaker or writer knows the audience personally, the **register** they use will usually be quite **informal**. It might include informal lexis, like slang and abbreviations.
- This may be more apparent in informal speech than in informal writing.

Purpose
- For example, a **report** will use a **formal register**, as its **purpose** is to convey information accurately.
- When the purpose is more **persuasive**, e.g. an advert, the register will often be more **informal** as the text needs to get the audience's attention in order to persuade them.

Field
- This is the subject being talked about.
- For example, if the topic is **football**, the **lexis** will include words linked to football, like *match, penalty,* etc.
- Some fields have a large specialist lexicon (stock of words), like **biochemistry**. Most workplaces have their own lexicon connected solely with that field, from car repair shops to hospitals (see p.34 for more on occupational language).

Form
- For example, business letters will be written in a **formal register**.
- Text messages, on the other hand, tend to use a more **informal register**.

> Whether the register is **appropriate** depends on the **context** it's used in — using an **informal register** in a **formal situation** is **inappropriate** because it could seem **disrespectful** or **rude**. Using **formal language** in an **informal situation** could sound **unfriendly** and **stuffy**.

Registers Vary in terms of Lexis, Grammar and Phonology

Different **registers** use different **lexis** and **grammar**, and the way they're **pronounced** can **vary** too. For example:

Lexis
- A conversation between two **specialists** would contain **technical vocabulary** that they would both understand.
- For example, the lexis in the registers used by **mechanical** and **medical** specialists would be very different.

Grammar
- **Register** can affect syntax — the **structure** of clauses and **complexity** of sentences.
- Some registers even have grammatical constructions that are **specific** to them, like the legal register (known as **legalese**), which uses lots of clauses and mainly passive sentences.

Phonology
- This is to do with how the words in a particular **register** are **pronounced**.
- The **informal register** people use when speaking to friends involves things like dropping the <h> from words like *have* and missing a <g> off words with the *ing* suffix, like *thinking*.
- Generally speaking, the more **formal** a situation is the more likely people are to **modify** their **accent** so it's closer to **Received Pronunciation** (see p.33).

Register and Mode

Modes can be Written or Spoken

Written modes

1) Written modes include letters, essays, novels, recipes and reports. Written modes tend to be the **most formal**.

2) In written modes the words have to make the **meaning** clear, because there's no opportunity for **non-verbal communication** between the writer and the reader.

3) Sometimes writers try to convey **prosodic features** like tone, intonation and pitch to make the meaning clearer, using **features** like *italicising*, underlining, CAPITALISATION, and **punctuation** like exclamation marks.

Spoken modes

1) Spoken modes are things like interviews, broadcasts and presentations. Spontaneous speech (like a conversation between friends) is normally the **least formal** mode.

2) In **spoken modes** speakers can rely on **non-verbal communication** like gestures and **prosodic features** (see p.52 and p.56) to get their point across.

3) The grammar of informal speech is often **disjointed** — it contains lots of **interruption** and **incomplete sentences**. It also contains **non-fluency features** (things that interrupt the flow of speech) like **self-correction**, **pauses**, **repetition**, **fillers** (*you know, sort of, I mean*) and **false starts**.

4) Speech also tends to contain **phatic expressions** (small talk expressions that have a **social function**, so their meaning isn't particularly important, like *hello* and *how's things?*).

Multi-Modal Texts contain Features of both Speech and Writing

Lots of texts are a **mixture** of **spoken** and **written** modes, especially electronic texts like **emails** and **text messages**.

1) These are **written modes** that can contain elements of **spoken language**, e.g. **phatic communication** like *hello* and *bye*.

2) Very **informal** emails or messages between friends contain **phonetic spellings**, like *b4* for *before*, and *u* for *you*.

3) **Formal** business emails still tend to be **less formal** than **letters** — they tend not to use **conventions** like writing the sender's address at the top. **Paragraphs** and **sentences** tend to be **shorter**.

For OCR, multimodal texts includes texts where different media are used at the same time, e.g. films, illustrated books and computer games.

Modes can be Classified in Different ways

Different modes can be **grouped** according to the following **approaches**:

1) **Continuum classification** — position on a **scale** that places written Standard English at one end and spoken informal speech at the other. In the middle are multi-modal texts like email.

2) **Typology** — grouping together types of language that have **characteristics** or **traits** in common, e.g. sports commentaries, music reviews, formal interviews, novels, poems, etc.

3) **The dimensions approach** — looking at different aspects of modes, e.g. lexis, grammar and structure to analyse the level of formality in a certain text.

Practice Questions

Q1 What impact can audience have on register?

Q2 Outline how registers can vary in terms of lexis and grammar.

Q3 Outline four typical features of spoken modes.

Q4 Classify these three types of language by placing them on a continuum from least formal to most formal: text message to family member, business letter, transcript of a conversation between friends.

Stod moding and ged od wid id...

When I was at primary school, we all thought it was a real treat if we were allowed to go and collect the class register from the office. Weird. Anyway, once you're sure you know everything on these pages, that's the end of the section. So you can give yourself a pat on the back, take a deep breath, and then you're ready to move on to the next section.

Choosing a Topic

*This is for AQA A, AQA B, WJEC, OCR and Edexcel. For your coursework you'll have to produce a **language investigation**. This involves looking at an area of language and saying how or why a particular issue affects it.*

You need to find a **Suitable Topic**

You need to have some idea about what **aspect** of **language** you want to study.

1) Think about your choice of topic so that you don't end up wasting time or getting stuck. This is probably the **most important** point of all — think ahead and be **realistic**. You'll need to produce **enough work** to satisfy the unit's requirements, but you don't want to choose too **wide-ranging** a task or one that ends up being **too demanding** and **impossible to complete**.

This section gives you some general advice about how to carry out an investigation. You should check the exact requirements for your exam board with your teacher.

2) It's best to pick something that really **interests you**. If you know the subject well, you should be able to work out whether it will offer enough **scope**, and if you'll be able to get **enough suitable information**.

3) Make sure you choose a topic where the data you need will be **accessible**. If you can't find **enough information** about your topic, then you're bound to struggle.

4) The **length** of your investigation will depend on the exam board you're doing, but it could be up to **2500** words.

Different Types *of* Investigation *look at different* Aspects *of language*

1) Being able to identify **different types** of language investigation and applying them to the area you're thinking of studying will help you to **narrow down** your topic.

2) It can also **highlight potential problems** (e.g. if your method is going to give you enough suitable information about your topic) before you get started.

3) This list of the different investigation types should help you focus on a more specific area for your study.

Language-based

An investigation that looks at a **particular type of language** in order to determine something about its distinctive features.

> **For example:**
> *Looking at regional variations in English by recording people from different parts of the country reading or speaking, and analysing these examples.*

Function-based

An investigation that focuses on the **use of language**, and how one type of language achieves a particular effect.

> **For example:**
> *The specific language techniques used in political speeches to persuade, convince or influence an audience so that they end up sharing the point of view of the speaker.*

Attitudes-based

An investigation that focuses on **reactions** and **responses** to a particular type of language.

> **For example:**
> *You could look at how people across different age groups feel about the language of teenagers, or their attitudes to slang words, or to neologisms that refer to new technologies etc. You'd have to identify specific groups to talk to in relation to this though.*

User-based

An investigation focusing on the **people** who use a particular type of language — how they use it and how it affects them and those around them.

> **For example:**
> *The jargon or sociolect used by people in a particular trade or profession, or in relation to a hobby or an area of personal interest.*

Choosing a Topic

*You might find it **Easier** to stick to something you've **Already Studied***

If you get the choice, here are a few things that you'll have covered at AS or A2 that you could investigate:

LANGUAGE IN SOCIAL CONTEXTS *(section 2 of this book)*	**LANGUAGE AND THE MEDIA** *(section 5)*	**LANGUAGE ACQUISITION** *(section 6)*
For example:	**For example:**	**For example:**
How are regional dialects perceived in schools?	How might newspapers appear biased?	What role does the caregiver play in language development?
Do men and women use language differently?	How is a relationship developed between a presenter and audience?	Is there an order in which children acquire features of language?

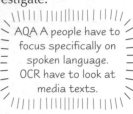

AQA A people have to focus specifically on spoken language. OCR have to look at media texts.

Think about **How** you're going to **Investigate Your Topic**

There are three main ways you can set up your investigation. You can suggest a **theory** that you want to try and prove or discredit, set yourself a **specific question** to answer, or go for a **study** based on discussing a certain area and its features.

1) **Hypothesis** based topics

- A hypothesis is a statement that proposes a **possible explanation** for some issue but doesn't offer proof, e.g: *If language changes through generations, then there will be identifiable language differences across three generations of the same family.*
- A hypothesis-based investigation tests the hypothesis by collecting data, and then by **evaluating** the **results**.

2) **Question** based topics

- Questions can be based on something you've **observed** about the way language functions, or how it's used, that can then be **explored** in more detail.
- Any question that you set yourself should be clear and make it **obvious** what you plan to look at, e.g: *To what extent is the language of children's television adapted to assist or influence their linguistic development?*

3) **Descriptive** topics

- A descriptive language investigation focuses on **comparing** and **evaluating** data without trying to prove a point or investigate a theory. Instead of analysing results, you **comment** on the features in the data you're looking at and **discuss** the **linguistic influences** that there may be on the text(s).

Think about how you'll **Get Your Information**

1) The **methodology** is the approach you use to **obtain your information**. It needs to be carefully planned in advance, because in your write-up you need to **describe** and **analyse** the process in detail and comment on what worked well — as well as what didn't.

2) These are the methodologies you might use for the types of topic listed above:

- For a **hypothesis based topic** you might **record** and **transcribe** samples of speech in order to prove a theory about certain speakers.
- For a **question based topic** you might look at **different types** of language and suggest which is most **effective** for its purpose.
- For a **descriptive topic** you might look back at the archives of selected newspapers to **compare** and **evaluate** the style of writing and presentation methods between old examples and up-to-date ones.

A seriously flawed methodology for studying the language of birds was about to teach Terry a very unpleasant lesson.

Time to pic a topic...

This stuff can all seem a bit daunting — you want to choose something vaguely interesting that isn't going to require shed loads of extra work, but isn't too easy either. Tricky. But it's not impossible. Just find a topic that isn't going to completely bore your brains out, and once you get stuck into it you'll soon become an enthusiastic linguist. That's the idea, anyway...

Collecting Data

AQA A, AQA B, WJEC, OCR and Edexcel. There are plenty of ways to collect data — but you need to make sure that your collection method gives you the best chance of getting what you need. If that happens to include the use of a sharp stick or forcing people to watch Noel Edmonds on TV for 6 hours, then so be it. Just kidding. Don't do that.

There are **Four** main types of **Data**

Data is the **raw material** that you'll be collecting so that you've got something to write about in your investigation.

1) Primary Language Data	This is language data that can be obtained **directly**. For example — **recordings** of spoken language, **samples** of written language, **lists** of words used in conversation or in writing, **examples** of slang or dialect, and **features** of pronunciation.
2) Secondary Language Data	Other sources, e.g. other people's research findings or newspaper articles about attitudes towards language.
3) Comparative and Contrastive Data	This is when **two or more** types of data are studied and you then analyse the **similarities** and **differences** between them. For example, you might compare and contrast the language of text messages with the language of emails.
4) Longitudinal Data	Longitudinal data from one source is gathered over a **period of time** so that comparisons or contrasts can be made. For an investigation of this kind, data is gathered by going back in time. For example, comparing the language of news coverage from the **past** with news coverage from **today**.

There are **Different Methods** of language data collection

1) Collecting Spoken Language Data

There are various different ways in which spoken language data can be collected.

- **Note-taking** — making notes as people are speaking.
- **Preparing a questionnaire on language use.** You can give a questionnaire to someone to fill in, or conduct an interview with them and fill in the answers yourself. You need to plan the questionnaire so that the person's answers demonstrate or discuss whatever feature of spoken language you've chosen to investigate.
- **Tape-recordings** — these could be of conversations between two people, or of a single person reading, speaking about a particular experience, or explaining their views or opinions on an issue. However, if you record someone without their knowledge, then you're **legally obliged** to obtain their **permission** afterwards, otherwise you can't use their responses as part of your investigation.

Collecting spoken language data is a **time-consuming** business. You might also have to transcribe recordings (in case you need a hard copy, or want to do a phonemic analysis). Doing this can be **useful** and will look really impressive, but you shouldn't spend loads of time doing it at the **expense** of the **other parts** of your investigation.

2) Collecting Written Language Data

Written language data is just any **written text**, e.g. fiction, media texts, emails. In theory, collecting written language data should be easier than collecting spoken language data, as long as it's fairly **concise** and **relevant** to your topic.

3) Combining Spoken and Written Language Data

You could also choose to analyse some of the **differences** between spoken and written language, either in everyday use or in the process of development. For example, if you're looking at how children begin to develop their language skills, you could **record** their conversations and get **samples** of their writing/drawings.

Collecting Data

Questionnaires need to be Carefully Designed

1) First of all, you need to have a **clear idea** of what you want to gain from your questions. It may be better to avoid questions that only have a 'yes' or 'no' response (known as **closed questions**) if you're looking for evidence of linguistic **features** or **opinions** on language.

2) You should ask **open questions** that will encourage people to talk for a while, e.g. asking them for their **opinion**, encouraging them to talk about themselves or getting them to tell **anecdotes** or **stories**.

3) You need to decide **who to ask** in order to get the information you want — this will be your **sample**. You need to make sure that participants fit into the group that your research question has specified (e.g. differences between **male** and **female teenagers**), and design your questions so **everyone can answer them effectively**.

You have to do some Planning before conducting an Interview

There are a number of decisions to make **before** you start:

1) **Who** are you going to interview — just **one person**, or a number of people so that you end up with a wider **range** of responses (but potentially more work)?

2) Are you going to **record** the interview, in which case you'll need to **transcribe** it later, or are you going along with just a notebook for **note-taking**?

3) Are you going to conduct your interview **face-to-face**, over the **phone**, or in some other way, for example via the **Internet**?

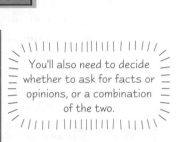
You'll also need to decide whether to ask for facts or opinions, or a combination of the two.

There are Problems with studying People

Whatever type of investigation and methodology you choose, collecting data from **other people** can be a bit tricky.

1) If they've been told exactly what a study is about, some participants can end up doing what **they think** the researcher wants them to, rather than **acting normally**.

2) Experimental situations aren't the most **normal experiences** at the best of times (it's pretty hard to just ignore a **camera** or a **microphone**, for example).

3) This is called the **observer's paradox** — the researcher can affect participants' reactions just by being present or making people aware they're being watched.

4) On the other hand, **not telling** participants what they should expect to experience can be **extremely unethical** — they have a right to be briefed on what the investigation is all about in case they're uncomfortable with the study.

The reaction to the 'language and the law investigation' was largely unfavourable.

Some Methods are better suited to certain Investigations

Language Based Investigation	You could collect **spoken** or **written** language data, or a **combination** of the two. **Transcriptions**, particularly phonemic transcriptions, give you lots of **detail** but can be very **time-consuming**.
Function Based Investigation	**Written data** is probably the most likely option here. You'll need to use a **variety of sources**, so you can make **comparisons** between them.
Attitudes Based Investigation	This is the most likely type of investigation for using **secondary language data** (see p.128), as it's all about how people respond to the use of language in a particular **context**.
User Based Investigation	This type of investigation could use **various methods** of data collection. It could focus on spoken language in a **particular context**, or on written language in a particular context, or on a **combination** of the two.

You'll get the most natural responses if you ask about data-day stuff...

... like holidays, or biscuits, or walking the dog. You need to make sure your participants (if you've got any) are at ease, so they'll act naturally and not just say what they think you want them to. That's what the observer's paradox is all about — influencing your own results just by being in the same room. When are they going to invent that invisibility cloak...

Recording Data

AQA A, AQA B, WJEC, OCR and Edexcel. When you've collected all the data you need, it's time to decide how you're going to present it in the context of your investigation. Maybe with a nice salad garnish, and a slice of lemon...

Be *Selective* with *Written Data*

1) If you're using **long pieces** of written data (like newspaper or magazine articles), then pick out some **shorter extracts** that **support** the point you're making. This saves you from having to do a detailed linguistic analysis of a huge amount of text, and should mean that the points you make are more **focused** on the topic.

2) Use **footnotes** to draw attention to **specific linguistic features** (see p. 134).

Spoken Data has to be *Transcribed*

1) Transcribing conversations is **tricky** — you'll probably need to listen to your recordings closely quite a **few times** before you write up your **final version**.

2) It's also quite **time-consuming**, so if you've recorded an **interview** or **conversation** as part of your data collection, you don't need to **transcribe** the whole thing. However, you do need to make sure that the extracts you choose are **relevant** to your investigation and that you **reproduce** what was said **accurately**.

3) Your data might include things like **pauses**, **repetitions** and **emphasis**. You should represent these features and include an **appendix** or **key** so the reader knows what it all means (e.g. like the key on p. 49)

For example:

If you decide to look at differences in language because of **gender**, you could **record** a **conversation** between a **mixed group** of students at school or college.

This short **sample conversation** shows the things you could focus on when transcribing spoken language:

> *This extract is of an unsupervised conversation between 2 male students (1M and 2M) and 2 female students (1F and 2F), all aged 18. They have been asked to talk about 'holidays'.*
>
> 1F: can't wait for mine (.) I haven't been away in <u>ages</u>
>
> 2F: I know (1) it'll be (.) just be <u>so</u> nice to be away
>
> 1M: // where you two going then
>
> 2F: er (.) France (1) like somewhere in the south I think
>
> 1M: // cool   // okay
>
> 1F: // the Dordogne
>
> 2F: it's well nice
>
> 2M: the <u>where</u> (1) what I've never heard of it
>
> 1M: that's because (.) because you're an idiot
>
> 2M: just because you're going camping in your garden

Don't use punctuation in your transcript — it isn't articulated, so it shouldn't be included. Use pauses or emphasis instead.

Key

(.) or (1) = *micropause or pause (number of seconds)*

// = *overlapping speech / interruptions*

<u>xxx</u> = *underlining — emphasis by speaker*

This transcript includes the following features to make it as **clear** and **accurate** as possible:

- Identifies each speaker **individually** (1M, 2M, 1F and 2F) and gives the **context** of the conversation.
- Uses a **consistent symbol** to denote overlapping speech and interruptions (//).
- Underlines words that were **emphasised** by the speakers in the conversation.
- Uses **micropauses** and **numbers** to show **pauses** in the conversation e.g. (.) and (1).
- Lists all the features in a **key**.

> If you're investigating **slang** or **dialect**, then you might want to include a **phonemic transcription** (see p.60-61). If you're looking at **intonation** or **stress** you could use **extra symbols** to highlight the differences. If you do decide to do this, remember that although it can be really impressive, producing a very detailed transcription can take **absolutely ages**.

Analysing Data

You need to Base Your Analysis on a Linguistic Framework

You don't have to present **all the data** you've collected in your analysis — select specific parts of the data to **focus on** instead. Make sure you choose the parts that are **most relevant** to the subject of your investigation, and the bits that will make your discussion as clear and focused on the topic as possible.

1) Before you start analysing the data, try to group it into **categories**. You might decide to place some items of data from different sources together to illustrate some **direct differences**. This will help you when you're making **comparisons**, and it might work better than going through each piece of data systematically from beginning to end.

2) Next you'll need to decide what kind of **framework** you're going to use for your analysis:

   - **Lexis** — words and phrases.
   - **Semantics** — the meaning of words.
   - **Grammar** — structural relationships.
   - **Phonology** — sounds and how they're produced.
   - **Pragmatics** — social conventions of language and its implied meanings.
   - **Graphology** — the physical appearance of language.
   - **Discourse** — how texts are structured and made cohesive.

See p. 108 for more on language frameworks.

Despair set in as they realised Dan had selected the wrong framework.

3) The framework you choose should be the one that you feel will **best demonstrate** the points you're trying to make. You should try to keep to whichever one you choose, although topics do inevitably **overlap**.

Make sure you choose the Right Framework

It's important to choose a sensible and relevant framework to work with when you're analysing data. For example, it'd be pretty stupid to look at the graphology of a conversation. Here are a few suggestions:

> **Comparing written data** — if you're comparing language use over a period of time you may be focusing on **lexis** or **grammar**. A function or user-based topic might focus on **pragmatics**, **discourse** or **graphology**.

> **Comparing spoken data** — a **phonological** framework would be an obvious choice for a topic focusing on slang or dialect, but you could use **lexical** or **grammatical** frameworks too.

> **Comparing spoken data to written data** — for language in everyday use, the question of **formality** versus **informality** is likely to come up, so you'll probably choose a **lexical / grammatical** framework. A topic on language development in the early years of childhood might also focus on lexis and grammar — you'd be looking for comparisons between **rates of development** of spoken and written language in those years.

Draw Conclusions from your Analysis

1) Ideally, you want to conclude your investigation by showing that you've found out **something new** and **worthwhile** that can be proved by the **evidence** you've presented.

2) There may be things you have to **leave open** because you can't fully prove them — e.g. with a hypothesis based topic you might find evidence that suggests a particular trend without providing **comprehensive proof**.

3) Your conclusions should always be **related** to your **evidence**, but they don't have to agree with your **original predictions**, or with any secondary sources you've looked at. The most important thing is that you **justify** what you say by showing how it's **supported** by your data.

Transcription might take ages, but it's worth sticking with it...

Do you think Rebecca Adlington invented swimming overnight? No — it took her years. The same goes for Lewis Hamilton and cars. Don't even get me started on how many rubbish breakfasts I had before I finally came up with the concept of putting milk on cereal. The point here, of course, is that it's worth it in the end. A thorough analysis will be too.

Writing Up the Investigation

AQA A, AQA B, WJEC, OCR and Edexcel. Now for the really important part — producing a write-up of your investigation. There's a pretty standard layout for all of this, so just be methodical and work through the sections.

Start by **Explaining** your **Work (Introduction)**

1) First of all, you need to **explain your reasons** for choosing a particular area of study, including any advice or guidance from **other sources** that helped you towards this decision.

> Zimmerman and West's (1975) dominance model suggests that male speakers are responsible for 96% of interruptions in male-female conversations. As this research is now over 30 years old, I wish to investigate whether the model they proposed still applies to today's mixed-gender conversations.

2) Then you'll need to explain what **type** of **topic** you've chosen, and whether it's hypothesis based, question based or descriptive — give **reasons** for these decisions too. You could also include some information about the data you've collected.

> This investigation will therefore deal with the following hypothesis: female students in mixed-gender conversations will compete with male speakers to dominate a conversation by non-supportive interruptions, not following rules of turn-taking, prolonging their own turns with non-verbal fillers, and instigating changes in conversation topic.

3) Finally you'll need to outline the **aims of your investigation**, specifically what you set out to **discover / achieve**, and what **type of language** you're investigating (e.g. spoken, written or multimodal).

Explain **How** You **Collected** your **Data (Methodology)**

1) In this section you'll need to explain how you **obtained your data**, and what **decisions** you made as part of the process. For example, whether your data is **written**, **spoken** or a **combination of the two**, and why this is.

> The data for this investigation comes from a series of unsupervised conversations between male and female students. In order to investigate the effect of gender on these conversations, the participants were informed that they would be recorded, and given the neutral topic "holidays" to discuss.

2) You should then explain how you **designed your investigation**, together with the **techniques** you used in your research and the **language frameworks** you chose, as well as why you thought they were appropriate.

> As this investigation deals with how male and female participants respond to each other, the principle framework that will inform the discussion is that of pragmatics — how the conventions of spoken language are respected, followed or broken according to the gender of different speakers.

Present your **Findings** clearly **(Results)**

1) This should be one of the **largest sections** of your investigation. You need to give a **detailed** and **systematic** **analysis** and **interpretation** of the data you've collected.

2) To make this section easier to follow (and write), divide it into **subsections**, with **relevant subheadings** to show how it all fits together.

3) Most of your results will be presented as a **discussion**, but you can also include **charts or diagrams** to support your points — they make the analysis **clearer** and more **systematic**.

> In this conversation between male and female students, there were 25 instances in which the speakers interrupted each other or overlapped. As the table and graph show, these instances were fairly evenly spread — the male speakers account for 14 of the interruptions (56%), and the females for 11 (44%).

Participant	M1	M2	F1	F2
Interruptions	8	6	7	4
As % of total	32	24	28	16

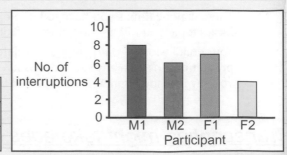

Writing Up the Investigation

Bring your Results and Analysis Together (Conclusion)

1) In your conclusion you should explain what you've been able to **work out** from your **analysis**. You should refer back to the **aims** in your introduction section and say if they've been met, and what you've found out.

(e.g.) This investigation tested the hypothesis that female speakers are as dominant as males in mixed-gender conversations. The evidence suggests that due to a similar frequency of non-supportive interruptions, topic shifting and disregarding turn-taking, female speakers are more similar to males than Zimmerman and West's dominance model suggests.

2) Whichever form of investigation you choose, you'll need to say if your **expectations** were met or not (if your hypothesis was correct). If your findings aren't what you expect, **don't be afraid to admit it** — you can **discuss** why this might be the case, and you'll still get plenty of **credit**.

3) The point of this investigation is to reveal something **new** or of **interest**. However, in **relative terms**, your sample size and resources won't be **very big**, so be careful about boldly claiming that you've worked out everything there is to know about female conversational habits (for example).

(e.g.) The evidence I have produced suggests that female speakers are just as likely as males to dominate conversations. This may reflect how gender roles in conversation are changing, and may mean that Zimmerman and West's (1975) dominance theory can be updated. However this is a very small sample so it is clear more research is needed.

4) If you can see a **potential** for **further study**, the end of your conclusion is a good place to suggest it.

Explain whether you could Improve your Investigation (Evaluation)

1) When you're evaluating your own work, **be honest** about the success of your investigation. Try and deal with some (if not all) of the following questions:

- Was the process of **data collection** easier or harder than you anticipated?
- How **effective** was your chosen method of **analysis**?
- Did you find you had **sufficient data** for your results to be **significant**?
- Did the information you came up with offer opportunities for **further research**?

(e.g.) I tried to avoid the observer's paradox in this investigation by giving the participants a conversation topic and some written instructions rather than being present in the room. However the presence of the recording equipment may have affected the participants' conduct and made them feel more self-conscious than they would normally.

2) It's never particularly easy to criticise yourself, but you should try to **evaluate** the whole process — it looks really good if you can say what worked well and what you would improve if you did the investigation again.

You might have to provide Copies of your Original Data (Appendices)

1) At the very end of your investigation, include any **extra information** that supports it, or that might be helpful to someone reading it. This could include **copies of questionnaires**, **transcripts of spoken data**, and **copies of written data**.

2) You should only include **primary research material** here — data that you've **collected yourself** during the course of your investigation.

3) Don't include **sources** that you've consulted or **articles** that you've read in relation to your work here — they need to be referenced in the **bibliography** instead (see p.134-135).

After spending 14 hours finding copies of her original data, poor Helen developed a nasty case of appendicitis.

Writing up is all very well, but make sure you write everything down too...

In fact, why is it called writing up? Just goes to show you can't trust the English language to make any sense whatsoever. On that revolutionary note, it's now your job to take a deep breath and start writing about your investigation (another 'write' preposition there). Remember — be thorough, methodical and accurate and the 'marks for' column will stack up just fine.

References and Bibliographies

AQA A, AQA B, WJEC, OCR and Edexcel. The last act in the investigation is to acknowledge your sources. There's a very specific way of doing this. Luckily for you, it's on these two pages. I wouldn't leave you hanging.

Include All your References

1) You have to include **references** in your investigation. It means that anyone reading or assessing your work can use the **same sources** as you have, and can check where you got your information from.

2) Referencing also provides **evidence** of the sources that you've consulted to widen your own **knowledge** and formulate your **hypothesis / research question**.

3) You have to include a list to show that you're not **plagiarising** — copying other people's work and/or ideas without **due acknowledgement**.

4) References let you **illustrate specific points**, and provide **support** for the arguments you're putting forward (or discrediting).

Make sure you Understand the Terminology

1) **Citations** and **footnotes** are the two main forms of *references*. They refer the reader to a **source** or **piece of information** that isn't in the **main body** of your text. If it's a citation, the information is highlighted **briefly** in the **same sentence**. If it's a footnote, the information is at the **foot of the page**.

2) A **bibliography** is the section at the end of the work where all the references are **drawn together** and listed in full. All examining boards specify that a bibliography has to be included in investigations — all sources **need to be acknowledged**.

3) People don't always use reference terms in the **same way** — for example, sometimes the word *references* is used to mean a bibliography. Make sure you **check** the exam board's terminology first.

You can make Citations in the Middle of your Writing

1) Citations **refer briefly** to a reference source in the **main body** of your writing.

2) If the citation mentions the **author's name**, you should include the **year** that the work was **published** in brackets.

> This model was found to be suitable at higher levels and was adopted by Alexander (1973).

3) If you do include a citation, you'll need to mention the source **again** at the **end** (in the bibliography, see p. 135), as the citation might not give the **full details**.

Footnotes allow you to Add Extra Information

1) Another way to make references is to use **footnotes**[1], where you place small numbers in the text that lead the reader to the **corresponding number** at the bottom of the page or at the end of the text.

2) Footnote references can refer to **any kind of source** — books, magazines, websites etc. They can also give **extra information** about the point you're trying to make[2].

3) The best thing to do is to keep footnotes **short and sweet**. Long or complicated footnotes take the reader's attention **away** from the main body of your writing and mean they might **lose** the flow of your argument completely.

They were furious that the footnote held no useful information whatsoever.

---

[1] Just like this one. What a fine example.

[2] Keep footnotes in order — the first one on a page is 1, the second is 2, and so on. On the next page you go back to 1.

References and Bibliographies

Bibliographies Reference *all your sources* **In Full**

Here's a **sample** of what your bibliography might look like. This example uses the **Harvard Referencing system**. However, there are lots of other systems for referencing, so **check** with your teacher exactly which one you'll be expected to use for your coursework. Whatever style you use, keep all the entries in **alphabetical order**.

Crystal, D. (1995) *The Cambridge Encyclopedia of the English Language*. Cambridge: Cambridge University Press p. 364.

Manches, A. (2008) *Language and Gender — TESOL Talk from Nottingham 07/08*. http://portal.lsri.nottingham.ac.uk/SiteDirectory/TTfN0708/Lists/Posts/Post.aspx?ID=21. Accessed 15/01/2009.

Zimmerman, D. and West, C. (1975) 'Sex roles, interruptions and silences in conversation', in Thorne, B. and Henley, N. [eds] *Language and Sex: Difference and Dominance*. Rowley, Massachusetts: Newbury House pp. 105-29.

Each type of source has to be **Referenced** in a **Certain Way**

1 *Published Books*

e.g. Crystal, D. (1995) *The Cambridge Encyclopedia of the English Language*. Cambridge: Cambridge University Press p. 364.

1) All the **published books** that you consulted during the course of your investigation **should be acknowledged**.
2) The correct way of doing this (in the **Harvard** system) is by giving the **name** of the author(s) first — their **surname** followed by the **first letter** of their first name (e.g. Crystal, D. above).
3) Follow the author's name with these details, in this order — **date** of publication, book **title** (in italics), the **city** it was published in and the **publisher**.
4) If you've only used a **section or certain pages** of the book, list these at the **end** of the reference (see above).
5) The bibliography should be arranged in **alphabetical order**, according to the first letter of the author's **surname**.

2 *Contributions* in *Other Books* / *Articles* in *Magazines* or *Journals*

e.g. Zimmerman, D. and West, C. (1975) 'Sex roles, interruptions and silences in conversation', in Thorne, B. and Henley, N. [eds] *Language and Sex: Difference and Dominance*. Rowley, Massachusetts: Newbury House pp. 105-29.

1) You still credit the **author and date** of the article first. Include the **title** of the article in **inverted commas**, and then the details of the **book**, **magazine** or **journal** in which it appears, in the same way as you would reference any other published book.
2) If you're referencing a magazine or journal, you'll need to include the **volume** and **issue number** (if applicable) **after the title** of the publication itself (e.g. *Journal of Applied Linguistics*, Volume 3, Number 2, pp. 422-436).
3) The general order for referencing **articles** is — **author**, **date**, **article title**, **title of journal** (italics), **volume number**, **part number**, **page numbers**. If an article appears in a published book you need to include the **publisher's details**.

3 *Websites* / *Online Resources*

e.g. Manches, A. (2008) *Language and Gender — TESOL Talk from Nottingham 07/08*. http://portal.lsri.nottingham.ac.uk/SiteDirectory/TTfN0708/Lists/Posts/Post.aspx?ID=21. Accessed 15/01/2009.

1) If you need to acknowledge a source from **the Internet**, then you have to bear in mind that this material can be **updated** and could have changed **after** you looked at it.
2) You need to give the **URL** (the website's address) so that your source can be **traced**. You can find it in the **address bar** of your web browser. If you're using a lot of websites, make sure you **keep notes** of the addresses.
3) You should reference the **entire address**, starting with *http://*, as above, and put the **date** you looked at the site.
4) On the other hand, if you've consulted a **digital version of a printed publication** (lots of journals etc. are available online), then you should reference these in the **same way** as you would if it was a printed text.

The only source I ever need is ketchup...

Why is it that there's never quite enough in those little pots you get? Why do they do that? If you're not going to provide enough ketchup, then serve fewer chips. Or, shock horror, provide more ketchup, and still serve fewer chips. You'd best learn all this stuff about referencing by the way, before I really go off on one about inverse chip-condiment correlations.

General Exam Advice

For your A2 exam, you'll need to understand and apply language frameworks, know how to analyse different types of discourse, organise your answers, write clearly and precisely, and join in on a jolly old language debate along the way. If that's all sounding a bit too much like hard work, then read these exam tips to get you started.

Make sure you know your **Language Frameworks**

Language frameworks can be thought of as **headings** to help you to **structure** your **analysis**. You need to be able to **identify them** in different kinds of texts and explain how the features are used to **create meaning**. So here they are:

> ### Language Frameworks
>
> - **Lexis** (vocabulary)
> - **Semantics** (the meanings that words convey)
> - **Grammar** (word classes, syntax and morphology)
> - **Phonology** (sounds)
> - **Pragmatics** (social conventions surrounding language use)
> - **Graphology** (the visual appearance and arrangement of the text)
> - **Discourse** (how sections of language are developed and structured)

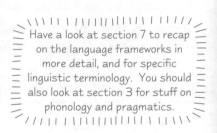
Have a look at section 7 to recap on the language frameworks in more detail, and for specific linguistic terminology. You should also look at section 3 for stuff on phonology and pragmatics.

1) You need to refer to as many of these as possible, as long as they're **appropriate**.

2) Remember to always give examples from the text to support your point, e.g. *Speaker A uses a formal 'title plus surname' address form to address speaker B: 'Mrs Biggs'.*

3) It **doesn't matter** whether you use **single** or **double quotation marks** when you're quoting from the text, as long as you're **consistent**.

4) Don't just be descriptive. You have to relate the frameworks to **purpose** and **meaning**, e.g.
The adjective 'unique' is persuasive, suggesting that the product is special.
      ↑ **purpose**   ↑ **meaning**

Think about how you're going to **Approach** the **Questions**

All of the exam questions you get will be based around **data**. You might have to write about **written texts**, **spoken material** or **tables** of **data**. When you first open the paper, think about the points on this checklist:

1) Read the **questions** so you know what kind of things to look out for in the texts. Read the texts **quickly** to get a feel for what they're about, then read them again **more carefully** and make notes.

2) The best way to prepare is to **underline key features** in the texts you're given.

3) For **written** texts, identify genre, register, likely audience and purpose.

4) For **spoken** texts, identify context, role of participants, register and pragmatics.

5) Find **examples** of the language frameworks — be selective and **link** linguistic features to purpose and meaning.

6) Look for features that **link** the texts (e.g. power, gender, occupation, technology, etc.).

Bear in mind the different **Assessment Objectives**

Assessment objectives are the **criteria** the examiners use to mark your answers.
The number of different AO marks you can get depends on the task.

AO1	You get AO1 marks for using **linguistic terminology** correctly and writing **accurately** and **effectively**.
AO2	You get AO2 marks for showing knowledge of **linguistic approaches**, and showing that you understand issues related to the construction and analysis of **meaning** in texts.
AO3	You get AO3 marks for analysing and evaluating the influence of **context** on the language used, and the **effect** the language has.
AO4	You get AO4 marks for using linguistic concepts to show **expertise** and **creativity** in your **own writing**.

General Exam Advice

Think about how to **Organise Your Answers**

These are **general guidelines** for how to best cover everything in your answers — if you're asked about something **specific**, you'll have to **tailor** what you say to the particular areas the question asks you to focus on.

Written Discourse	Spoken Discourse
Write a **couple of paragraphs** on: Genre, purpose, register, formality, likely audience.	Write a **couple of paragraphs** on: Context, content, function, participants.
Write in **more detail** about: **Lexis** (e.g. lexical fields, figurative language) **Grammar** (e.g. word classes — nouns, adverbs etc.) **Discourse structure** (e.g. beginning, development, end) **Phonology** (e.g. alliteration, assonance, repetition) **Graphology** (e.g layout, fonts, images)	Write in **more detail** about: **Non-fluency features** (e.g. pauses, false starts, fillers) **Non-verbal aspects of speech** (e.g. stress) **Pragmatics** (conversational theory) **Phonology** (e.g. pronunciation features) **Lexis**, **grammar** and **discourse structure**.

The A2 exams are **Synoptic**

1) The paper you sit for A2 is **synoptic** — it tests you on the subject as a **whole**.

2) This means that you need to **build on** what you've learnt from **AS**, to show a **broader understanding** of the subject, and recognise when it's **appropriate** to use which bits of information.

3) This is especially the case with your use of **linguistic terminology**. You'll need to be really **familiar** with **specific linguistic terms**, because you're expected to **build** on what you learnt at AS.

4) All of the questions you'll get will be based on **data**. You need to stay **focused** on this, but use it as a **springboard** for discussing **wider points** about topics you've covered in the rest of the course. For example, you might get a question where you're looking at **genre** in two texts from **different periods**. You should focus on genre, but because the texts also show evidence of **language change** over **time**, you could also bring this into your **analysis** of **lexis** and **grammar**.

Make sure you know the **Difference** between **Analysis** and **Evaluation**

1) If you're asked to **analyse** a text, you need to look at the language in **detail**. You'll have to **identify** and **explain** the **key components**.

2) You do this using the **language frameworks** — e.g. you can analyse a text **specifically** in terms of lexis or phonology, or you can do a **broader** analysis where you look at all the relevant frameworks.

3) If you're asked to **evaluate** a text or **discuss** the **issues** in it, you have to make **judgements** about it. For example, you might comment on the **ideas** that a text raises about a **language debate**, like the superiority of Standard English.

4) For a full evaluation you should analyse specific ideas in the text, using **quotations**. You should then bring in evidence to **support** these ideas, as well as **contrasting points of view**.

"Then Little Red Riding Hood addressed the wolf using the second person pronoun..."

It's **Important** to write **Clearly** and **Precisely**

The points you make need to be as **precise** as possible. There's no need to use **big words** for the sake of it, but it's really important that you use **linguistic terms** appropriately.

1) Spend a few minutes jotting down a **plan** so your answer has some **structure**. Your writing should be **fluent**, so **don't** use **bullet points** in your essay.

2) Write in **paragraphs** and make sure that each paragraph has a clear focus. For example, you might do separate paragraphs on lexis and grammar. **Short sentences** and **paragraphs** are better than long rambling ones.

3) Always use **quotations** and **examples** to **back up** your points. **Short quotations** are better than long ones, and it's good to **weave** them into sentences rather than present them as big separate chunks.

AQA A Exam

*If you're doing **AQA A**, the A2 exam is **Unit 3**, **Language Explorations**. It's possible that the information here could change, so make sure you check the details with your teacher, and read the instructions on the paper carefully on the day.*

The exam has **Two Sections**

The exam lasts **two and a half hours** and is split into **two sections**. You need to answer **one** question from **each section**. You should spend **half** an **hour** reading and preparing the sources, and an **hour** answering each question.

Section A — Language Variation and Change

1) You'll have a choice of **two questions**, each with **two** sets of **data**. The data could be written texts, transcripts of spoken language, tables of data, word lists, illustrated texts or texts representing ideas about language.

2) Your essay should **evaluate** ideas and issues around language **variation** and **change**. For example, you might have to compare the language of an 18th Century diary with a 21st Century blog.

Section B — Language Discourses

1) You only get **one question** in section B. The focus is on how **ideas** about language are **represented** and **debated** in society. You'll be given **two** passages, which are aimed at **non-expert audiences**.

2) The passages could be about **attitudes** towards different **varieties** of English, **language change**, **gender and interaction**, and **political correctness**.

3) You need to **analyse** and **evaluate** how the writers **present** their **views** on language, how these views **contribute** to language **debates**, and whether you think they're **valid**.

Here's an **Example Question** and **Answer** to give you some tips:

> 3   **Text D** is from a letter to a newspaper, written in 2009.
>   **Text E** is from Lowth's *A Short Introduction to English Grammar*, written in 1762.
> -   Analyse and evaluate the ways the two writers convey ideas about the English language.
> -   Evaluate these ideas using your knowledge of language change.
>
> *The texts you'll get in the real exam will be longer than this.*
>
> **Text D**
> As a recently retired teacher, I have seen first hand how the conventions of spelling, punctuation and grammar have, over the years, become seriously eroded. Features of 'text speak' such as phonological spelling (or should that be *fonological*?) perverse punctuation (!!!?) and gruesome grammar (*is u awright, innit?*) show language in decline, and history has shown us where language is in decline, civilisation is too!
>
> **Text E**
> The English Language hath been much cultivated in the last two hundred years. It hath been considerably polished and refined; its bounds have been greatly enlarged; its energy, variety, richness, and elegance, have been abundantly proved, by numberless trials, in verse and in prose, upon all subjects, and in every kind of style: but, whatever other improvements it may have received, it hath made no advances in Grammatical Accuracy.

The introduction isn't too long and has a good overview of the writer's opinions →

The writer of Text D expresses a negative view of text language, indicating that it has had a harmful effect on the literacy of young people. He or she uses negative adjectives such as 'perverse' and 'gruesome' to describe the features of text speak.

← *Good use of language frameworks*

This shows a prescriptivist view of language — the idea that Standard English is superior to other varieties, so it shouldn't be 'eroded'. The writer doesn't recognise that text-messaging can be seen as a kind of dialect which is appropriate to informal electronic communication. It is a form that has developed out of a need to communicate quickly and informally.

← *Challenges the writer's view, offers an alternative perspective and gives reasons for it*

Good linking word →

Similarly, the writer of Text E also takes a prescriptivist view of language. His high regard for English is shown in the use of abstract nouns such as 'elegance'. He thinks of English as something that has been nurtured (like a plant) over time, evident in his use of the past participle 'cultivated'. This text shows a number of features that are typical of the eighteenth century. Lowth uses the inflection '-th' in the third person singular form of the verb 'to have', while the writer of Text A uses Present Day English 'has'...

The quotations are well-integrated into the main body of the text →

← *Good use of language frameworks*

This answer addresses both **parts** of the question — how the writers convey their attitudes, and some evaluation of these attitudes. There are **good examples** and **well-integrated quotations**. There is good use of a range of **linguistic terms**. The candidate engages with the **prescriptivist-descriptivist debate**, arguing for the status of all varieties of language according to context. Further discussion of this is needed in response to Text E. This is only a partial answer, but the essay would get at least **36 marks** out of **45** if it kept up this standard all the way through.

AQA A Coursework

What the **Exam Board Wants**

You have to produce **two** pieces of work for the **coursework** part of the A2 exam. (You should check these details with your teacher, in case anything's changed.)

	Type of Writing	Description
Piece 1	Language Investigation (**1750-2500 words**, excluding data)	An investigation of spoken language, either spontaneous or scripted.
Piece 2	Language Intervention (**1250 words**)	One or two pieces of original writing based around a language debate.

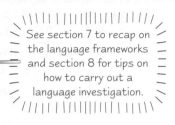
See section 7 to recap on the language frameworks and section 8 for tips on how to carry out a language investigation.

You can do **Different Types** of **Language Investigation**

You need to carry out an investigation of **spoken language**, which can be **scripted** or **spontaneous** (e.g. a transcript of a political speech or a real conversation).

There are 4 different types of investigation you could do

1) An investigation that focuses on the **language features** of a spoken discourse. For example, you might look at the grammatical features used in conversations between two close friends.

2) An investigation that focuses on the **function** or **use** of a spoken discourse. For example, you might look at the persuasive features used in political speeches.

3) An investigation that focuses on people's **attitudes** to an aspect of spoken language. For example, you might record a conversation between people from different generations about attitudes to swearing.

4) An investigation that focuses on the **user** or **speaker**. For example, you could explore how men and women talk to each other when they're given a problem to solve.

Different investigations require **Different Types** of **Data**

Your investigation should be based on **original primary data** — scripted or spontaneous speech that you've collected yourself. You'll use **different types** of primary data, depending on the focus of your investigation.

1) **Longitudinal data** — data collected over a **period of time**, e.g. recordings of conversations taken around the dinner table for a week.

2) **Comparative data** — data that has a similar **context**, **theme** or **purpose**, e.g. two dramatic monologues that discuss the idea of loneliness.

3) **Contrastive data** — data that has different **contexts**, **themes**, or **purposes**, e.g. an after-dinner speech and a recorded conversation between a group of friends.

You also need to use **secondary data** to **support** what you've found out in your **primary data**. This should show that you've done some **wider reading** about the **theories** and **attitudes** towards the **language issue** you're looking at. For example, you might use a newspaper article about the importance of teaching Standard English at school to support the attitudes that you've recorded in a conversation between teachers.

The **Language Intervention** piece should be part of a **Language Debate**

For this part you're **creating** the text rather than **analysing** it. You can write **one** or **two** texts that focus on one of the **language discourses** you've covered in **Unit 3**, e.g. attitudes towards language change.

1) You need to write something for a **non-specialist audience**, e.g. an article, an editorial or a radio script.

2) Do a bit of **research** first — e.g. if you're writing a newspaper editorial about text speak then make sure you read some editorials to find out the style of language they use. You could also research **popular ideas** about text speak, to give you some hints about what kind of things to say.

3) You need to **contribute** to a popular **debate** about language, so your writing needs to be **persuasive** — you're trying to get people to see your point of view. Remember that you're writing for a **non-specialist audience**, so don't use too many **technical terms** that might **alienate** them.

4) Concentrate on who your **audience** are, **what** you want to say, and using **appropriate techniques** to say it.

AQA B Exam

*If you're doing **AQA B**, the A2 exam is **Unit 3**, **Developing Language**. It's possible that the information here could change, so make sure you check the details with your teacher, and read the instructions on the paper carefully on the day.*

The exam has **Two Sections**

The exam lasts **two and a half hours** and is split into **two sections**. You need to answer **one** question from **each section**. You should spend **half** an **hour** reading and preparing the sources, and an **hour** answering each question.

Section A — Language Acquisition *[48 marks]*

1) You'll have a choice of **two questions**, each based on a selection of **data**. The data could be things like transcripts of spoken language, or texts written by or for children. It will be based on child language acquisition from **birth** to **eleven years old**.

2) Your answer should **analyse** the children's language development shown in the data. For example, you might analyse the language of two three-year-old children playing.

Section B — Language Change *[48 marks]*

1) For section B you also have a choice of **two questions**, each based on a selection of **data**. The data will be taken from the **Late Modern Period** (from **1700**) to the **present day**.

2) The texts will show evidence of **historical** and **contemporary change** to English, so you need to **analyse** changes in lexis, semantics, grammar, orthography and graphology.

3) You'll also have to **evaluate** what they show about **issues** like attitudes to language change, the impact of standardisation and how social and political forces can lead to language change.

Here's an **Example Question** and **Answer** to give you some tips:

3 **Text E** is from an article called *Observations in Gardening for January* which appeared in *Gentleman's Magazine* (1731).
Text F is from a website that gives gardening advice: www.allotment.org (2008).
• Describe and comment on what these texts show about language change over time.

The texts you'll get in the real exam will be longer than this.

Text E

Lop and top Trees, cut your Coppice and Hedge Rows; in open weather remove and plant Trees and Vines, lay up your Borders, uncover the Roots of Such Trees as require it, putting Soil under them, also prune Vines and Trees, nail and trim wall Fruits, cleanse Trees from Moss and Succors; gather Cions for grafts about the latter end of this month before the Bud sprouts which stick in the ground for some time, because they will take the better for being kept some time from the Tree, graft them the beginning of next month.

Text F

We all know not to plant when it's too wet or too cold, but when we have had a few good days its very difficult to resist popping in a seed or two. How can we be a little more certain whether or not it's ok to start sowing? Well one sure test is the "**baby water test**". Yes, place your elbow in the soil and if it's too cold you will soon know it. Just like baby's bath water your elbow makes a great tester to check if the soil is suitable or not. Your fingers and hands are just not suitable for either task.

Text E has some eighteenth century orthographical features, for example the capitalisation of proper nouns: 'Vines and Trees'. The syntax is complex and contains lots of subordinate clauses. Lexical change can be seen in the division of the now compound noun 'hedgerows' into two separate words: 'Hedge Rows'.

Good use of language frameworks

Identifies similarities in the texts

Both texts address the reader directly with the second person pronoun 'you'. This draws readers in and makes them more likely to take the advice. Text F also uses the plural pronoun 'we', to make readers feel included, and uses interrogatives: 'How can we be a little more certain whether or not it's ok to start sowing?'.

Makes direct contrasts between the two texts

Discusses the effect of certain language features

Text F has a less formal tone than Text E. It uses features of spoken language, for example the informal present participle 'popping'. The syntax is less complex — there are fewer subordinate clauses and sentences are shorter. It's also less authoritative than Text E — there is only one imperative ('place your elbow...') compared to numerous ones in Text E (e.g. 'nail and trim'). It's typical of the period Text E was written in that it sounds more authoritative than friendly....

This answer covers **lexis** and **grammar** well. There is effective use of **linguistic terminology**, particularly when discussing **grammar**. There's **good comparison** between the two texts. **Quotations** are used to support most points, and the examples are **well-integrated** into the main body of the answer. Some parts of the answer, e.g. the point about complex syntax, need to be **supported** by **quotations** from the text. The essay should go on to discuss other language frameworks, such as semantics and discourse structure. This is only a partial answer, but the essay would get about **39 marks** out of **48** if it kept up this standard all the way through.

AQA B Coursework

What the Exam Board Wants

You have to produce **two** pieces of work for the **coursework** part of the A2 exam. (You should check these details with your teacher, in case anything's changed.)

	Type of Writing	Description
Piece 1	Language Investigation (**1750-2500 words**, excluding data and appendices)	A topic-based study of an aspect of language.
Piece 2	Media Text (**750-1000 words**)	A piece of original writing about the topic studied in the language investigation.

See section 7 to recap on the language frameworks, and section 8 for tips on how to carry out a language investigation.

Your Language Investigation can be on Any Topic You Like

1) You can choose **any topic** for your language investigation. It could be something you've **already studied** for AS or A2, or **another topic** that you're particularly interested in (it has to be about English language though...).

2) Broad topic areas include things like **gender and representation**, **language and power**, **language and new technology**, the **language of children** and **language change**.

3) The investigation should be based on **primary data**, which could include written texts or transcripts of spoken language.

4) You also need to use **secondary data** to **support** what you've found in your **primary data**. This should show that you've done some **wider reading** about the **theories** and **attitudes** towards the **language issue** you're looking at. For example, you might use a newspaper article about the importance of teaching Standard English at school to support the attitudes that you've recorded in a conversation between teachers.

5) Your investigation should be presented as a **report**, and **structured** under these **headings**:

> **Introduction** — the aim of the study
> **Methodology** — how you carried it out
> **Analysis** — what the data tells you
> **Conclusion** — what the results showed you
> **Evaluation** — the implications of the results
> **Bibliography** — a list of secondary sources
> **Appendices** — all the primary data you used

Don't make your Topic too Broad

1) You need to give your topic some thought and **check it out** with your **teacher** before you start.

2) It's probably best to start off with a **broad** topic of study and gradually **narrow it down**. **Detailed analysis** is more important than cramming loads of different points in.

3) For example, you might start with a **broad** idea for a topic like "**language and new technology**". You could then make this more **specific** by narrowing it down to look at **text messages**. You might then decide to look at the text messages sent between two people over the course of two days. This means that your investigation will be much more **focused**.

4) Another way to make sure your investigation stays focused is to just look at **one language framework**, e.g. "**phonological** differences in the speech of men and women".

The Media Text is for a Non-specialist Audience

1) You need to write a **media text** for a **non-specialist audience**, e.g. a newspaper or magazine article, an editorial or a web page.

2) It should be **based** on the topic you studied in your **language investigation**.

3) For example, if your language investigation was about text messaging, you could write a serious newspaper article on attitudes to text speak, or a humorous magazine article on what people's texts really say about them.

4) Do a bit of **research** first, e.g. if you're writing a newspaper editorial about text speak then make sure you read some editorials to find out the style of language they use. You could also research **popular ideas** about the topic, to give you some hints about what kind of things to say. You have to include a **bibliography** with your investigation (see p. 135), so make a note of where your research came from.

5) Remember that you're writing for a **non-specialist audience**, so don't use too many **technical terms**.

Edexcel Exam

*If you're doing **Edexcel**, the exam is **Unit 3**, **Language Diversity and Children's Language Development**. This information could change, so check the details with your teacher, and read the instructions on the paper carefully.*

The exam has **Two Sections**

The exam lasts **two hours forty-five minutes** and is split into **two sections**. It's marked out of **100**.

Section A — Language Diversity

1) In this section you'll probably get two questions — **1a** and **1b**.
2) For **1a** you might have to choose two significant linguistic features of a text and analyse them. This could include **spelling**, **grammar**, **syntax**, **lexis** and **phonology**.
3) For example, you might be asked to look at a historical text and identify how two language features differ from present-day English.
4) This question will probably be worth **10 marks**.
5) For **1b** you might have to **analyse two texts**, exploring how language is used and what it says about the writer, the purpose of the text, the audience and the subject matter.
6) For example, you could be asked to look at the writing of two medical experts.
7) This question will probably be worth **40 marks**.

Section B — Children's Language Development

1) In this section you'll probably get two questions — **2a** and **2b**.
2) **Question 2a** may be made up of a number of **short questions**, where you'll have to describe some of the **key linguistic features** in one or more spoken or written texts.
3) For example, you might be asked about children's grammatical development based on a transcript of two children playing.
4) This question will probably be worth **10 marks**.
5) For **2b** you have to write a **longer answer** about **one or more** spoken or written texts.
6) For example, you might have to look at some examples of a child's writing and analyse how it develops over time.
7) This question will probably be worth **40 marks**.

Here's an **Example Question** and **Answer** to give you some tips:

The texts you'll get in the real exam might be longer than the extract here.

2 (a) (i) Identify and describe two things in Text 4 that suggest that what we might think are mistakes are really examples of the child understanding particular grammatical rules.

Text 4 — a conversation between Jake (age 3) and his dad.

Jake: dadad

Dad: all right there mate (1) where have you been

Jake: park (1) I seed a doggie

Dad: oh great (1) you saw a doggie (.) woof woof

Jake: you not doggie (.) dadad

Dad: yes I am (1) woof woof

Jake: [laugh] you silly dad

Dad: and now I'm a sheep (1) baaa (1) baaa

Jake: [laugh] I like sheeps (1) baaa baaa

The first feature that shows Jake has understood a grammatical rule is when he says 'seed'. This is an irregular verb which becomes 'saw' when it is used in the past tense. In saying 'seed' Jake has created the past tense of this irregular verb as if it were a regular verb, where the past tense is formed by adding '-ed'. This shows that he understands how the past tense is normally formed, so it's an example of what Cruttenden (1979) would call a 'virtuous error'.

Good use of linguistic terminology

Uses a theory to support the point

Jake also says 'sheeps', which shows that he understands that nouns in the plural usually take an '–s' inflection at the end. However, he over-generalises and applies this rule to an irregular plural, as the plural of 'sheep' is 'sheep'.

This is good because it gets to the point straight away, which is what you need to do in short-answer questions. The grammatical issues are **identified** and **explained** using **appropriate linguistic terms**. The answer also identifies a relevant **theorist**, which gives it more weight. The language used is **clear** and **fluent**, so this answer should get full marks in the exam (**6 out of 6**).

Edexcel Coursework

What the Exam Board Wants

You have to produce **two** pieces of work for the **coursework** part of the A2 exam. (You should check these details with your teacher, in case anything's changed.)

	Type of Writing	Description
Task 1	Article, talk or presentation **(600-750 words)**	An article, talk or presentation that explains the topic of the language investigation (below) for a non-specialist audience.
Task 2	Language Investigation **(2000-2250 words)**	A topic-based study of an aspect of language.

You have to write a **cumulative word count** at the **bottom** of each **page** of your coursework (a **running total** of how many words you've used on each page). It's **really important** that you **don't** go **over** the **word limit** — if you do then the marker will **stop marking** at the point where you reached the word limit, meaning you could **miss out** on loads of marks.

See section 7 to recap on the language frameworks and section 8 for tips on how to carry out a language investigation.

Task One is a Preparatory task

1) For **Task 1** you have to write a short **article**, **talk** or **presentation** on the topic you're investigating in Task 2.
2) You're meant to do this **before** you've done any **detailed research** into the area you're studying. The idea is to show you can **explain** the **concepts** in your investigation to a **non-specialist audience**.
3) This means that you shouldn't use too many **technical terms** that might **alienate** the audience.
4) There are **24 marks available** for this task.

Your Language Investigation can be on Any Topic You Like

1) You can choose **any topic** for your language investigation. It could be something you've **already studied** for AS or A2, or **another topic** that you're particularly interested in (it has to be about English language though...).
2) Broad topic areas include things like **gender and representation**, **language and power**, **language and new technology**, the **language of children** and **language change**. You need to pick something **specific** to study from one of these broad headings.
3) The investigation needs to be based on **primary data**, which could include written texts or transcripts of spoken language.
4) You also need to use **secondary data** to **support** what you've found in your **primary data**. This should show that you've done some **wider reading** about the **theories** and **attitudes** towards the **language issue** you're looking at. For example, you might use a newspaper article about the importance of teaching Standard English at school to support the attitudes that you've recorded in a conversation between teachers.
5) Your investigation should be presented as a **report**, so you could **structure** it under these **headings** (see section 8 for more on this):

Introduction — the aim of the study
Methodology — how you carried it out
Analysis — what the data tells you
Conclusion — what the results showed you
Evaluation — the implications of the results
Bibliography — a list of secondary sources
Appendices — all the primary data you used

There are Different Types of Language Investigation

There are **three** different kinds of investigation topic to choose from:

1) **Hypothesis based topics** — the investigation **tests** the **validity** of a **hypothesis** (an **assumption** about language), e.g. *If children of the same age but from different backgrounds show similar grammatical features in their speech, then grammatical development does not depend on input from caregivers.*
2) **Question based topics** — the investigation answers a specific question, e.g. *What are the distinctive grammatical features of the Lincolnshire dialect?*
3) **Descriptive topics** — the investigation tests a **statement** about language, e.g. *Young people's attitudes to swear words are substantially different from those of their grandparents.*

OCR Exam

*If you're doing **OCR**, the A2 exam is **Unit F653, Culture, Language and Identity**. The information here could change, so make sure you check the details with your teacher, and read the instructions on the paper carefully on the day.*

You have to answer Two Questions

The OCR paper lasts **two hours** and is split into **four sections**. You have to answer **one** question from **section A**, and then **one** question from **any** of the **other three sections**.

1) **Section A (compulsory) — Language and Speech.** In this section you'll have to **analyse** spoken or written data, and **evaluate** issues relating to spoken language (e.g. attitudes towards variation). There will be a list of **phonemic symbols** printed on the exam paper.

2) **Section B (optional) — The Language of Popular Written Texts.** You'll have to **analyse** and **evaluate** the texts provided, which might be fiction, non-fiction or media texts.

3) **Section C (optional) — Language and Cultural Production.** You'll have to **analyse** and **evaluate** the texts provided, which might be from genres such as broadcasting, advertising and cinema.

4) **Section D (optional) — Language, Power and Identity.** You'll have to **analyse** and **evaluate** the texts provided, which might be from the media, political and professional writing or PR and advertising. The texts will relate to language and identity, especially in terms of gender, class and status.

5) There is a total of **60 marks** available for the paper.

Here's an Example Question and Answer to give you some tips:

The texts you'll get in the real exam will be longer than this.

1 **Passage (a)** is an edited transcript of a 50-year-old Mathematics lecturer talking about his accent.
Passage (b) is an extract from a website that promotes Norfolk and its heritage.
By close reference to BOTH passages analyse some of the arguments raised by the authors. You should also evaluate contextual factors, like time and mode of production and, where appropriate, refer to your wider studies of this topic.

Passage (a)

I grew up in Norfolk in the 1950s (1) you'd think I'd have some sort of Norfolk accent wouldn't you (2) the reason I haven't of course is simply because I wasn't allowed to (2) my mother made us speak the Queen's English because at the time people outside Norfolk thought people who spoke with a Norfolk accent sounded funny and silly (.) a bit (.) well they thought country bumpkins didn't they (1) she thought if you wanted to get on (.) get on in life you needed to speak proper (3) so I suppose regional accents were seen as inferior (.) maybe still maybe they still are (1) but it's interesting er now that local radio has done a lot in keeping the Norfolk accent alive and giving it respectability (.) course you'd never hear a Norfolk accent on the radio in the fifties

Passage (b)

Just like the Norfolk coastline, the Norfolk dialect is under constant attack. However, it's not from the destructive effect of the North Sea but from the spread of 'estuary English'.

Norfolk's relatively isolated location has meant that Norfolk dialect has survived when many other local speech patterns have been subsumed. Yet, since the publication of *The Vocabulary of East Anglia* by the Rev. Robert Forby in 1830 many Norfolk words have undoubtedly been lost. Fortunately though, Norfolk dialect, or more accurately the Norfolk accent, is still alive and well thanks in large part to champions such as Keith Skipper who helped to found F.O.N.D. (Friends of Norfolk Dialect).

The Norfolk accent has also helped to preserve and nurture the county's unique sense of humour. In fact, the Norfolk accent lends itself perfectly to humour and particularly to that shrewd, under-stated type of rural wit.

Summarises the main points in the text →

Both texts focus on the Norfolk dialect and attitudes to it. In Passage (a) the speaker focuses on the Norfolk dialect being an obstacle to social advancement in the 1950s. This is shown by the noun phrase 'country bumpkins' — people were thought of as uneducated and unrefined if they didn't speak Standard English. He states that regional accents were 'inferior', because the 'Queen's English' (RP) carried the most prestige. He speculates that this is 'maybe' still the case. However, Workman (2008) studied people's perception of different accents and found that Yorkshire accents were rated the most intelligent. This suggests that the 'Queen's English' isn't the most prestigious accent anymore.

← *Refers to relevant research to evaluate the text*

Uses own knowledge of wider issues →

Over the last 100 years or so, regional dialects have become diluted, partly because of the influence of TV and radio. This is called dialect levelling. However, the speaker here argues that local radio has actually helped to revive the Norfolk accent and increase its prestige.

Good linking sentence →

Passage (b), in contrast, sees the Norfolk accent as still under threat. This is indicated by the use of the noun 'attack', while those who defend the Norfolk dialect are described as 'champions'. It argues that the threat comes from 'estuary English' — a relatively new accent which combines features of RP and features of cockney. This is thought to be a shame because of the association of the Norfolk accent with humour. This shows a contrast with Passage (a), which sees the association with humour as something that has been used in a negative way — people with a Norfolk accent 'sounded funny and silly'.

← *Uses quotes from the text to support a point*

This answer refers to **wider research** to **evaluate** the attitudes in the texts, and shows **wider knowledge** of **issues** relating to accent and dialect. It also **compares** and **contrasts** the two passages well, and shows good use of **linguistic terminology**. To get higher marks it should discuss **contextual factors** in more detail. This is only a partial answer, but the essay would get about **23 marks** out of **30** if it kept up this standard all the way through.

OCR Coursework

What the Exam Board Wants

You have to produce **two** pieces of work for the **coursework** part of the A2 exam. (You should check these details with your teacher, in case anything's changed.)

	Type of Writing	Description
Task 1	Independent Investigation (**20 marks**)	A comparison and analysis of three media texts from the three different modes (spoken, written and multimodal).
Task 2	Original Writing and Commentary (**20 marks**)	A piece of original media writing in one of the three modes. A discussion of the linguistic features in the original writing.

You should **include** the **three texts** you're comparing for the language investigation in your coursework folder.

You have to Compare Three Texts for the Language Investigation

1) For this task you have to **compare** and **analyse three media texts** — one from the **spoken mode**, one from the **written mode** and one **multimodal** text. You should try to have a mixture of **traditional** media texts, e.g. a newspaper article, and ones from **developing** media like the internet.

2) The texts should be **linked** by a **common theme**. For example, you could compare a transcript of a radio discussion, an editorial from a tabloid newspaper and an informal blog, where the **linking theme** was *Knife crime in the UK*.

3) You need to compare and contrast the language in each text, using the language frameworks — **lexis**, **semantics**, **grammar**, **phonology**, **pragmatics**, **graphology** and **discourse**.

4) You also need to think about the **purpose** and **audience** of each text, and its **social** and **cultural context**.

5) For example, the main purpose of the tabloid newspaper editorial will be to persuade, and it will have a mostly working-class audience. It will probably have appeared in **response** to a **social context** where knife crime is said to be increasing.

6) If appropriate, you should look at some **secondary sources**, e.g. other linguistic research.

7) You should write up your coursework as an **essay**.

Your Original Writing has to be a Media Text

1) For the **original writing** task you have to write a **media text** for a **specific audience**, **purpose** and **context**.

2) It can be a **spoken**, **written** or **multimodal text**.

3) Possible types of **media text** include articles for newspapers or magazines, editorials, scripts for TV or radio, adverts and electronic texts (e.g. websites or blogs).

You have to write a Commentary about your Original Writing

The commentary is where you get the chance to **explain** the language choices you made in your **original writing**.

1) The commentary shows the examiner that you knew what you were doing in the **writing process**, and that you thought about the effect that your **language choices** would have on the piece of writing you produced.

2) You should analyse your language choices using the **language frameworks** that you'd use for any other text. For example, you might analyse your grammatical choices like this: *I used modals and adverbs to create a sense of urgency: 'You must do something now!'*.

3) Your commentary should explain how your language choices in your coursework are **appropriate** for the genre, mode, purpose, audience and subject matter of your text. For example: *I made the text typical of the genre of editorial writing by using the first person pronoun 'I' and addressing the reader directly.*

4) You'll also need to **evaluate** how effective your writing is. For example: *This technique is successful because it engages the readers from the start, and asks them to question their own beliefs.*

> With commentaries, there are **two** important things to remember:
> 1) **Support** every point you make with **examples**.
> 2) For every linguistic choice you discuss, say what **effect** it has on the audience and **how** it does this.

WJEC Exam

*If you're doing **WJEC**, the A2 exam is **LG4**, **Analysing and Evaluating Language Modes and Contexts**. The information here could change, so check the details with your teacher, and read the instructions on the paper carefully on the day.*

The exam has **Two Sections**

The WJEC paper lasts **two and a half hours** and is split into **two sections**. You need to answer **all** the **questions**.

Section A — Analysis of Spoken Language *[40 marks]*

1) In this section you'll get **more than one** spoken language text.

2) You need to **analyse**, **discuss**, **compare** and **evaluate** the language of the texts in your essay. For example, you might be asked to discuss the language of interviews or political speeches.

Section B — Analysis of Written Language Over Time *[40 marks]*

1) In this section you'll be given **more than one** text from **different periods** of time. The texts will probably be from the **same genre**.

2) You need to **analyse**, **compare** and **evaluate** the texts in terms of the impact of **time** and **context** on the type of language used.

Here's an **Example Question** and **Answer** to give you some tips:

The texts you'll get in the real exam will be longer than this.

> **B** **Text A** is from *The Life of Samuel Johnson* by James Boswell — 1791.
> **Text B** is from *The Life of John Clare* by Frederick Martin — 1865.
> Analyse and compare the use of language in Texts A and B as examples of biographical writing from two different periods. In your answer you should consider the different concerns of the writers, the way they use the biography form, and the influence of context on their use of language.

Text A

One night when Beauclerk and Langton had supped at a tavern in London, and sat till about three in the morning, it came into their heads to go and knock up Johnson, and see if they could prevail on him to join them in a ramble. They rapped violently at the door of his chambers in the Temple, till at last he appeared in his shirt, with his little black wig on the top of his head, instead of a nightcap, and a poker in his hand, imagining, probably, that some ruffians were coming to attack him. When he discovered who they were, and was told their errand, he smiled, and with great good humour agreed to their proposal: 'What, is it you, you dogs! I'll have a frisk with you.' He was soon drest, and they sallied forth together into Covent-Garden, where the greengrocers and fruiterers were beginning to arrange their hampers, just come in from the country.

Text B

When the spring came, Clare had gathered sufficient strength to be able to leave the house. But he now, to the infinite surprise of his family, refused to leave it. He seemed to have lost, all at once, his old love for flowers, sunshine, and green trees, and kept sitting in his little study, silently writing verses, or poring over his books. In vain his children begged him to go with them into the smiling fields, spread out temptingly on all sides around their pretty cottage. He went, now and then, as far as the garden; but quickly returned, sitting down again to his books and papers. Some theological works in his collection, which had been presented to him years ago, but at which he had scarcely ever looked before, now chiefly engrossed his attention.

Good use of language frameworks →

Text A is typical of a biography because it is written in the third person. The episode is humorous, partly because of the way Johnson is described: 'black wig on the top of his head, instead of a nightcap'. There are quite a few examples of archaic lexis seen in nouns such as 'tavern' and 'chambers', and in verbs such as 'supped'. There are also examples of archaic spelling in the formation of the past tense — 'drest' takes a '-t' inflection as opposed to the present day '-ed'. In contrast, the language of Text B is closer to present-day English in both its lexis and spelling.

← *Uses examples to support points*

← *Needs to include some examples here*

Shows awareness of the different contexts →

The setting of Text B is rural compared to the city setting of Text A. Consequently, there is a lexical field we would associate with country life in nouns such as 'flowers', 'trees', 'fields', and 'garden'. The other lexical field concerns books and reading, particularly poetry and religious works. The passive voice is used to show how Clare has lost his energy — the 'theological works...now chiefly engrossed his attention'. This is a contrast with the active voice in Text A, which shows Johnson's enthusiasm for going out: 'I'll have a frisk with you'.

← *Good use of language frameworks*

This answer has some good **detailed analysis**, especially of **lexis** and **grammar**. It **compares** and **contrasts** the texts well in terms of **linguistic features** and **context**. It also discusses the **effect** of these **linguistic features** well. However, some of the points need to be **supported** by **quotations** to get more marks. This is only a partial answer, but the essay would get about **32 marks** out of **40** if it kept up this standard all the way through.

WJEC Coursework

What the Exam Board Wants

You have to produce **two** pieces of work for the **coursework** part of the A2 exam. (You should check these details with your teacher, in case anything's changed.)

	Type of Writing	Description
Task 1	Language Investigation (**1500 words**, excluding appendices)	A topic-based study of an aspect of language.
Task 2	• Writing for Specific Purposes (**800-1000 words**) • Analysis (**500 words**)	• A piece of functional writing in a specific genre. • A discussion of the linguistic features in the original writing.

See section 7 to recap on the language frameworks and section 8 for tips on how to carry out a language investigation.

You can Choose the Topic of your Language Investigation

You should choose the **topic** of your language investigation from this list:

- Language acquisition
- Accent and / or dialect
- Attitudes towards an area of language
- Language and gender
- Language from the past (language change)
- Black English or Ebonics

- Language and political power
- The language of parliamentary debate
- Political correctness
- Spelling reform
- Other 'Englishes'
- American and British English

1) Your investigation will probably be based on **primary data**, e.g. written texts or transcripts of spoken language. This won't be added to the word count and doesn't have to be sent in with the rest of your coursework.

2) You could also use **secondary data** to **support** what you've found in your **primary data**. This should show that you've done some **wider reading** about the **theories** and **attitudes** towards the **language issue** you're looking at. For example, you might use a newspaper article about the importance of teaching Standard English at school to support the attitudes that you've recorded in a conversation between teachers.

3) See **section 8** for information on how to **structure** your **write-up**.

For Task Two you decide the Genre and Target Audience

1) For this task you have to write a text with a **specific function** in a **specific genre**. This means you'll need to have a thorough knowledge of the **genre** you'll be writing in.

2) You also need to think about the **target audience** of the text.

3) There are lots of **possibilities** for what you could write, e.g. travel writing, diary entries, newspaper reports, sports writing, biography or autobiography, guides, magazine articles, speeches, reviews or obituaries.

4) However, you **can't** write **narrative fiction**, **dramatic monologues** or **scripts**.

5) You should also **avoid** writing about **yourself**, even if you're doing an autobiography or diary. Instead, base your text on **someone else**, e.g. a famous person or historical figure (if it's appropriate to the genre).

You have to write an Analysis for Task Two

1) The analysis shows the examiner that you knew what you were doing in the **writing process**, and that you thought about the effect that your **language choices** would have on the piece of writing you produced.

2) You should analyse your language choices using the **language frameworks** that you'd use for any other text. For example, you might analyse your grammatical choices like this: *I used modals and adverbs to create a sense of urgency: 'You must do something now!'*.

3) Your analysis should explain how your language choices in your coursework are **appropriate** for the genre, mode, purpose, audience and subject matter of your text. For example: *I made the text typical of the genre of editorial writing by using the first person pronoun 'I' and addressing the reader directly.*

4) You'll also need to **evaluate** how effective your writing is. For example: *This technique is successful because it engages the readers from the start, and asks them to question their own beliefs.*

Answers to Exam Questions

This answer section gives you some tips about what to include when you have a go at the sample exam questions at the end of sections 1 to 6. We haven't written complete essays (everyone writes essays differently), but these points are suggestions for the things you should think about including in your answers.

Section 1 — Language Change

Page 26-29

1   The question asks you to analyse both texts in terms of what they show about the changes in written language over time. Here are some points you could make in your answer:

Text A — from *The First Book of Manners*

- The syntax in this text is quite complex, which is typical of English from the Victorian period. It contains a lot of subordinate clauses: *should it be your duty, perform it reverently, with a due feeling of devotion*. The opening sentence appears archaic to a modern reader because it begins with a subordinate clause and is in the passive: *When the hour for meals draws nigh*. However, because this was written for children, the language isn't as complex as a text written for adults from the same period. Most of the clauses are quite straightforward, even though the sentences are long: *You will find the knife and spoon at your right hand*.

- The lexis is also formal compared with Present Day English. It contains more Latinate words than text B, e.g. *ascribed*, *unmannerly*. There is also nineteenth century spelling, e.g. *Shew* (in modern texts it would be *show*) and *unfrequently* (instead of *infrequently*).

- The text is quite heavily punctuated and semi-colons are frequently used, whereas in more modern texts they are quite unusual, e.g. the writer uses one in *shew no unbecoming haste to sit down; but take your place*. Placing a semi-colon before a coordinating conjunction is rare in modern texts.

- By addressing the reader directly using the second person pronoun *you* and possessive pronoun *your*, the writer creates a sense of a formal lecture. It's as if the reader is being directly spoken to by the writer. If it had been in the third person then the writer would seem more detached.

- The writer assumes the role of an expert, using imperatives like *Sit upright* to instruct the reader. He is very prescriptive about the way the reader should act, for example, the use of the modal verb *will* in *You will find the knife and spoon* creates an authoritative and definite tone.

- The text aims to educate the reader about a strict hierarchy —there is a *head of the family* or *clergyman* in charge, and the *youngest present* is expected to perform their duties *reverently*.

Text B — from a website for parents

- This text is an extract from a twentieth century website giving advice to parents about how to get their children to conduct themselves at mealtimes.

- As in text A the writer addresses the reader directly using *you* and *your*: *Find out which rules work for you*. They also use imperatives like *serve*, *give*, and *assure* to come across as knowledgeable and authoritative.

- The writer uses direct statements to persuade the reader into accepting a shared understanding of proper behaviour (*No one wants to see what's in their mouths*).

- The lexis in text B is not as formal as it is in the nineteenth century text (it includes informal terms like *kids* and adjectives like *crazy*) and includes exclamatory sentences: *piling a plate with a mountain of food is a recipe for frustrations!*). This is intended to show the process as having an element of entertainment and fun about it, as well as making it seem like the writer is using the voice of experience. The text contains metaphor (*ravenous monsters*), which makes it more entertaining and informal. This effect is emphasised by the use of phonological features, e.g. assonance in *Chow Down* and alliteration in *Chew and Chat*.

- The sentences in the text are of varying complexity. The writer uses conditional clauses to pre-empt how the children in question might behave, e.g. *If they need to remove something from their mouth*, which also suggests they've experienced the same thing. It puts them at the same level as the reader, rather than dictating strict rules like the author of text A.

- The punctuation of the text reflects the lack of semi-colons in modern written English compared to the Victorian English in text A. The writer in text B uses commas, full stops and colons.

- Rather than being in linked paragraphs like text A, this text is broken down into sections with individual headings, and uses bullet points to make lists. This is intended to make it easier for the reader to digest the information as it's in smaller, manageable blocks.

2   This question also asks you to comment on how the language in each of the texts reflects the development of language over time. Here are a few things you could discuss in your answer:

Text C — a letter by Byron (1819)

- Text C has a very personal, intimate tone, and includes terms of endearment like *My love*, and *dearest Teresa*, suggesting that the purpose of the letter is to convey Byron's affection.

- The personal nature of the text is intensified by the frequent use of the personal pronouns *I*, *me* and *you*. They show the reflective nature of the letter, as it's all about Teresa or them as a couple.

- The letter mainly uses the simple present tense, which also intensifies the sentiments contained in it. There is a sense of immediacy to Byron's writing, e.g. *I feel, I love, I wish that*. This makes the reader feel as if they're being spoken to directly.

- There isn't much archaic lexis in the letter, other than the use of *hereafter*, which is a compound that isn't often used in English any more. The lexis is occasionally complex, e.g. *comprised*, *cease*, but is generally the same as you would expect from any letter

Answers to Exam Questions

written in Standard English for a known audience.

- However one common feature of older texts is that they have quite complicated syntax, making them seem much more formal than modern texts. For example, this letter contains several coordinate or subordinate clauses in one sentence, e.g. the sentence that begins *But you will recognise....*

- Byron also uses a shorter sentence to conclude the letter and some shorter clauses towards the end of it. The final sentence begins with an imperative / instruction *Think of me*, which has a very direct impact and ensures the letter stays in the reader's mind.

Text D — a letter from 2009

- This text seems less emotive than text C, despite also having a very personal tone. It's similar to text C in that it also uses the second person pronoun *you* to directly address the reader.

- The letter is in a different style from text C. It engages with the reader in a familiar, conversational manner without any of the wild or intense declarations of love or feelings that mark Byron's letter.

- The lexis is not quite as formal as Byron's, and has some quite informal turns of phrase like the noun phrase *right wuss* (using *right* as an intensifying adjective), and the colloquial verb phrase *stuck in to*. A lot of the lexis is in the lexical field of travel, e.g. adjectives like *jetlagged*. This shows the impact of technology on Present Day English, as this word wouldn't have been available to Byron in the early nineteenth century.

- The writing is conversational and regularly self-referential (e.g. *yes, that's me talking*). It maintains its informal style with contractions like *I've, I'm, can't* and *till*. This marks it out as a Present Day English text, as contractions were used much less in the nineteenth century. It also contains ellipsis: *will write again soon*.

- Text D is similar to text C in its ending — the writer also uses imperatives to make the sentiments more direct (*Give my love, tell them I'm fine*).

3   This question asks you to evaluate the ideas contained in the two texts using your knowledge of language change. Here are some points you could pick out to talk about in your answer:

Text E — from the Preface to Johnson's Dictionary

- Johnson's ideas about language change were based upon the fact that he thought English needed to be recorded, regulated and controlled. He recognises how important the role of language was in the *cultivation* of literature, but then says that as the language grew it became *neglected* and corrupted by people not using it properly (*ignorance*), and the unpredictable ways that people created new phrases (*caprices of innovation*).

- This shows that Johnson was a prescriptivist — his aim was to create an *established principle* by which words or phrases used in English could be *rejected or received*. This shows how he aimed to document the English language so that it could be widely used and learnt.

- Johnson recognises that there's a difference between distinguishing the *irregularities that are inherent* in English from the features that have come about through *ignorance or negligence*. This shows some agreement with text F, as there's an acceptance that languages always change and will never be completely consistent,

- However, text E differs from text F because Johnson makes value judgements about which features are *improprieties* and *absurdities* that he feels it is his *duty... to correct or proscribe*.

- The language of this text is typical of eighteenth century English. The sentences are long and the syntax is complex — there are lots of subordinate clauses separated by commas and semi-colons. The lexis is formal and there are a lot of Latinate words, e.g. *perplexity, tyranny*. There is also some archaic spelling, e.g. *energetick*.

Text F — from *The language web*, by Jean Aitchison

- In contrast to Johnson, Aitchison is in favour of describing linguistic change, rather than trying to regulate it. She states that *Naturally, language changes all the time*, and contrasts this descriptive approach with the more extreme attitude that change represents *decay*.

- Aitchison makes her feelings about the linguists who identify aspects of language as *deformed or bad* pretty clear, comparing them with out of touch *cranks who argue that the world is flat*. This suggests that she thinks prescriptivism is archaic compared to the descriptive approach of the majority of modern linguists.

- She attributes the concerns other people have about language change being a bad thing to *traditional* feelings, and says it's a stage that each new generation seems to pass through as they become worried about protecting the conventions of language that they learned as they grew up.

- Aitchison also highlights how the notion of *correct* English was often related to how the members of the *upper- and middle-class* would speak, as well as the influence of Latin. She mentions how Latin was prestigious at the time of the first prescriptivists, due to its fixed grammar. There is evidence for this view in text E — Johnson talks about *writers of classical reputation or acknowledged authority*, showing how the idea behind prescriptive attitudes was to copy what was seen as a rigid model of language that guaranteed prestige.

- Aitchison's language is generally quite informal, and she tries to balance both sides of the argument by giving the history and motivations behind prescriptive views. However she disagrees with them through direct statements like '*correct English*' was as hard to define then as it is now, and by asking rhetorical questions, e.g. *Is our language really changing for the worse, as some people argue?*

4   This question asks you to think about language and context, and how the context surrounding the texts might have affected the way that the ideas in them were communicated.

Answers to Exam Questions

Here are a few points you could think about when writing your answer:

Text G — from a blog written by an American man

- The context of this text affects the language used because blogs can be very personal. They're written as if the writer is speaking to the reader in person. This means that the writing style is often informal, and not bound by the spelling and grammar rules of more formal written texts.

- The writer uses non-standard punctuation and orthography, e.g. multiple exclamation marks and capital letters for emphasis: *GET THE HELL OFF OF HER!!!!!* There is also non-standard phonetic spelling, e.g. *cuz* for *because* and *watchin*.

- The writer uses double negatives e.g. *I'm no hero or nothing*, and often starts sentences with the conjunction *and* or linking adverbs like *well* or *anyway*. He also uses colloquial words and phrases, e.g. *real shaken up*. This makes the text seem informal and more like the writer is engaged in spoken discourse with the reader, which reflects the perception that you don't have to adhere to standard rules in the context of blogging.

- This text is also affected by its geographical context. The writer is American, so the text includes American lexical and grammatical variations. For example, it includes standard American words like *groceries* and *sidewalk*, as well as American colloquialisms like *dude*, *goofing around* and *I had no clue* (as opposed to Standard English *I hadn't got a clue*).

- The use of the historical present tense to report something that happened in the past is typical of informal American speech: *next thing I know I've grabbed him and pulled him off her*. It also adds to the drama of the piece by making the action seem more immediate.

- The writer engages the reader by using a very personal tone. He uses personal pronouns like *I* and *you* and asks rhetorical tag questions: *Nothing so weird in that right?* Including *right* at the end of the question makes the reader engage further with the text as they are encouraged to form an opinion about what the author's saying and put themselves in his position.

Text H — from a story written by a pupil of Caribbean descent

- Because of the speaker's descent, the text includes lots of words from Afro-Caribbean English, like *spar* (friend), *donsi* (money), the *wicked* (police) and *yard* (home).

- The syntax is also non-standard. This is best shown by the third person plural pronoun *dem*, as in *me and my spars dem was coming*.

- Singular verb forms are used instead of plural e.g. *dem was coming* instead of *were coming*.

- The writer also uses double negatives e.g. *we didn't have no donsi* (we didn't have any money).

- There are lots of examples of phonetic spelling, e.g.

manin, de/dem/den, ting, mout, pon and *wid*.

- The writer uses the kind of informal sociolect that people use when they're talking to friends. The writer shows awareness of different types of speech by recording the police officer's speech in Standard English: *Save all that until we get to the station*. This technique highlights the social differences between the police and the other characters, and makes the police officer seem like a stuffy authority figure.

Section 2 — Language in Social Contexts
Pages 46-49

1   The question asks you to analyse and compare the use of language in the four texts, how the texts portray attitudes towards accent and dialect, and how the language choices convey these attitudes. Here are some points you could think about covering in your answer:

Text A — extract from *Sons and Lovers*

- This is an extract from a novel, so it's important to look at how the author has used accent or dialect features to tell the reader more about the characters in the text.

- Morel and his wife speak differently. He speaks in a broad regional accent and uses regional dialect: *nowt b'r a lousy hae'f-crown*. His wife, on the other hand, speaks in Standard English with no noticeable accent. This contrast suggests that they're from different social backgrounds, and perhaps that he's more working-class than she is. It could also be intended to highlight the fact that he's drunk and she's sober.

- You could argue that Lawrence shows some of the negative stereotypes attached to regional variation — that it suggests people are lower class, and that they are not 'properly' educated. Lawrence has even used it in conjunction with Morel being under the influence of alcohol, opposing it to his sober wife speaking in Standard English. He uses accent to make a distinction between 'correct' and 'incorrect' behaviour.

- However, Lawrence also acknowledges some of the more positive perceptions of regional variations — Morel's *voice went tender* as he told his wife about what he'd brought for her and their children. This reflects the other kind of attitude towards regional accents and dialects, that they're representative of down-to-earth, caring people, who are good-natured and generous. You can also see this attitude reflected in Morel's enthusiasm (*he chattered on*) and in how pleased he is to tell his story.

Text B — from *Twelfth Night*

- The short quote from Shakespeare refers to a *swaggering accent*, suggesting that an extra confidence or sense of identity can be achieved by the use of an accent or variation.

- The text has a very positive attitude to this — as a whole it suggests that swearing in a *swaggering* accent denotes his toughness and masculinity. This shows how people can gain covert prestige by using non-standard forms.

Answers to Exam Questions

- However, *sharply twanged off* swearing does not seem to be appropriate for polite or formal conversation. Shakespeare aligns it with an accent and therefore associates swearing with a less standard aspect of the English language.

Text C — extracts from a blog on English in schools

- The first reply is careful to make the distinction between written and spoken English, suggesting that spoken English has *fluidity*, but that a standard variety must be taught in schools so that students can use formal written language: *imagine writing a letter to the bank in your dialect — ridiculous.*

- A source like this might enable you to talk about some research or theory in this area. You could mention John Honey (1997) and the fact that he thinks Standard English should be taught in schools so all the children have equal opportunities. Standard English is still the most prestigious form of English, so children could be discriminated against, e.g. by employers, if they weren't taught how to use it. This view is reflected in the comments by 'lyssy20' and 'i_love_lamp', who argue that it would put some children at a disadvantage if teachers weren't consistent: *Teaching a standard variety of a language ensures that everyone is learning the same thing.*

- Only the third poster voices concerns about children struggling in school if they are forced to learn a variety of English outside their own regional variation: *Why should he be corrected all the time just because his teacher thinks he is wrong?* You could mention Milroy and Milroy's (1985) argument that Standard English is no more 'valuable' than other varieties, so children shouldn't be discouraged from using non-standard forms. They also argued that because regional dialects are linked to social class, it's often working-class children who are put at an immediate disadvantage because they're told that the language they use is wrong.

Text D — a conversation between two friends

- This is an informal conversation between friends, so the language is colloquial and they overlap each other a lot: *total rubbish man.* The speakers use dialect words and non-standard grammar, which is typical of informal speech, e.g. speaker S misses the *-ly* suffix off the end of the adverb *properly.* The variety of English they use suggests that they're from the Newcastle area, e.g. they use *gan* as the past participle of the verb *to go*, and address each other as *man.*

- The language that speaker S uses changes according to the context of his conversation. What speaker R describes as a *phone voice* is speaker S adopting a more standard variety of English that he feels is appropriate for phone conversations, which tend to be more formal than face-to-face dialogue. He uses formulaic conversational markers, e.g. he answers the phone by saying *hello.* He also uses more formal politeness strategies than in the face-to-face conversation, his lexis becomes more formal and the grammar is more

standard: *she's not here at the moment I'm afraid*, compared with *soz mate*. This shows that the speaker is seeking overt prestige — he believes the best way to come across well on the phone is to use a more standard form of English.

- Speaker R mocks speaker S for sounding *well posh* on the phone, showing that he associates Standard English with being overly formal. There's a sense that speaker R feels that speaker S is putting on an act. This shows that he seeks covert prestige — he asserts his identity by using non-standard forms, which gives the impression that he doesn't care about talking *proper*.

2 The question asks you to analyse the use of language in texts concerning gender and relationships. Here are some points you could make in your answer:

Text A — Extract from *The Yellow Wallpaper*

- The attitudes towards gender roles portrayed in this extract are the result of its historical context. The narrator comes across as dutifully obeying the men who are involved in her domestic life and refusing to question them out loud or in public: *If a physician of high standing, and one's own husband, assures friends and relatives that there is really nothing the matter with one... what is one to do?* This shows how the narrator feels oppressed by her husband and brother.

- The repetition of rhetorial questions like *And what can one do?* highlights the social context in which she's writing — readers at the time would know that there was no answer to this question, which is why it's rhetorical. There's no solution to her problem because she has a lower status than the men. The use of the third person pronoun *one*, rather than the first person pronoun *I*, emphasises the fact that this is a universal situation that many married women faced at the time.

- The narrator seems aware of her lack of control over her situation, and uses writing as her only outlet: *this is dead paper and a great relief to my mind.* The fact that she can't express these feelings to her husband suggests that she's afraid of being met with *opposition* from him, and knows that she won't be listened to. She also uses sarcasm to express her bitterness about the situation: *John laughs at me, of course, but one expects that in marriage.*

- The narrator's helplessness and lack of control over her own condition is shown in the fact that she isn't made fully aware of the treatments she's given: *So I take phosphates or phosphites — whichever it is.* This factual information, that she doesn't seem to really understand or care about, is juxtaposed with sentences that begin with the adverb *Personally*, and describe how she would like to deal with her condition. This emphasises the contrast between her husband's outlook, which is *practical in the extreme* and concerned with things that can be *put down in figures*, and her own feelings about how she should be treated, which she isn't allowed to express.

Answers to Exam Questions

Text B — extract from a humorous magazine feature

- The main purpose of this text is to be entertaining and humorous, so you should look at how the language achieves this by playing on popular sexist stereotypes or preconceptions that are often portrayed in the media.

- The text pokes fun at the stereotypes held by each gender about the other — mainly that (first of all) men's speech seems to be based around saying one thing to achieve a different goal. According to the text, even when they appear to be offering support or interest (e.g. *Your hair looks really nice* or *That one looks really nice*) they are instead trying to gloss over something or influence the behaviour of the person they're with.

- The portrayal of female language is slightly different — it is mainly based on opposites, (e.g. *I don't mind* meaning *I do mind*), conforming to the stereotype that female language is difficult to understand because women rarely say what they mean.

- You could apply this selection of 'translations' to wider attitudes about relationships — that men are often quite non-committal and try to escape responsibility (*can we take your car?*), whilst women can be unreasonable and difficult to understand.

- You could also bring in research into language and gender here. For example, Tannen's (1990) difference model suggested it was men who didn't mind conflict whilst women were more likely to talk less and agree more with men. However, the language patterns portrayed here loosely (as they are meant to be exaggerated and humorous) suggest that it is the men who would prefer to avoid conflict and *watch the football with my mates*, while women are not always inclined to seek compromises.

Text C — conversation between friends

- There are aspects of interaction in this extract that support widespread stereotypes about male and female conversation. For example, the male and female speakers seem to form two separate 'teams', where the female speakers support each other and disagree with the male speakers, and vice versa: *yeah right be quiet Chris (1)good on you Kate*.

- Some of the speech in this interaction supports Zimmerman and West's (1975) dominance model, which states that men interrupt more than women, and are especially likely to interrupt when a woman is speaking. For example, speaker 1F is interrupted by 1M and doesn't finish her utterance: *we've only been here...* However, there are also instances in the conversation when the women interrupt the men, and interrupt each other, showing how this model might not be completely accurate.

- There are examples that support Tannen's (1990) difference model as well, as the female speakers offer support to other speakers in the conversation, e.g. *good on you Kate*. However, there are also instances when the male speakers do this, e.g. *unlucky mate*. This

suggests that 'male' conversation is just as much about support as it is about dominance or one-upmanship.

- The text also supports Lakoff's (1975) theory about male and female speech, as 2F is hesitant when she thinks she hasn't got the right food. Her hedging and non-verbal fillers (*um, er*) are aimed at avoiding a confrontation, while one of the male speakers is more direct and aims to find a solution to the problem at the risk of conflict: *I think this is wrong can you change it.*

- Some aspects of the conversation don't support Tannen and Lakoff's ideas — rather than talking less and agreeing more, the female speakers contribute more to the conversation and take an equal role in controlling and maintaining the exchanges. For example, 1F interrupts 2F to say *no I think you should get the right [food]*, showing that it's not just male speakers who interrupt or speak directly.

Section 3 — Analysing Spoken Language
Pages 62-63

1   The question asks you to analyse and compare the use of language in the texts, in relation to confrontation, pace and standard or non-standard English. Here are some points you could include in your answer:

Text A — a manager confronts an employee

- In text A, the manager uses an aggressive approach to get their point across. They use prosody to stress adverbs like *precisely* and *really* to emphasise their point. The employee reacts to this aggression by asking the manager direct questions: *are you threatening me.*

- There are very few pauses in this dialogue, which show that the speakers are speaking quickly and suggests that they're both angry. There's a lot of interruption and overlap, which shows that the speakers are trying to exert power over each other.

- The language is typical of colloquial speech — it contains mostly standard forms with some informal phrases, e.g. *going off home* and *decking you.*

- The language of both speakers contains fillers and non-fluency features such as back-tracking and repetition, which are common in spontaneous interaction, e.g. *like* and *you think (.) you (.) right basically you need to pull your socks up*. However, their speech is more fluent and contains fewer fillers than in text B, which suggests that the speakers in text A aren't thinking about what they're saying as much.

Text B — a manager and an employee have a discussion

- The manager in text B is more hesitant and reluctant to confront the other employee than the manager in text A. The dialogue is more disjointed than in text A. This is mostly because of the long pauses, which suggest that the manager is hesitating and thinking about what to say. Their speech contains more fillers and non-fluency features like false starts, e.g. *(2) right (.) okay Josh well basically (.) basically.* This suggests to the other

Answers to Exam Questions

speaker that the manager doesn't feel completely in control and is uncomfortable with dominating the conversation. The manager also hedges to try and soften the criticism, e.g. *that's all I'm saying*.

- The employee, on the other hand, seems less reluctant to exert power, e.g. by interrupting: *so they've gone behind my back*. Both employees in text A and B directly question the managers in an accusatory fashion, e.g. *sorry what's not acceptable* and *what's wrong with it*.

- The manager's language is more formal and contains more standard forms than the other speakers' language in texts A and B. This suggests that the context is quite formal and the manager is trying to be professional. It fits in with the use of occupational sociolect such as *output* and *review*. The employee uses more informal lexis, which suggests that they're not taking the situation as seriously and aim to gain covert prestige, e.g. *cool*.

Text C — a conversation between a motorist and a traffic warden

- In contrast to the other sources, in which the participants know each other, text C is an exchange between strangers. The traffic warden tries to remain polite and professional and keeps to formal standard language, always addressing the motorist as *sir* — a formal politeness strategy. This is similar to the manager's language in text B — blunt statements are preceded by phrases that are actually superfluous to the meaning of the statement, to soften their impact e.g. *I've called you in today* and *the thing is*.

- The motorist's language is less formal — he uses colloquialisms such as the verbs *popped* and *snooping*. He also addresses the traffic warden as *mate*, which could be used to try and create a friendly bond between them. However, because the traffic warden has already addressed the motorist as *sir*, this creates an imbalance in the formality of address terms used. It shows that the motorist aims to assert his dominance over the other speaker by addressing him as if he has a lower social status. This technique is also used by the manager in text A to show that he's in control and not taking the employee's threats seriously: *very scary mate*.

- The motorist's language shows typical conversational features such as ellipsis: *Knew you'd see sense*. This type of phrase also gives him power in the conversation — it doesn't contain any features that invite a response, so it's uttered to suggest that the speakers have reached an agreement and signal closure to the conversation.

Section 4 — Analysing Written Language

Pages 72-73

The question asks you to analyse the linguistic devices in the texts, and the effect of their social and historical contexts. Here are some points you could make in your answer:

Text A — extract from *The Adventures of Sherlock Holmes*

- Texts A and B were written about 100 years apart, so text A contains more archaic lexis, e.g. archaic colloquialisms like *capital* and *rather*. The lexis is also quite formal and more complex than in text B — it contains more Latinate vocabulary, e.g. *deduce* and *endeavouring*.

- There is more figurative language in text A than in text B, e.g. Holmes describes Germans as being *uncourteous* to their *verbs*. This is typical of the time in which the text was produced, as modern detective fiction tends to be more factual and scientific.

- The narrative in text A is in the first person — the reader is told the story from the point of view of Holmes's assistant. This creates a sense of mystery around the character of Sherlock Holmes. The assistant provides the layman's interpretation of events, before Holmes comes up with an insight that his assistant (and therefore the reader) doesn't expect. This is a technique used to create suspense, as the reader doesn't know what's going to happen next.

- The dialogue between Holmes and his assistant reveals the power balance in their relationship. Holmes addresses his assistant as *my boy*, which is affectionate, but shows that Holmes is his superior. He also uses direct questions and imperatives: *What do you deduce from it?* and *Hold it up to the light*. This shows that he is in control in the dialogue, and his assistant obeys his requests. He speaks to his assistant in the supportive way that a teacher might speak to a pupil — he uses statements to give him information, asks questions to guide him towards an answer, and agrees with him when he's right: *Peculiar — that is the very word*.

Text B — extract from a modern short story

- Text B contains more scientific terms and lexis from the semantic field of forensics than text A, e.g. *ESDA* and *Ninhydrin*. This demonstrates the more hi-tech approach to modern detective work. The narrator doesn't offer an explanation of these terms, which suggests that the reader will be familiar enough with the genre to understand the jargon.

- The lexis in text B is less formal than text A, which is typical of Present Day English. It contains features of spoken English, such as contractions like *didn't* and *he'd*. The sentences are short and often made up of one clause: *Her mind was racing*, which makes the pace of the text much quicker than text A. This device is used to emphasise the fact that the Inspector is in a hurry and *desperate* to solve the case.

- Text B is written in the third person, but from the point of view of Inspector Langham. It's similar to text A because it means that information is held back from the reader until the protagonist discovers it: *Someone must have had a reason for contaminating the evidence*. This technique is typical to the genre of detective fiction, because it builds more suspense.

- The exchanges between the characters in text B show a more hostile relationship compared to the characters' relationship in text A. Inspector Langham asks direct questions because she's in a rush: *What did the ESDA bring up?* Dr Verne doesn't respond with the same sense of urgency or use occupational sociolect. Instead he answers using informal language, which suggests that he isn't taking the case seriously: *Beats me.* This highlights the friction between the characters.

2 The question asks you to analyse the linguistic devices in the texts, and the effect that their context has on the language used. Here are some points you could make in your answer:

Text A — extract from online encyclopedia entry

- The text follows lots of the conventions of an informative piece — it is split up into sections separated by subheadings to make it easier to read. It's written in the third person and uses the third person pronoun *he* to talk about the subject.

- The text is typical of its genre because it's written using Standard English. The tone is quite formal and it contains long sentences with complex syntax, e.g. subordinate clauses: *he was a constant thorn in the side of the Conservatives, and was seen as something of a maverick even by members of his own party, often having to be brought to order by the Speaker of the House of Commons.*

- It also contains some figurative language: *thorn in the side.* This use of a cliché makes the tone seem less formal, which fits with the fact that this is a web-based text, as they tend to contain more features of spoken English than printed texts do. It also contains figurative language that makes his political career seem like a battle against evil, e.g. *the fight against racism.* This is also evident in text B, where words from the semantic field of war are used to make the issue seem important and the speaker seem powerful, e.g. *frontline.*

- Text A contains lexis from the semantic field of politics, such as *House of Commons*, *Speaker* and *left-wing.* It assumes knowledge from the reader because it doesn't explain these terms, which suggests that the target audience for the text is people who already have an interest in politics. Text B also contains lexis from the semantic field of politics, e.g. *Government*, *immigration*, *debate.*

Text B — from a political speech

- Like text A, text B has a clear discourse structure. The speaker uses discourse markers to introduce the next point he's going to make, e.g. *There are 4 themes to our work.* This breaks it up for the listener and makes the points easier to follow.

- The primary purpose of text B is to persuade. This is evident in the use of pronouns, e.g. the speaker uses the first person pronoun *I*, which gives the sense that they are taking responsibility for direct action. The audience is directly addressed using the second person pronoun

you: *It's a debate that many of you are marshalling.* The first person plural pronoun *we* is also used to make the audience feel included in the debate.

- Because it's designed to persuade, text B is more subjective than text A, e.g. there's more emotive language such as *victims* and the adjective *vulnerable.* The speaker creates a sense of urgency through the use of adverbs like *crucially* and *emphatically.* This is a contrast to the more reflective tone of text A.

- Text B is typical of political writing because it uses lots of rhetorical devices. Lists are used to create momentum and build to a climax, e.g. the final point in the bullet-pointed list is introduced by the adverb *crucially*, suggesting that the most important and powerful piece of information has been saved for last. Phonological features such as alliteration are used to emphasise important phrases, e.g. *vulnerable victims.*

- It's likely that there will be 'spin' in political speeches. This text reiterates and repeats the urgency and necessity of the reforms it is proposing. There's evidence of hyperbole (exaggeration) in the speech — it's unlikely that the *public... demand for a different system* the speaker talks about was actually 'demanded' by everyone. However, suggesting that it was makes it more difficult to disagree with the speaker, as it implies that logically the only people who disagree are those who endorse the *21st century slave trade.*

Section 5 — Language and the Media
Pages 86-89

1 The question asks you to analyse this holiday advert in terms of the persuasive devices it uses. Here are some points you could make in your answer:

- The advert uses terms from the lexical field of travel, e.g. *journey* and *destination.* The tone is quite formal and Standard English is used throughout. The syntax is relatively complex and contains subordinate clauses: *Our team of dedicated Voyages Du Monde call handlers, based in our purpose-built office in the New Forest, are here to take you through our wide range of travel options.* This gives the text an authoritative voice that is designed to inspire confidence in the readers and make them feel secure about choosing the company.

- The advert also uses imperatives like *pack up your bags* and declaratives like *you have reached your perfect destination*, so that it sounds confident and expert. The reader is addressed directly using the second person pronoun *you*: *you can rest assured...* This creates the sense that the company knows the reader personally, and understands what they want. The first person plural pronoun *we* and the possessive pronoun *our* are used to create a sense of belonging to an exclusive club: *our family.*

- Text A is also very flattering to the readers — it 'strokes' them by using language that makes the company and its customers seem exclusive, e.g. *special*

Answers to Exam Questions

people, discerning and demanding traveller.

- The discourse structure is typical of an advert. Its purpose is to persuade, so it contains a lot of rhetorical devices. The company is introduced using rhetorical questions to grab the reader's attention: *Are you looking for a company that has seen the world and wants to share it with you?* The company is 'sold' in the main body of the text (*trips of a lifetime...*), and this is followed by imperatives to instruct the reader on what to do next: *Visit our website*. The advert ends with a hook to make the company more memorable: *We look forward to your holiday as much as you do*.

- Text A also uses graphological features to keep the reader's interest, e.g. the company name is repeated in every paragraph and printed in a distinctive typeface from the rest of the copy to make it stand out.

2 The question asks you to analyse the language of this text in terms of the conventions of a television news broadcast. Here are some points you could make in your answer:

- The text follows the conventions of television news. It begins with an introduction in formal, serious language, and is followed by a link to a more informal, personal analysis by a reporter.

- The lexis is in the semantic field of finance, e.g. *figures*, *global markets* and *recession*. It assumes a certain level of knowledge from the audience, e.g. it refers to a *think tank* and the *Department of Trade and Industry*, but doesn't explain what they are.

- The tone is formal and serious in the first part of the broadcast: *the recent downturn was linked to a global recession*. Formal language and Standard English are used to give the newsreader authority, so that what they say sounds credible. Standard English is also used to make sure that everyone can understand the broadcast, which they might not be able to do if it was in another variety of English.

- The second part of the broadcast is less formal because it gives a more in-depth picture of how the issue has affected individuals. For example, it uses colloquial phrases like *back end* and *comes as a huge relief*. The reporter refers to himself personally: *I visited one site in Sunderland*, to seem more accessible to the viewer. He also includes the viewer by using the first person plural pronoun *we*.

- News broadcasts are usually scripted, so the text doesn't contain features of spontaneous speech, e.g. non-fluency features and fillers. Instead, it's very fluent and contains pauses to break up the sentences into small units that are easy to understand, e.g. *the global markets were starting to show success (1) the recent downturn was linked to a global recession...*

3 This question asks you to analyse the language of an extract from a radio talk show, in terms of the conventions of radio language. Here are some points you could include in your answer:

- This extract shows how radio talk show hosts use pragmatics to control the direction of conversations.

The presenter introduces the topic and invites the speakers to talk: *now Brian (.) what have you got to say to us*. He also sums up what the speakers have said and introduces new topics: *would you say that's true of people like (.) say the wives and girlfriends of the Royal Family*. The other speakers are willing to let him take charge of the conversation, e.g. he interrupts speaker B to move the dialogue along: *what would you like to say*.

- The host's speech contains some non-fluency features, such as repetition and pauses: *give us a call on (.) on (.) the (.) usual (.) number (1)*. This instance shows how the host draws out his speech to give himself time to think, but because it's radio he still has to fill the gap with something. This is why the dialogue generally contains very few pauses. He also stumbles over his words in response to speaker D's phatic communication (asking him how he is): *oh er yes good thanks good thank you*. This is possibly because he is in control of the dialogue, so didn't expect to be asked a question.

- The callers' speech contains a lot more non-fluency features, because their speech is spontaneous and they're possibly quite nervous: *er (.) erm well they're not the same (.) no*.

- The expert is addressed by their title+surname, while the host and the callers are addressed by their first names. This shows respect for the expert and gives them more power in the conversation. Addressing people by their names is also necessary on the radio to make it clearer who's speaking, as there are no visual clues for the audience.

- The expert's high status is also evident by the fact that they are given more air time than the callers, showing that their opinion is thought to be worth more. Their speech is more confident than the callers' — it includes fewer fillers like *er*, *erm*, or *well*. The expert's language is also more formal and complex than the other speakers', which shows they are a more authoritative voice, and have had the chance to prepare some answers, e.g. *consider the whole issue in the context of changing standards*.

4 This question asks you to analyse the language of an extract from a magazine film review, in terms of the conventions of journalism. Here are some points you could cover in your answer:

- The article follows a conventional layout for a film review. It's immediately recognisable as it highlights the title of the film, and accompanies it with the age classification in brackets. It lists the director and running time (the length of the film), and then the main members of the cast. It assumes some readers will be familiar with some of the names included.

- Most of the language used in the text is suitable only for a specialist audience. The author uses the specific lexical field of film-making, including terms like *cinematography* and *shot*. The writer addresses the reader as a peer with some previous knowledge or interest in cinema and the film that is being reviewed.

Answers to Exam Questions

- The reader's assumed knowledge is reflected in the writing — as this film is a sequel, the writer talks about its predecessor with lots of familiarity, e.g. *continue their long march*, *the sweeping views we were treated to* and *as precise as we have been led to expect*. The writer also doesn't feel it necessary to introduce the characters or elaborate on the plot, and includes the reader in their opinions and experience of the film by using the first person plural pronoun *we*.

- This text is designed to persuade as well as inform, e.g. it contains emotive adjective phrases like *undeniably captivating*. It also uses rhetorical devices to sway the reader, e.g. hyperbole (exaggeration): *It's been this year's most hotly awaited sequel*.

5 This question asks you to compare extracts from an online music news page interview and a newspaper article, in terms of the language of the media. Here are some comparisons you could make in your answer:

- Text A is a multimodal web-based text, so it contains features of spoken and written English. This means that the language is more informal than the language of text B, containing features like elision (e.g. *gonna*) and contractions (e.g. *'cos* and *someone'll*). It also contains incomplete clauses: *I mean, we've had to practise loads but...*

- Text B is written in Standard English, which is typical of texts in the written mode. It contains more polysyllabic, Latinate words than text A, e.g. *compositions*, *ascent* and *professionally*.

- Text A is less confined by the structure and conventions that text B sticks to, e.g. standard lexis, grammar and syntax. Text B has more complex sentences such as *She's rapidly gathering a following on the live circuit in London, and it's her straightforward, no-nonsense style the audiences like*, which suggests it may come from a review in a broadsheet rather than a tabloid paper.

- The interviewees in both texts use slang, e.g. *belted out* and *bloke* in text B. The texts also both contain jargon, because they're about people from similar occupational backgrounds, e.g. *FreshRock*, *gig*, *set* (text A) and *Music Scene show*, *live circuit* (text B).

- Text B displays more cohesion than text A, because it's a prepared, written piece designed to be easy to follow. By contrast the tone of text A conveys a bit more of a sense of occasion and spontaneity, as it's a transcription of a direct question and answer session.

- Text B makes use of allusion, in its reference to the Human League song 'Don't You Want Me' (*She was working as a waitress in a cocktail bar...*) and a reference to the blues singer Bessie Smith — these sentences rely on the reader's prior knowledge and suggest that the audience for the article is people with a wide musical knowledge. Text A could be written for a specialist audience because it mentions *FreshRock* in its introduction, but is also suitable for people who don't have much background knowledge and want to find out about the band being interviewed.

- Text A demonstrates examples of pragmatics, especially in the interviewees' turn-taking. The two women interrupt and talk over each other equally, and they also end up finishing each other's sentences. They take it in turn to speak and neither dominates the conversation at the expense of the other. The interviewer asks some open questions to gather as much information as possible from them.

- Text B uses some of the rhetorical devices of newspaper language, to keep the reader's attention. For example, the headline is a pun on the singer's name, which alludes to a well-known song and suggests that she's going to be a star: *Starry starry Knight*. There are also rhetorical questions (*how did this Edinburgh-born unknown make her rapid ascent to the top?*) and anecdotes from the interviewee to break up the story and maintain the reader's interest.

Section 6 — Language Acquisition
Pages 106-107

1 The question asks you to analyse the texts in terms of language acquisition and discuss how the child is being helped to understand and remember what happens in the story. Here are some points you could include in your answer:

Text A — conversation between Ellie and her mother

- In text A, Ellie's mother is making sure that Ellie understands the story. Ellie's mother is the main contributor, which is to be expected, as early conversations are usually initiated and maintained by adults. Ellie's contributions to the conversation are mainly short statements that her mother responds to.

- Ellie's mother uses questions (e.g. *so what do they do*) and phrases followed by an imperative (e.g. *it's an owl (.) look*) to encourage Ellie to respond either with short phrases, repetitions of her own, or actions.

- The mother also repeats the structure of her utterances to maintain the conversation. Towards the end of the conversation she gives Ellie positive reinforcement and feedback, starting her turns with *that's right* as Ellie answers a question or spots something in the story. The mother also expands on Ellie's short utterances that relate to the story, repeating or recasting what she's said and then telling Ellie the next part of the story.

- The conversation is also kept in the present tense, so that Ellie can engage with what is happening 'now' rather than in the past: *and then they hear another noise*. This means that Ellie can directly relate what's being said to what they're looking at, and begin to understand what the words and pictures represent.

- Ellie's mother also directly corrects her at the opening of the conversation — *no (.) they're getting out of bed*, but even though she seems abrupt at first she also provides Ellie with what's right (i.e. they're *getting out of bed* instead of being *in bed*).

Answers to Exam Questions

Text B — a second conversation between Ellie and her mother

- In this conversation Ellie's mother is encouraging her to talk. She uses Ellie's name twice while she's maintaining the conversation and asks her direct questions about what happened in the story in chronological order, e.g. *and what happened next*.

- Ellie's mother still prompts her in the right direction (*they were frightened weren't they*) but doesn't give her anywhere near as much help as she did in text A. She tries to let Ellie come to the answers by herself and only speaks to support her (e.g. *that's right*) or keep the conversation going.

- By repeating and expanding on what Ellie says in both their conversations, her mother keeps the conversations going and encourages her daughter's language development. You could call this child-directed speech (CDS), caretaker speech or even motherese — reinforcing and feeding back on what Ellie says in conversation encourages her to carry on interacting, and is thought to benefit child language development as a whole.

2 The question asks you to comment on the development of a child's writing as shown by three different texts. Here are some points you could include in your answer:

Text A — written aged 6

- You can talk about Barclay's (1996) and Kroll's (1981) theories about stages of writing development in this question.

- In text A David appears to be around stage 5 of Barclay's model. Most simple words are spelled correctly but the more complex words (whether in length or spelling) are not. David tries to spell them based on how they sound (e.g. *opound* for opened, *stele* for still, *launge* for lounge and *notes* for notice). He also shows some evidence of getting slightly confused and repeating a spelling unit (*ep*) in *lepeped*, which is supposed to represent leaped.

- David's writing also shows features that are identified in Kroll's consolidation stage — his written language is not punctuated and as a result is similar to the way that David might tell the story if he was speaking to someone. However despite the lack of punctuation the story is made up of short declarative statements that are all from David's point of view (they all start with *I*). He's able to express a sequence of ideas but doesn't know how to finish off a sentence.

- David also uses capitalisation consistently for the first person pronoun *I* but then quite randomly for the verb *Jumped* twice.

Text B — written aged 7

- The main development in David's writing is the fact that he is now able to basically punctuate sentences. This makes it a lot easier for him to develop a longer story rather than it just being a stream of thoughts on the page.

- He has progressed in terms of Barclay's stages of development. His sentences have become more complex and now involve more than one character as well as trying to include the interactions between them. However he doesn't use speech marks or other punctuation apart from the full stops at the end of a sentence and the capitalisation at the beginning of a new one.

- David's attempts at spelling follow a more logical pattern e.g. in his spelling of *clime* (instead of climb). He's attempted to represent the word phonologically by using an *e* on the end of *clime* (trying to replicate the sound in *time*, where an *e* creates a long vowel inside the word). This can also be seen with *frew* instead of threw, which would suggest that David is currently *th*-fronting when he speaks.

- David's writing is still developing — for example he gets confused between using first person pronouns and third person narration in this extract. Although he starts off writing in the first person (*On the way I met an old man*) he then switches between referring to himself as *I* and using his own name, e.g. *Yes I said so David went off with the magic beans*.

- However, he does use an apostrophe for contraction — *when I got home my mum said where's the money*. This is quite advanced for a child writing at 7 years old and might be an imitated form from another text.

Text C — written aged 9

- At 9 years old David has developed even further. He's now at Barclay's seventh stage in which most words are spelled correctly, even if the punctuation and grammar aren't totally correct.

- He also shows some of the features of Kroll's differentiation stage — he is consistent with characters and his use of tense and person as well as marking out the characters' speech with speech marks.

- His punctuation is also more consistent, although he doesn't put an apostrophe in *lets*. His syntax is still simple — none of his sentences are more than a main and coordinate or subordinate clause. Where the clauses in the sentence are a bit more complicated David hasn't yet managed to include any commas. He also sometimes misses out conjunctions, e.g. *We jumped in [and] when we got to the bottom we were inside a cave*.

- David shows more of an awareness of the creative nature of stories. There is a sense of creating an atmosphere, e.g. starting a sentence with the adverb *suddenly* to create surprise and urgency. This shows an awareness of how language can influence the reader. It also suggests that his vocabulary is continuing to increase.

Glossary

abstract noun A **noun** that refers to a concept, state, quality or emotion.

accent The distinctive way a speaker from a particular region pronounces words.

acronym A new word made from the initial letters of all the words in a name or **phrase**, e.g NASA.

active voice When the **subject** of the sentence is directly performing the **verb** e.g. *Steve burst the bubble.*

adjacency pair Dialogue that follows a set pattern, e.g. when speakers greet each other.

adjective A class of words that can appear before (attributive) or after (predicative) a **noun** to describe it, e.g. *pretty.*

adverb A class of words that modify **verbs** according to time, place, manner, frequency, duration or degree. They can also sometimes modify nouns and adjectives too.

affixation The process of adding an affix before (**prefix**) or after (**suffix**) an existing word to change either its meaning or grammatical function.

alliteration When two or more words close to each other in a **phrase** begin with the same sound, e.g. *down in the dumps.*

allusion When a text or speaker refers to a saying, idea, etc. outside the text or conversation.

amelioration When a word develops a more positive meaning over time.

anaphoric reference When a word, usually a pronoun, refers back to something or someone that has already been mentioned, e.g. *Barrie can't come because he's ill.*

antithesis Type of **rhetorical language** where contrasting ideas or words are balanced against each other, e.g. *it's just too good from Green, and just too bad for the goalkeeper.*

antonyms Words with opposite meanings.

archaism An old-fashioned word or phrase that isn't used in Present Day English, e.g. *forsooth.*

article A kind of **determiner** that shows if the reference to a **noun** is general (*a / an*) or specific (*the*).

aspect A **verb's** aspect shows whether the action it refers to is already completed, or if it is still taking place.

assimilation When sounds next to each other in a spoken word or **sentence** are pronounced in a different way to normal to make them easier to say.

assonance When the main vowel sounds of two or more words that are close together in a text are similar or the same, e.g. *low smoky holes.*

audience A person or group of people that read, view or listen to a text or performance. A writer or speaker can aim to appeal to a certain type of audience by using specific literary techniques and language choices.

auxiliary verbs Verbs used before the **main verb** in a sentence to give extra information about it, e.g. *I have seen him.*

babbling The production of short vowel / consonant combinations by a baby acquiring language.

back-channelling A kind of **feedback** in spoken language that supports the person speaking and shows that what is being said is understood.

back-formation In word formation, back-formation occurs when it looks like a **suffix** has been added to an existing base form to create a new word, but in fact the suffix has been removed to create a new term e.g. the **verb** *enthuse* was formed from the **noun** *enthusiast.*

behaviourism A theory of language acquisition that suggests children learn language through a process of imitation and reinforcement.

bidialectism The ability of speakers to switch between two **dialect** forms, the most common being between **Standard English** and a speaker's regional variety.

blending When parts of two words are combined to make a new one, e.g. *netizen.*

borrowing When words from one language fall into common usage in another as a result of contact.

broadening When a word that has quite a specific meaning becomes more general over time (also called generalisation, expansion or extension).

cataphora A reference in a text to something that follows in later **phrases** or **sentences**, e.g. *These are the directions...*

characterisation The way that a writer conveys information about a character relating to their appearance, speech, etc.

child-directed speech (CDS) The way that caregivers talk to children — usually in simplified and / or exaggerated language.

clause The simplest meaningful unit of a **sentence**.

cliché An expression that has lost its novelty value due to being overused.

clipping When a shortened version of a word becomes a word in its own right, e.g. *demo, phone.*

cluster reduction When a child only pronounces one consonant from a consonant cluster, e.g. saying *pay* instead of *play.*

code-switching When speakers use different varieties of English depending on where they are and who they're with.

cognitive theory A theory of language acquisition that suggests children need to have acquired certain mental abilities before they can acquire language.

cohesion The linking of ideas in texts to ensure the text makes sense.

coining The general term for creating new words.

collective noun A **noun** that refers to a group of people, animals or things, e.g. *team.*

Glossary

collocation Words that commonly appear together in order, in specific lexical units, e.g. *done and dusted*.

colloquialism An informal word or phrase that wouldn't normally be used in formal written English, e.g. *How's it going, mate?*

common noun A **noun** that refers to a class of things or a concept. Every noun is a common noun except those that refer to unique things, e.g. the names of particular people or places.

comparative An **adjective** that makes a degree of comparison, normally by adding an -*er* **suffix**, e.g. *faster*.

complement A word or **phrase** that gives more information about the **subject** or **object** in a sentence, e.g. *the boy is actually a cow*.

compound A new word created by combining two or more existing words, e.g. *skyscraper*.

concrete noun A **noun** that refers to things you can physically touch or see, e.g. *chair*.

conjunction A linking word that connects **phrases** and **clauses** to each other to form **sentences**, e.g. *but*.

connotation The associations that are made with a particular word.

context The circumstances that surround a word, **phrase** or text, e.g. time and place produced, intended audience.

contraction A word that's formed by shortening and combining two or more words, e.g. *can't, might've*.

convergence When one accent or dialect begins to use features that are common in another, as a result of **language contact**.

conversion When a word becomes part of a different **word class** in addition to its original sense (e.g. *text* is now both a **noun** and a **verb**).

cooing The earliest sounds children are able to make as they experiment with moving their lips and tongue.

coordinate clause An independent **clause** that's linked to another independent **clause** in the same **sentence**.

coordinating conjunction A linking word like *and, but* and *or* that connects independent phrases and **clauses** to each other, e.g. *He was handsome and she was jolly*.

count noun A **noun** that can be preceded by a number and counted, e.g. *one book, two books* etc.

creole A **pidgin** that has developed into the main language in a community.

critical period hypothesis A theory popularised by Lenneberg (1967), which states that if a child does not have any linguistic interaction before the ages of 5-6, their language development will be severely limited.

declarative sentence A **sentence** that makes a statement to give information, e.g. *she enjoyed her scampi*.

deixis A reference to something outside of the text or conversation (e.g. location, time) that can't be understood unless you know the **context**.

deletion When a child misses out consonants in words, e.g. saying *sto* instead of *stop*.

demonstrative Words that refer to specific objects that only those involved in the discourse can see. They can be **pronouns**, e.g. *I like this*, or **adjectives**, e.g. *I like this bike*.

denotation The literal meaning of a word.

descriptivism The attitude that no use of language is incorrect and that variation should be described rather than corrected.

determiner A word that goes before a **noun** to show possession or number (e.g. *his, two*).

dialect The distinctive **lexis**, **grammar** and pronunciation of a person's spoken English, usually affected by the region they're from and their social background.

dialect levelling A process of **language contact** where differences between **dialects** in proximity to each other are gradually lost.

dialogue Any exchange between two or more characters or speakers.

difference model Tannen's (1990) theory about gender and conversation which states that men and women have different objectives when they interact.

diphthong Two vowel sounds that are joined together to form one sound, e.g. the *a* in *late* is a diphthong as it starts with an /e/ phoneme and finishes on an /ɪ/.

discourse An extended piece of written or spoken language.

dominance model Zimmerman and West's (1975) theory that gender differences in conversations reflect male dominance in society.

double comparative Using an **adjective** that makes a degree of comparison, normally by adding an -*er* **suffix**, with the word *more*, e.g. *more faster*.

double negative When negatives are used twice in a phrase, e.g. *I didn't do nothing*.

Early Modern English The language spoken in England from the late 15th century onwards, when Caxton's printing press began the process of **standardisation**.

egocentric The early mental state of a child in which they can only understand things existing in relation to themselves, i.e. things they can see or touch, etc.

elision When sounds or **syllables** are slurred together in speech to make pronunciation easier and quicker.

Glossary

ellipsis When part of a grammatical structure is left out of the **sentence** without affecting the meaning.

Estuary English An **accent** that was originally from the Thames Estuary area in London but is now heard outside the area and may be replacing RP as the country's most widespread form.

euphemism A word or phrase that is used as a substitute for harsher or more unpleasant sounding words or concepts.

exclamative A **sentence** that has an expressive function and ends with an exclamation mark.

exophoric reference Referring to something outside a text, e.g. *that* tree over *there*.

feedback Verbal and **non-verbal** signs that a person is listening to a speaker.

figurative language Language that is used in a non-literal way to create images and form comparisons, e.g. metaphor and simile.

filler A sound produced by speakers to keep a conversation going and avoid silence, e.g. *mm*.

fricative A group of consonant sounds in English produced by forcing air through a restricted passage (e.g. between the lips or teeth). Some of the English fricatives are *th* sounds, *f, v, s, z, j* sounds, and *sh* sounds.

generic term A **marked term** that is used to refer to men and women, e.g. *chairman*.

genre A group of texts with a particular form or purpose, e.g. letters, poems, adverts.

glottal stop A sound produced when the vocal cords interrupt the flow of air, often to replace a /t/ sound (e.g. *water* becomes *wa-uh*).

grammar The system of rules that govern how **words**, **clauses** and **sentences** are put together.

grapheme The smallest unit of writing that can create contrasts in meaning, e.g. individual letters or symbols.

graphology The study of the appearance of a text, how it looks on the page and how the layout helps to get the meaning across.

Great Vowel Shift A phonological change that took place in the Early Modern English period where long vowels shifted their place of articulation to be higher and further forward in mouth e.g. *hoos* became *house*.

head word A word that has the same grammatical function as the **phrase** that has been built around it, e.g. in a noun phrase, the head word is a **noun**.

hedging Word choices that show uncertainty in conversations, e.g. *probably, maybe*.

holophrase In language acquisition, a single word that expresses a complete idea, e.g. *ball*, which could mean the child wants it, or has found it, etc. Caregivers need contextual clues to interpret holophrases.

hyperbole When exaggeration is used for effect.

hypernym A general word that is a term for many **hyponyms**, e.g. *vehicle* is a hypernym of *car, bus, lorry*, etc.

hyponym A word that refers to a specific type of a **hypernym**, e.g. *car, bus, lorry* are hyponyms of *vehicle*.

ideology A set of ideas and beliefs.

idiolect An individual's **accent** and **dialect** features, which are a result of their personal upbringing and experiences.

idiom A saying that doesn't make sense if interpreted literally but is understood because it's commonly used e.g. *I could eat a horse*.

imagery Describing something in a way that creates a picture of it in the mind of an audience.

imperative A **sentence** that gives orders, advice or directions. It starts with a **main verb** and doesn't have a **subject**.

implication When a meaning is suggested, rather than explicitly described.

infinitive The base form of a **verb**, preceded by *to*, e.g. *to sing*.

inflection An **affix** that is attached to a base word and gives extra information about it, e.g. its tense or person.

initialism Where the first letter of a word stands for the word itself as part of an abbreviation e.g. *FBI* (for Federal Bureau of Investigation). Initialisms are always pronounced letter by letter.

internalisation When a child learning language starts to apply one of the language's rules consistently, even to words they've never seen before.

interrogative A sentence or utterance that asks a question.

intertextuality When a text makes reference to another existing text for effect.

intonation The pitch of a speaker's voice, e.g. rising intonation shows it's a question.

jargon **1**. Specialist words that are used by a particular social or occupational group that may not be understood by a non-member.
2. The chattering sounds that babies make before they start using proper words. It sounds like a made-up language.

juxtaposition Positioning words, ideas or images next to each other in a text to create certain effects.

koineisation When two existing **dialects** come into contact and create a third variety that then exists independently, containing features of both the original dialects.

language acquisition device (LAD) The innate ability of children acquiring language to take in and use the grammatical rules of the language they hear, according to Chomsky (1965).

Glossary

language acquisition support system (LASS) The system of support from caregivers to children that helps them to acquire language and become sociable, according to Bruner (1983).

language contact Occurs when speakers of different languages or varieties of the same language interact for prolonged periods.

Late Modern English The more **standardised** form of the English language, used from around 1700.

lexical asymmetry When two words that appear to be direct opposites of each other actually have different connotations, e.g. *to father* means to conceive a child, *to mother* means to look after it.

lexical field A group of words that relate to the same topic, e.g. *hotel* and *destination* are in the lexical field of travel.

lexis A general term for the words of a language.

liaison When a consonant is pronounced between words or **syllables** to make them run together.

lingua franca A language used for communication between speakers who don't have the same native language. **Pidgins** and **creoles** are both examples, but a lingua franca can be distinct from the speakers' native languages too.

loan words Words that are taken from other languages.

main verb Words that identify the action of a **sentence**.

management speak A way of communicating in the workplace designed to sound up-to-date and formal, but usually overly complex.

marked term A word that reveals a person's gender, e.g. *mistress*, *postman*.

mass noun A **noun** that can't be counted and doesn't have a plural, e.g. *information*.

metaphor Words or phrases that describe something as if it actually was something else, e.g. *the heart of the matter*.

metonymy Using a part of something, or one of its attributes, to describe the whole thing, e.g. *the press* to refer to journalists and the news industry.

Middle English The language spoken in England from 1150 AD until the late 15th century.

modal auxiliary verbs Verbs that give more information about the **main verb**, but can't occur as main verbs themselves, e.g. *can*, *will*.

mode A way of classifying texts (e.g. written or spoken or a combination of the two).

modifier A word, usually an **adjective** or **adverb**, that changes (modifies) the meaning of a **head word**.

monologue The utterances of one speaker or performer to an audience.

monosyllabic Words with only one **syllable**.

morpheme The individual meaningful units that make up words (although they don't always make sense on their own).

morphology The study of the internal structure of words.

multimodal text A text that involves elements of different **modes**, e.g. text messages are a mixture of written and spoken language.

narrative voice The point of view a text is written from, e.g. a first person narrator tells the story from their personal point of view.

narrowing When a word that has a general meaning becomes more specific over time (also called specialisation or restriction).

negatives Words like *not* and *no*, that turn positive statements into negative ones, e.g. *I'm not here tomorrow*.

neologisms New words that enter a language.

non-fluency features Features that interrupt the flow of talk, e.g. hesitation, repetition, **fillers**, interruption and overlap.

non-verbal communication Any method of communication that isn't words, e.g. gestures, facial expressions, body language and tone of voice.

noun A word used as the name of a person, place, thing or concept.

object The part of the **sentence** that the **verb** acts upon, e.g. in *I broke a plate*, the plate is the object and ends up *broken*.

Old English The earliest form of the English language, spoken in England from around 450 AD - 1150 AD.

omission When sounds are left out from words. If a lot of speakers do this over a prolonged period of time, the sound can end up being lost from the word altogether.

onomatopoeia A word that sounds like the noise it's describing, e.g. *buzz*.

orthography The writing system of a language — how the language is represented through symbols (letters) and spelling.

overextension When a child acquiring language uses a word too generally to refer to different but related things, e.g. calling everything with four legs a *dog*.

oxymoron A phrase that brings two conflicting ideas together, e.g. *bittersweet*.

parallelism The repetition of structural features in a sentence or throughout a text, e.g. repeated use of the past tense in a sentence — *he came home, ran up the stairs and jumped in the bath*.

parentheses Another word for brackets.

parody Subverting traditional expectations of a text's features to produce humour or satire.

passive voice When the **object** of the verb is described first, rather than the **subject** (e.g. *the bubble was burst by Steve*).

Glossary

pejoration When a word develops a more negative meaning over time.

personification When an object, concept or situation is given human qualities.

phatic language Expressions that have a social function rather than expressing serious meaning, e.g *hello*.

phoneme The smallest unit of sound.

phonetics The study of how speech sounds are made and received.

phonology The study of the sound systems of languages, in particular the patterns of sounds.

phrase A meaningful unit of language built around a **head word**.

pidgin A language that develops so that speakers of different languages can communicate with each other, normally with limited vocabulary and simplified **grammar**.

plosive A consonant sound in English produced by completely stopping the flow of air from the lungs and then releasing it. English plosives include *p, b, t, d, k,* and *g*.

politeness strategy A way of phrasing something to avoid causing offence, e.g. apologising or being evasive.

political correctness Avoiding using language or ideas that might be offensive about members of a particular group (e.g. ethnic, gender, or age groups).

polysyllabic Words with more than one **syllable**.

post-modifier Words that come after the **head word** in a **phrase** and tell you something about it.

pragmatics The study of how language functions in social situations.

pre-modifier Words used before the head word of a **phrase** (often **determiner** + **adjective**) that tell you something about it.

prefix An **affix** that comes before the base form, e.g. *un*fortunate.

preposition A word that defines the relationship between things in terms of time, space or direction, e.g. *the toy was in the box*, *he's behind you*.

prescriptivism The attitude that language should have a strict set of rules that must be obeyed in speech and writing.

primary auxiliary verbs **Auxiliary verbs** that can also occur as **main verbs** (*do, be* and *have*).

pronoun A word that can take the place of a **noun**, e.g. *he, she, it*.

proper noun A **noun** that is the name of a specific person, place or brand.

prosody **Non-verbal** aspects of speech like pace, stress, pitch, intonation, volume and pauses.

proto-word A combination of sounds that a child uses that actually contains meaning, rather than just being a random utterance like **cooing** or **babbling**.

pun Replacing a word or phrase with one that sounds the same or similar for creative or humorous effect.

punctus A punctuation mark used in Early Modern English that functioned like a full stop (•).

quantifier A word that gives information about the quantity of a **noun**, e.g. *there are few cardigans*.

Received Pronunciation (RP) An **accent** traditionally associated with educated people and the upper class. It's characterised by lots of long vowels and the pronunciation of /h/ and /t/ in words where people with regional accents might leave them out.

referential language Spoken language that gives information by referring to objects or concepts. It usually only makes sense if the listener understands the context, e.g. *the vase is over there*.

register A type of language that's appropriate for a particular audience or situation, e.g. formal language is appropriate for a political speech.

rhetorical language Language with phonological or structural features used to provide extra effects or meanings.

sans-serif typeface A typeface where there aren't any fine 'strokes' attached to the tops and bottoms of letters.

schwa A generic vowel sound ([ ]) that is usually pronounced in unstressed syllables e.g. the *e* in *system* or the *a* in *alone*.

semantics The study of how the meanings of words are created and interpreted. ə

sentence An independent grammatical unit made up of one or more **clauses**.

serif typeface A typeface where fine 'strokes' are attached to the tops and bottoms of letters.

similes Comparisons that use the words *like* or *as*.

simplification When a child learning to speak drops consonants or consonant clusters to make words easier to pronounce, or swaps the consonants for others that are easier to pronounce.

slang Informal, non-standard vocabulary used in casual speech.

sociolect A variety of language used by a particular social group.

split infinitive When the base form of a verb is separated from the word *to* by an adverb, e.g. *to quickly run*.

Glossary

Standard English A **dialect** of English considered 'correct' and 'normal', because it has distinctive and standardised features of spelling, vocabulary and **syntax**. It's the form of English usually used in formal writing.

standardisation The process by which grammarians and prescriptivists attempted to structure and influence English usage according to what constituted 'correct' or 'incorrect' usage of the language.

sub-genre A group of similar texts that combine with others to create a complete **genre**, e.g. tragedy and comedy are types of drama.

subject The focus of a **sentence** — the person or thing that performs the action described by the **verb**, e.g. *Billy* ate a sandwich.

subordinate clause A **clause** that gives extra information about the main clause, but can't stand alone and still make sense.

subordinating conjunction A linking word like *although* or *because* that connects a subordinate clause to the main clause, e.g. *I'm off work because I feel sick.*

substitution When a child replaces a consonant in a word with one that's easier to say, e.g. saying *dot* instead of *got*.

subtext The implied meaning behind what's actually being said or described.

suffix An **affix** that comes after the base form, e.g. *sadness*.

superlative An **adjective** that states the **noun** it's describing is beyond comparison, usually by adding *-est*, e.g. *fastest*.

syllables A word's individual units of pronunciation.

symbolism When a word or phrase represents something other than its literal meaning.

synonyms Words that have the same or very similar meanings.

syntax The order and structure of sentences.

tag question A question added to the end of a statement to encourage a response, e.g. *don't you think so?*

telegraphic stage The stage of language acquisition at which children begin to create three- or four-word utterances containing mainly subjects, verbs, objects and complements.

tense Grammatical **inflections** on verbs that show the time an action took place, e.g. in the past or present.

th-fronting When a speaker replaces *th*-sounds with *f* or *v*, e.g. *think* as *fink* and *them* as *vem*.

transactional language Spoken exchanges aimed at making some sort of deal.

turn-taking A feature of orderly conversations when the chance to speak switches back and forth between the participants.

underextension When a child uses words in a very restricted way, e.g. using a word like *hat* to refer only to the one the child is wearing, not to other hats too.

uptalk / upspeak When the intonation rises at the end of statements rather than just questions.

verb A word that describes the action or state that a **sentence** refers to.

verisimilitude The appearance of something as being true to life.

vernacular The commonly-spoken language of a country or region.

virgule A punctuation mark used in Early Modern English that functioned like a comma (/).

word classes How words are categorised according to the function they can perform in a **sentence**.

World English The international varieties of English, and the English that non-native speakers use to communicate with each other.

Zone of Proximal Development Vygotsky's (1978) theory that when caregivers help children with verbal responses, they provide a model that the child can copy and apply when they're in other situations.

Index

Index

Index